**Dr T. Scarlett Epstein** is a Professor at the Institute of Development Studies, University of Sussex. She was previously Senior Fellow in the Department of Economics at the Australian National University.

She is the author of *Economic Development and Social Change in South India*, to which this is the successor volume, and *Capitalism, Primitive and Modern*.

# SOUTH INDIA:
## Yesterday, Today
and Tomorrow

# SOUTH INDIA:
## Yesterday, Today and Tomorrow

### Mysore villages revisited

T. Scarlett Epstein

Macmillan

312464

*First published* 1973 *by*
THE MACMILLAN PRESS LTD
*London and Basingstoke*
*Associated companies in Toronto Dublin*
*Melbourne Johannesburg and Madras*

SBN 333 13389 7

*Printed in Great Britain by*
A. WHEATON & CO.
*Exeter*

To
Max Gluckman
my guru and friend

# Contents

## PART THREE: TOMORROW

# List of Tables

# List of Maps

# Foreword

## TO HIM THAT HATH MUCH...

THE literature of village India is immense, and immensely varied in style and temper, from the workaday pioneer studies of Gilbert Slater in Tamiland to the matchless 'Rural Rides' of Malcolm Darling in the Punjab and the inspired journalism of Kusum Nair's *Blossoms in the Dust*. This book, with its predecessor, *Economic Development and Social Change in South India*, will take an honourable place in goodly company. It belongs also to another company, smaller but not less distinguished, for few anthropologists have the good fortune, like Raymond Firth, to return to the places and people they had known intimately but long ago. I stress the 'long ago', since, valuable as it is to return repeatedly to the same field over a period of years, there can hardly be the same 'shock of recognition' as when absence has been prolonged: changes observed during the very process of change can rarely be grasped with the immediacy and force which come from seeing the beginning and the end as distinct isolates rather than as barely separable points on a continuum. Of course, they are in very fact points on a continuum; but their sharp separation, as observed, provides a challenge, and a base, for exploration and explanation. This, I think, is implicit, and often enough explicit, throughout Dr Epstein's book.

The book is closely observed and closely argued; the constant counterposing both in space and time – of Dalena and Wangala, of 1955 and 1970 – is basic to the argument and the structure, and is carried out with skill: what could have been mechanical and obtrusive is neatly and efficiently done. Although there is no 'fine writing', the result is a very vivid and even at times evocative landscape of rural India; much of this is due to the sketches of individual lives, Beregowda and Chennu and Yeera – and even, presented with a splendid economy, Honamma. The villages themselves come before us as one might say clearly and dustily at the same time, and that is as it should be. India is like that. There are so many vignettes of the reality of life, so different from the models of bureaucrats and idealists.

This is not a geographer's book; yet it rejoices the heart of a geographer to see how much flows from the simple fact that Wangala is wet and Dalena dry, with all that that implies in the way of differing economic opportunity and consequently of differing response in the same general region – to much the same general factors of change – electricity and the motor bus, education and *Panchayati Raj*. Dr Epstein seems to claim that in a modest way her two villages are in some sense a microcosm. There are dangers in this, dangers of extrapolation; and it is sometimes forgotten that any number of traverses do not add up to a triangulation. But there can be no doubt also that the micro-approach is not merely a valuable but a necessary complement to the macro-approach of the planners, and this also is often forgotten. There is also much to be said for the middle term – why is the useful concept of meso-regional analysis so often overlooked? – but for this too a firm basis of detailed local studies is necessary.

*Jit ke pas jitna hai, utana use milta hai*: precisely, in Biblical phrase, To him that hath much, shall much be given. The proverb comes from northern India, but its reference and its validity are world-wide; it seems, unfortunately, the First Law of Development – and in a sense Dr Epstein's book is simply an elaborate gloss, acutely and meticulously worked out, on this melancholy verity in the context of Indian rural development.

The voluntary (or quasi-voluntary) labour of the whole village may build the local dam or the feeder road; it is the *malik*, the big farmer, only who has the bullocks and carts to use them. It is therefore somewhat naïve when planners complain pitifully that rural folk as a whole are much more enthusiastic for amenity projects than directly productive ones. There is no need to labour this matter nor to cite examples from Dr Epstein's work: the burden of the book is quite simply that the poor are getting poorer and the rich richer; the point is illustrated forcibly, by apt example and in concrete detail, in almost every chapter. There are of course many other studies, throughout the Third World, which enforce this dreadful moral. Almost as frightening, perhaps more so, is the attitude of those macro-planners, themselves more than comfortably off, who shrug their shoulders and murmur (usually *sotto voce*), 'Well, what would you, the price of progress . . .' It is very greatly to Dr Epstein's credit that she has the heart and the courage to try at least to break away from this doctrine of despair. She is also honest enough to label her suggestions frankly 'palliatives', and she is aware of likely objections, some valid, some dubious.

It is predictable that her suggestions will not find ready acceptance; but they appear to me worthy of the most serious consideration, and indeed – despite obvious difficulties – likely to be much more workable than many Third World panaceas. It is clear that in this case of chronic deterioration of the living standards of the poorer rural masses, some form of favourable discrimination is necessary : the suggestion that the criterion for receiving such favour should be landlessness rather than low caste is well worked out and seems practicable. Even more interesting, because more imaginative, is the proposal, in the closing pages of the book, that minimum rural wages should be expressed, and often indeed paid, not in cash but in kind. As Dr Epstein admits, 'It may be argued . . . that to make rural economies revert to barter is a retrogressive step.' But the *expression* of wages in kind, the tieing of the reward to labour to a tangible quantum of food, does not mean a general reversion to barter even in the wages field; and in any case, if this is retrogression, can the constant deepening of the already desperate poverty of so many millions of men, women, and children be called a progression?

Such are the questions raised by this book, which I recommend as an acute and authentic portrayal of a very fundamental aspect of Indian life.

O. H. K. SPATE

*Australian National University*

# Acknowledgements

My FOREMOST thanks are due to Mr Schönherr without whose initiative my return to South India might never have come about. He, together with his colleague, Mr Sen Gupta, and Professor Wurzbacher of the University of Erlangen-Nürnberg, not only encouraged me to revisit in 1970 the Mysore villages I had studied in 1954–56 but also facilitated the collection of the data on which this book is based. They made available to me their experienced research assistants, Mr B. R. Dwaraki, Miss Leela, Miss Rekha Subbiah and Mr B. V. Raman, whose help I gratefully acknowledge. They also let me have some of the preliminary results of their overall village census which enabled me to concentrate on collecting case material during the short period I could spend in the villages. Moreover, they arranged with the German Academic Exchange Service to finance my visit from England to Germany so that we could discuss our findings. My thanks are also due to Professors J. G. Crawford and O. H. K. Spate for their encouragement in my research as well as for making available funds from the Research School of Pacific Studies, Australian National University, which enabled me to get to India.

The difficulties and discomforts of my short field trip were greatly eased by many friends of whom I can mention only a few. The two research assistants who had helped me previously were both keen to join me again : Mr M. S. Sharma managed to spend one day in the villages with us while Mr A. P. Suryanarayana took two weeks' leave from his present employment and assisted in the collection of the data. For me it was a pleasure to work together once more with my two eager and capable assistants of earlier days. Mr B. G. Dasegowda, the retired General Manager of the Mandya sugar refinery, as well as his successor, Mr Krishnagowda, allowed our research team to stay in one of the refinery guest houses; they also kindly arranged for a few factory clerks to spend about two weeks digging up past records relating to the sale of cane by Wangala farmers. On my fleeting visits to Bangalore I was always welcome to stay with Dr and Mrs Stöcker or take a meal with Mrs Schönherr which she miraculously prepared at a moment's notice whenever I arrived unexpectedly. Mr John D. Van Ingen and his brother Joubert offered me hospitality whenever I turned up in Mysore; moreover they allowed me to use their jeep which made my field work a lot easier and more efficient.

I am heavily indebted to Dr Rosemary Barnard and Mrs Audrey Cornish who helped in processing my field data and to Mr E. K. Fisk, Dr D. H. Penny and Dr R. M. Sundrum for their constructive comments on earlier drafts. I also want to thank Mr T. S. McMahon, who prepared the photographs, Mr H. E. Gunther, who drew the maps and Mrs Erica Harriss, who diligently kept to a tight time schedule in typing the manuscript.

My debt is greatest to my many village friends whose warmth of welcome made my return such a memorable as well as stimulating experience.

Finally I have to thank my family : my husband and two little daughters, who cheerfully put up with the inconvenience of my absence while I was away in South India and who, throughout the period of preparing this book, never complained about my preoccupation with writing. My husband in particular deserves my thanks for his continuous interest in my work and for the painstaking way he carefully worked through my manuscript and offered constructive criticism. Words fail me to express in full how much I appreciate being able to discuss with him my research problems and how grateful I am for his constant help and love.

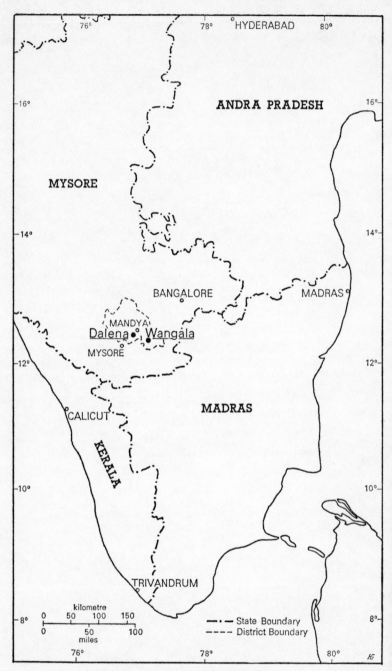

Dalena and Wangala in South India

# 1 Introduction: The Study of Socio-economic Development

## MACRO-LEVEL STUDIES

The problem of 'under-developed countries' still looms large on the international horizon. The various armed conflicts, which have flared up in recent years in the poorest regions of the world, bear witness to this. The changing terminology applied to the poorest parts of our globe illustrates the change in approach by the advanced countries to their poverty-stricken neighbours. In colonial times and right up to the Second World War, there was talk of 'backward regions' which at once implied a paternalistic approach and a somewhat moral condemnation. But the emergence of a number of new nations in the post-war period led, in the first flush of self-confidence provided by independence, to strong objections to the stigma of backwardness. They then came to be referred to as 'under-developed areas'. In this context Myrdal remarks perceptively that 'the tendency to think and act in a diplomatic manner when dealing with the problem of the under-developed countries has, in the new era of independence, become a new version of the "white man's burden". . . . The common agreement to change over to various euphemistic expressions for the term "under-developed countries" is an indication of this. . . . One such is "developing countries". This term is, of course, illogical' (1971:25),[1] for it implies that the poorest countries are all necessarily involved in the process of economic growth.

To seek to initiate a *universal* process of economic development, let alone ensure its cumulative growth, is still only wishful thinking. It will take a lot more research and understanding of the importance of socio-political variables in economic growth before we can hope to know enough to introduce in all the societies of the world the process of cumulative development.

[1] These and similar figures in brackets throughout the book refer to the Bibliography, p. 265.

The study and planning of economic growth in under-developed countries is generally regarded as the preserve of economists, most of whom still pay no more than lip service to the important role of non-economic variables in development. Myrdal is one of a small though growing number of leading economists who stress the futility of approaching development problems from a purely economic viewpoint. He says explicitly : 'the non-economic factors, broad attitudes, institutions and productivity consequences of very low levels of living, are of such paramount importance in under-developed countries that they cannot be abstracted from in economic theory and in planning'. Moreover, he goes on to say that 'the very act of clarifying what should be meant by "economic" problems or "economic" factors must, in fact, imply an analysis that includes all the "non-economic" determinants. From a scientific point of view the only permissable demarcation – the only one that is fully tenable logically – is between relevant and less relevant factors' (1971:30).

Constructing development models in purely 'economic' terms for economies which are not yet industrialised makes them devoid of all reality. Admittedly, all models are abstractions from reality, but they must at least bear some resemblance to real life otherwise they amount to no more than playing an intellectual game. Myrdal's suggestion that development studies and planning must be all-embracing of social variables, though laudable in itself, is not very helpful either. Unfortunately, social science is still in its infancy and is not yet in a position to advance a general theory of socio-economic development. Significantly, in this context, Myrdal himself complains that other social scientists have never had the courage really to challenge the economists' main approach, still less to work out an alternative macro-theory to deal with these problems (1971:37).

As yet our understanding of social processes is too limited to allow for general socio-economic theories to be developed on a macro-level. We are only beginning to appreciate the heterogeneous nature of different societies, of sections within them and of individuals within each group. It is relatively easy for social anthropologists or other social scientists to prick holes in the economists' development bubbles and burst them, but it is much more difficult, in fact it seems still impossible, to suggest all-embracing development theories which may be universally applicable. Social anthropologists realise much more clearly than do economists the severe limitation the vast scope and range of human societies sets to their research. Myrdal illustrates this by saying 'place the economist in the capital city of an under-developed country and give him the necessary assistance and he will in no time make a Plan. In this regard we are unique among the social scientists. No sociologist, psychologist or anthropologist would ever think of trying to do such a thing' (1971:37).

The professional economist normally confines himself to study-ing measurable phenomena. By using sampling methods he can study a larger universe and make broader generalisations. Rarely, if ever, do economists study a system of interconnected economic and social variables to see how the different aspects of social life affect each other. The social anthropologist, on the other hand, tends to select a small universe (usually a village or tribe) which he studies intensively for a lengthy period in order to analyse its intricate system of social relations. His universe is rarely selected on the basis of scientific sampling, and indeed this would be difficult because of the complexity of social life and the cultural variations that exist even within a small region. Therefore the social anthropologist cannot generalise easily beyond the bound-aries of his universe.

Macro-analysis in purely 'economic' terms is a much more valid procedure in advanced than in under-developed countries: in the former, attitudes, institutions and other such variables are frequently more in harmony with development or easily adjust to it, whereas this is far from so in the latter. Social institutions and attitudes in under-developed countries are not tuned to forces of economic growth and therefore quantitative analysis purely in terms of markets is unrealistic in such an environment.

This does not mean that studies and planning in under-developed countries on a purely 'economic' basis are altogether useless. All I am trying to say here is that economists working with blinkers in under-developed countries are not likely to produce realistic macro-level development plans or theories. Planning, too, remains essential. The fact that it errs on the over-optimistic side matters less than that the people concerned should try to understand why it does err; too often they deceive themselves and the general public by the way in which the data have been collected and the statistics presented to point to what are in fact spurious achievements. It would be foolish to suggest that development planning should wait until social anthropologists and other social scientists have gathered sufficient knowledge to help produce a general growth model applicable to even only one particular country, let alone to society at large. It is only to be hoped that in the meantime planners in under-developed countries always bear in mind the following considerations : first, that mere financial and fiscal plans cannot cover the great variety of development problems; second, and as a consequence of the first point, they should be intellectually honest enough to present their plans in the form of rough estimates of what they think might be achieved rather than as accurate targets that must be fulfilled; and third, that they should try and learn as much as possible at grass roots level about the problems and difficulties of the people for whom they plan development. To satisfy this last condition planners in particular and development economists in general will have to acquaint themselves with many social anthropological and other micro-studies relating to the under-developed regions of the world.

Development planning on a national scale has adopted highly sophisticated techniques. Yet there is still a big gap in our understanding of the various social and psychological variables which affect economic motivation. In this context there is an urgent need for micro-level studies to be conducted within a standardised framework of research in different parts of the under-developed world; it is to be hoped and expected that regularities emerging from these various reports will ultimately result in a general theory of socio-economic development encompassing all relevant factors.

## MICRO-LEVEL STUDIES

Economists rarely conduct studies at micro-level; if they do so they usually investigate individual units, or groups of them, which have been randomly selected as part of a statistical sample; the collected data is then presented in the form of averages, or other, often much more sophisticated statistical concepts, which allow for wider generalisations. This general statistical approach precludes the study of social systems as such. Moreover, it does not encourage the re-examination of the very same objects of study after a lapse of time – any other purely randomly selected sample serves equally well for purposes of statistical comparisons. Therefore, very few economic studies exist which examine data collected from the same individuals or economic units at different points in time.

By contrast, social anthropologists almost always study small-scale societies where they are able to examine the interaction of the different social variables. However, few anthropological studies deal specifically with economic phenomena. Many modern anthropological reports do include a great deal of economic data, but these are generally only a by-product of the study of social relations. In this respect Firth's works (e.g. 1929) constitute a pioneering effort in the field of economic anthropology; they show the interaction between economic and other variables within a social system. More recently, there has been an increasing number of such economic anthropological studies at micro-level as in the writings, for instance, of Bailey (1957), Barth (1967), Douglas (1962), Salisbury (1962) and Watson (1958). These various studies clearly illustrate the problem of applying to a subsistence or barter economy many of the concepts developed from a cash economy; they also point out how some western economic concepts may have to be modified to suit the conditions of subsistence economies.

Firth (1956:72) has remarked how in modern industrial societies economists have worked out an elaborate technique for the study of economic organisation, and have produced a body of generalisations upon it, but he adds that it is still a matter of argument how far this technique and these generalisations can be applied to the study of primitive societies and their economic development. Only micro-level studies in under-developed areas can throw light on how far modern economic concepts are universally applicable and in what way they may have to be modified to fit the different socio-economic conditions operative in some of the world's poorest countries. Collecting the kind of statistics with which economists in industrial countries work is made possible only by the existence of a complex social system, dominated by the market, whereby all values can be expressed in terms of a common denominator – money. Comparable institutions are of course frequently absent in under-developed societies. There is therefore the problem of collecting the kind of information in

these societies which the economist regards as the *sine qua non*
of economic analysis, but it is not impossible. First, it must be
realised that in many largely subsistence-dominated economies
there are at least some links with markets. Where this is so, it is
possible to evaluate subsistence activities at market rates. Second,
even in societies which have no links with the wider market
system, there are criteria of value other than money – time may
serve as such – which permit the study of choice.

The number of micro-level social anthropological studies is
continually growing. Many of these concentrate on what to the
economist may appear odd aspects of society such as ritual and
religion or kinship terminology and to which he pays little or no
attention. However, it is likely that even the most esoteric social
anthropological report will produce at least some information of
interest to development economists. For instance, an understanding of the complex of Hindu religious beliefs as they operate at
village level in which the caste structure and the sacredness of
cattle occupy an important place is directly relevant to the problem of developing India's economy. This is but one of numerous
examples which can be quoted to support the claim that development economists work in the dark unless they acquaint themselves
with the relevant socio-political literature.

Field studies of small-scale societies have become accepted as
a necessary part in the discipline of social anthropology. Even the
return by anthropologists to their earlier area of fieldwork after
years have passed has now become commonplace. Some have
gone to fill gaps in their earlier material, but others, such as Mead
(1956) and Firth (1959), have set out to study the changes that
have occurred since their first visits. Firth, in particular, has tried
to express in quantitative terms some of the economic changes he
found among the Tikopia since 1929 when he first did his research there (1959:134). However, since his major interest was in
social structure and social organisation (1959:19) his study is not
basically concerned with economic development. Yet much can
be gleaned about the process of socio-economic change from these
monographs describing and analysing social changes over a period
of time.

In my own interdisciplinary approach to the study of development at micro-level I have tried to examine the interaction between economic and other variables within a social system. I

conducted my first field work in South India in 1954–6, when I studied the impact of irrigation on the economic and social organisation of two villages within a regional economy. *Dalena*, a dry, and *Wangala*,[1] a wet village are situated close to each other within the same culture area near Mandya town in Mysore State, South India. I selected these particular villages because of their multicaste composition, and because they were then still outside the sphere of the Community Development Project. The results of my findings were published in 1962.

## MYSORE VILLAGES REVISITED

Following an invitation and assistance from colleagues at the University of Nürnberg, who had recently been conducting sociological research in Wangala and Dalena, it became possible for me to revisit these villages after a lapse of fifteen years. This second study enables me not only to pinpoint the trends of change in these two South Indian villages, and within the different sections and economic strata in each of them, but also, more importantly, to analyse the various economic, political and social factors and their interactions responsible for the observed changes.

I would have liked to be able to spend much longer in the villages on my return visit; for personal reasons this proved to be impossible. I also seriously considered delaying publication of my findings to allow more time to digest all my material and to bring myself up-to-date with the literature on India, an area with which I was now rather out of touch, having been concerned more in recent years with research in New Guinea. After further reflection, however, I decided in favour of early publication because I felt it my duty to make my findings available as soon as possible to readers concerned with development problems in general and to Indians in particular, even if this meant committing errors that delay might have avoided.

Much has been written on the process of economic growth in under-developed countries and the increasing economic differentiation despite the egalitarian policies so ardently pursued by the

---

[1] I have changed the names of the two villages in order to conceal the identity of my informants. To remind readers of the difference between wet and dry land, I have called the *wet* village *W*angala and the *dry* D*alena. All names given in the text are fictitious.

governments concerned. But very few empirical studies can evince such detailed evidence as will be found here, of the degree to which the wealthier sections managed to become richer while the poorer became poorer not only relatively but also in absolute terms. It is this aspect of my research which I regard as the most interesting and it is in this respect that I hope my study will help to advance at least a little our understanding of the process of economic development in South India as well as other under-developed areas.

Chapter 2 sets out in detail the techniques I employed in my first research as well as in my re-study of Wangala and Dalena. Part One: *Yesterday*, begins with a summary of my earlier findings so that this book should be self-contained, and not require readers to refer back continually to my earlier study (1962). Chapter 4 outlines the new economic opportunities which have come within reach of Dalena and Wangala since 1956. Part Two: *Today*, describes and analyses in detail the response to these new changes up to the time of my re-study in 1970 and how it was affected by, and in turn itself impinged on, the socio-political organisation of the villages. In Part Three: *Tomorrow*, I project the trend of past developments into the future and work out in detail a few suggestions which, if implemented, may help India to approach her present major goals of rural uplift and a more egalitarian society.

# 2 Research Methodology

## 1954–6 STUDY

On my first visit to South India I had a long spell of two years' field work in the two villages I studied. I learned sufficient of the vernacular to be able to conduct some of my own enquiries; moreover, I had two Mysore graduate research assistants who worked diligently to help me collect the data I set out to gather. In this way I had sufficient time and opportunity to carry out systematic enquiries to accumulate a lot of quantitative and qualitative information on life in the villages.

I started my field work by preparing a sketch map of the settlement, a large-scale version of which I hung on a wall of my house. As I continued to gather more and more details of the various households I inserted these on the map – the different castes were denoted by different coloured horizontal lines and the different Peasant lineages by coloured vertical lines. For each house I wrote on the map my census serial number or numbers of its occupants. The map proved an invaluable help in identifying villagers. My informants enjoyed pointing out specific homes on my map. This process of identification with serial numbers was a tremendous help in a society where many different villagers have identical names. I copied out the land registers for Wangala and Dalena and with the aid of the sketch maps identified the recorded holding of each farmer in the villages. Moreover, I conducted a census of all resident households in the villages in which I included not only basic demographic data, but also some general details on the households' economics, such as occupation, landholding, etc. I also conducted a 100 per cent census of animal ownership in the two villages. Thus I collected a number of details from the total population of the two villages. However, most of my 1954–56 statistics were based on a sample.

## (a) Stratified random sample

This sample was systematically compiled in the following way. First, I took a full census of population and landholding of all households in the village. Thus my first enquiry completely covered the village universe.

Secondly, I gave each household a point value according to the size of wet and dry landholding. For Wangala the price relationship of wet and dry land was three to one : I allocated twelve points for one wet acre and four points for one dry acre to allow for holdings of a quarter acre; for Dalena the price relationship between dry and wet land was one to four, so for that village I allocated four points for one dry acre and sixteen points for one wet acre. Land was the only major source of income in Wangala whereas in Dalena residents derived income from various sources. However, since my census was one of the first jobs I did after I moved into Dalena, I did not then know the full range and extent of the various incomes other than from cultivation of crops. The only incomes I knew for certain at that stage were wages earned by men working regularly in Mandya. I allocated eight points for each wage-earner, because his annual wages equalled about half the annual yield in farm wages and profits of one wet acre under cane. My point allocation in Dalena therefore underestimated the income of a number of middle-farmers and magnates, but least affected the poorest because they had few alternative sources of income.

Thirdly, I tried to eliminate the impact of the different size and age composition of households by allocating different weights for males and females of different age groups. In Wangala I had no access to library facilities and therefore was restricted to the books I had with me for advice on research problems. Searching for an appropriate authoritative index I discovered in the *Report on an Enquiry into the Conditions of Agricultural Workers in the village Archikarahalli, Mysore State* (M.O.L. 1951:15) Lusk's coefficient (see p. 144). I decided to accept it and consequently divided the number of allocated points per household by the number of consumption units each contained. Thus I arrived at a point allocation per consumption unit per household. I then proceeded to list these point values into several categories at a group interval of five, which gave five categories for Wangala and seven for Dalena. I subsequently joined together the first two and the second two in Wangala and the first three and the next three in Dalena, leaving three economic strata in each of the two villages. In Wangala about 40 per cent of the households belonged to the poorest section, 57 per cent belonged to the middle-farmers and 3 per cent to the magnates; the respective percentages in Dalena were 76 per cent poorest, 19 per cent middle-farmers and 5 per cent magnates.

On the basis of households grouped according to their economic status I selected a third in each category completely at random. Thus my sample was random in so far as the actual households in the sample were selected at random, but it was at the same time stratified in as much as households had been previously put into economic categories on the basis of landholding and the size and age composition of the household. My Wangala sample was made up of 64 of the 192 village households; of my sample of 51 of Dalena's 153 households I had to discard 3 because I soon discovered that the data received from them was not reliable. Each of the sample households was subjected to intensive enquiry. From each I collected details of the production of the major crops, and of property as well as of income and expenditure.

## (b) *Crop statistics*

For each crop I prepared separate schedules which included all the operations involved in its cultivation. These schedules have separate columns for each operation to show who performed the work, i.e. whether it was the farmer or his own household labour, or exchange or hired labour; then there were columns to indicate the daily rate for hired labour and how many men or women had been employed for how many days. The data on labour time were collected in units of labour days or fractions thereof.

The schedules also showed the number of bullock- or implement-days each operation required and indicated whether these were the farmers' own assets or whether they were hired; if they were hired the rate was indicated. Furthermore the schedules included questions relating to the quantity and price of seeds, manure and fertiliser. I also collected details of all tools and equipment the farmer employed in the cultivation of each crop, by noting the price of each item of equipment, how old it was and its annual maintenance charge. As regards output, I enquired the yield of the major crop as well as all subsidiary crops grown on one plot and the yield of hay.

Each informant was asked to give details of his cost of production of each crop for an area he actually cultivated: thus if a farmer cultivated half an acre of paddy, he gave details for that half-acre, if he cultivated two acres he gave details for two acres.[1] For purposes of exposition I converted all data into a common denominator of one acre. Such conversion assumed constant costs to scale, which within the range of acreage involved seemed a reasonable enough assumption judging from the data I collected. In most cases I found that one acre required about twice the input that half an acre did. For sugar-cane the conversion problem hardly arose, because most sample farmers cultivated cane in units of one acre.

After I had converted all schedules into one-acre figures in real terms, I faced the problem of evaluating subsistence inputs. I decided to evaluate labour at the ruling daily wage rate in the village : home produce such as manure, seed, cattle fodder I priced at the rate ruling in the village. All money figures throughout the book are expressed in rupees.[2] But although I decided to evaluate subsistence labour at the ruling wage rate in the village, I always calculated farmers' wages and profits together, which is the important item each farmer most wanted to know. He never thought of evaluating his subsistence inputs in money terms. Many of my informants were very keen to supply input and output data correctly, for they themselves wished to find out how much they made by cultivating the different crops. For output figures, too, the information seemed fairly accurate. I managed to check a number of details myself by observation and in each case the details were almost identical with those the farmer had supplied. Because of my close knowledge of the farmers and local conditions at the time of my first study I assume that the error in my basic data was then only small.

In my calculation of agricultural capital I did not include landed property, nor did I include an interest charge on investment in land among my items of overhead expenditure. I omitted these items because, since land was sold only rarely, it was very difficult to estimate the price of any particular piece of land. In order to calculate overhead expenditure I collected details on maintenance, depreciation and interest. I calculated depreciation

---

[1] Those readers who are interested in seeing the exact layout of my schedules may refer to a paper I published in 1967 (164).

[2] The exchange rate for one rupee was Stg. 1s. 6d. in 1954–56 and Stg. 1s. 1d. in 1970.

at 7 per cent per annum because 15 years was roughly the work-ing life of a pair of bullocks, a cart and ploughs, and I calculated interest at 12 per cent per annum, the ruling rate in the villages.

Another problem I encountered in the preparation of crop statistics was the allocation of subsistence and cash overhead expenditure of the individual farm among its acres under the various crops. Farmers had supplied me with details of their estates' overhead expenditure, but, of course, they could give me no idea of how to allocate this expenditure to the different crop acres. I consulted different Agricultural Authorities in India on the question, but received no satisfactory answers. At length I realised that draught animals, ploughs and carts are the major items of agricultural capital. Since I had collected data on their use for the various crops, I could calculate the average relation-ship between the utilisation of these major items of agricultural capital on the four major crops grown at the time. I found this relationship to be 60 per cent for cane, 20 per cent for paddy, 10 per cent each for dry or wet ragi and jowar (types of millet). If a farmer cultivated one acre each of the four major crops and his total cash and/or subsistence overhead expenditure was Rs. 100, Rs. 60 would be allocated to his acre of cane, Rs. 20 to his acre of paddy, and Rs. 10 each to his one acre of wet or dry ragi and jowar. Thus the weights given to the acreage under the various crops were 60 for cane, 20 for paddy, and 10 each for wet or dry ragi and jowar.

Thus as part of my first study in South Indian villages I com-piled information on the major crops per acre, as well as data on the whole farm. Output totals of food crops were evaluated at the average price farmers received in the year of my survey. Prices of food crops varied throughout the year; there was about 15 per cent variation per *palla* of paddy[1] between the harvest season when paddy prices were at the lowest and the autumn when paddy prices were at their highest.

## (c) *Property data*

The collection of data on property, which also covered non-productive property, was relatively easy: all I had to do was to

---

[1] A *palla* is a measure of volume which contains 100 *seers*. One seer of paddy or ragi weighs about 2 lb.

compile a list of all the possible items that a villager might possess and then enquire how many he owned of each, how long he had owned them, at what price he had purchased them and, if he knew, at what price he could purchase them in 1955–6. I enquired also how he had acquired all the items he possessed. Thus I got a complete picture of a household's property; but the difficulty arose when it came to evaluating the items of property, for I had to allow some rate of depreciation on old items, or appreciation in the case of jewellery. What I did in fact was to find out the market rate of old items, so as to check the accuracy of my informants' estimates of the present value of their old possessions; in most cases I found that they had been correct. In the nearest town bazaars I could relatively easily ascertain prices of old jewellery and old safes and I verified my informants' estimates there. The market price of old houses was a little more difficult to verify. But although there were only few sales of old houses, a number of householders who had built new houses and sold their portion of the house they had previously jointly occupied to their brothers, could act as guides in the determination of the market prices of houses in the villages. Here again I found that informants' estimates did not differ significantly from the actual price paid for similar houses, or portions thereof. In view of the reasonable accuracy of my informants' data, which I had been able to establish, I decided to accept as the value of the property the price stated by the informants as being the present market price for each of the items they listed.

Since I had decided to take the household as my unit of enquiry, I had to collect property details for each of my sample households and therefore included households of different size, age and sex composition. For purposes of comparison I again utilised the concept of the consumption unit and divided the total property of each household by the number of its consumption units. Thus the figures I showed for non-productive property were all based on consumption units.

Many of my informants were keen to find out the value of their property and, apart from those few who were eager to brag of their riches or to impress their poverty upon me, they were on the whole honest about the number of items they possessed. But in each case I tried to cross-check informants' data with observations as well as by enquiry from their spouses, relatives and neighbours. The interest of my informants in having an idea of the total value of their own non-productive property, and my extensive cross-checking of the data they had supplied, led me to believe that the error in my basic data on property was only small.

I divided the various items of non-productive property into three categories, namely, personal property, household chattels and houses. Subsequently I calculated sample averages and also showed the frequency distributions.

### (d) *Household budgets*

In the compilation of household budgets I encountered much greater difficulties than in the collection of data on property. Here villagers were torn between two conflicting interests : they wanted to impress me with their great expenditure while at the same time they were keen to show their extreme poverty by underestimating their incomes. In the first instance many budgets showed a considerable deficit. However, I collected three separate monthly budgets for Wangala's sample and two for Dalena's sample so as to cover seasonal variations throughout the year; in this way I believe I managed to get a more accurate picture of household income and expenditure. Usually we got husband and wife to act jointly as informants on their household's expenditure : for all items of regular consumption, such as food and firewood, I noted how much they used of each item during the unit of time the villager himself indicated; thus, for example, for rice it was so much per meal, for vegetables and other items they bought at the Mandya fair, it was so much per week, while for other items such as clothing it was so much per month or per year. I carefully checked the prices householders indicated by regularly visiting Mandya fair and bazaars during the periods I collected budgets and systematically compiled a price list for all items of villagers' expenditure. There was only slight divergence between prices stated by informants and those I found ruling at the market. On the basis of all this information I calculated monthly totals of expenditure for the sample households.

I probably did not manage to get complete information on all items consumed : for instance, I know I failed to get full data on the consumption of watersnakes or field rats, which were also eaten, but which people did not like to confess they consumed and which had no market value. I do believe though that I covered most marketable items of expenditure in my schedules. I tried to check informants' data on expenditure by personal observation and by enquiry from relatives or neighbours, but the many different items of expenditure and the different length of period during which each item was supposed to be consumed made an accurate check extremely difficult. However, the three months of budgets in Wangala and two in Dalena collected from each of the sample households exposed the worst of the inaccuracies. Prices were taken as those ruling at the time of the collection of the budgets. Thus the three monthly budgets evened out the seasonal price fluctuations throughout the year. The budgets collected at different times in the year for each sample household were finally averaged and the monthly total per household calculated. Again, in order to express the different monthly household totals in terms of a common denominator, I calculated monthly expenditure per consumption unit.

The collection of income details was even more difficult than that of expenditure. I could not very well expect the farmer to state his monthly income, when his subsistence and cash income was derived from his crop harvests once or twice a year. It was relatively easy to gather details of the household's subsistence income by enquiring for each item of consumption whether it was self-produced, bartered, received as gift or bought with cash. But to arrive at the household's cash income I had to fall back on my crop statistics collected for each sample household. Also I had access to the Wangala records of the sugar factory, which enabled me to establish what money farmers received from the sale of their cane. By these means I worked out fairly accurately the major source of cash income of sample households. It was much more difficult to collect details of minor sources of cash income, such as the occasional sale of paddy, and it was most difficult to collect details about the income of women from the sale of milk and butter. But by checking the income of each sample household more than once in a year I think I fairly well covered all sources of income and items of expenditure, and if I failed to collect all the details correctly, I suspect the error can only have been small. In order to balance income with expenditure I calculated income per consumption unit per household. The difference between household income and expenditure was either savings or net borrowing. However, this was not just a balancing item, but I tried in each case to verify if the household actually saved or borrowed money. In most cases details of savings and indebtedness bore out the budget data.

I presented the budget data in the form of monthly averages per consumption unit of all sample households for each of the two villages I studied. Moreover, I gave details of the distribution of the different items of income and expenditure in sample households.

## (e) *Wedding expenditure*

I did not include wedding expenditure in the budgets of my sample households. Had I included it this would have unduly exaggerated the expenditure of the household concerned; moreover, incorporating wedding expenditure in this way would hardly have thrown much light on the economic differentiation it illustrates.

Instead I collected details of wedding expenditure for all the fourteen marriages in Wangala and six marriages in Dalena which took place during my stay there. Then it was sufficient to gather information on wedding expenditure from the groom's parents only, for among peasants it was the groom's party that had to foot the bill. I utilised four 'typical' wedding budgets to illustrate how wedding arrangements reflected economic differentiation.

I tried very hard to process most of my basic data before leaving the villages. This was not only important to satisfy the curiosity of individual informants about the economics of their own household but also enabled me to check on any discrepancies or shortcomings in data which emerged in the course of processing it.

## (f) *Qualitative data*

As far as my research was concerned I regarded the collection of quantitative data as constituting the skeleton of my material; the qualitative data provided the flesh. I found that only by combining numerical with behavioural data could I get full insight into the socio-economic organisation and its change in Mysore villages. The disappearance of the hereditary labour relationship between Peasant[1] masters and their A.K.[2] dependents in Dalena illustrates this well: I discovered in the course of collecting crop statistics among Dalena Peasants in 1955–6 that by contrast with their Wangala counterparts they no more gave annual rewards in kind to their local A.K.s. This led me to watch out carefully to see if the non-economic links, which had been part of this labour relationship, still existed. I soon discovered on the occasion of a Peasant funeral, when the A.K. refused to perform his customary role of carrying a torch ahead of the funeral procession for his Peasant master, that the ritual aspects had also disappeared. It is this sort of fusion between quantitative and qualitative methods of enquiry which I find most instructive.//

I collected genealogies for all residents in Wangala and Dalena; I attended all marriages, meetings and altogether all functions which took place during my stay in the villages. When it was not expedient to take notes while observing the social interaction between villagers I tried to memorise the essential facts and then, after I got back to my house, sat over my typewriter often into the early hours of the morning to write it all down while it was still fresh in my mind. It was a fascinating exercise to fit together like a jigsaw puzzle the various data collected on different occasions by different means to present an overall picture of village life in South India and to analyse its changes meaningfully.

*1970 RE-STUDY*

Many research workers dream of the opportunity to return some day to their field of study after years have elapsed just to see how the people and the place have changed. I too cherished the dream of re-visiting South India but had little hope that it would come true. The invitation to return to Wangala and Dalena, which I received from Mr Schönherr, my German colleague, early in 1970, gave me the unexpected chance to realise my secretly-held ambition and return to the very same villages where I had done my first piece of field work during 1954–56. In the meantime I had conducted socio-economic studies among a New Guinea

---

[1] Caste names are denoted by an initial capital letter; thus a Peasant is a man belonging to that caste, a peasant is a farmer.

[2] A.K. is the abbreviation used for Adikarnataka, the village Scheduled Caste in the Mandya region. In my earlier writings I referred to these people as Untouchables, now I call them by their caste name.

tribal people. I had dropped much of my interest in India and lost such command as I had had of the language, and therefore I was worried that it would be a long and difficult task for me to re-establish *rapport* in South India after an absence of fifteen years. Much as I would have liked to spend another two years in Wangala and Dalena, personal circumstances made a long spell of field work impossible : I could spend no more than five weeks in the field.

As I left for my re-study I took with me a lot of the data I had collected earlier : the tattered maps which used to decorate the walls of my village home, a list of my sample households and the processed details I had calculated for each of them, sets of blank schedules, which I had used in 1954–56, one copy of all the notes I had collected then and so on. I also took along a copy of the volume I had published in the meantime to prove to my village friends that I had kept my promise and written a book about their way of life. This was how I had explained to them my interest in their villages and managed to get their willing co-operation in the study. When I left South India in 1956 none of my village friends was literate in English. I could not communicate with them in writing nor did I see any point in sending them a book about their villages which none of them was able to read. When I returned in 1970 I had my first chance of showing it to them.

Travelling to South India I began to feel very nervous. I tried to remember words in the vernacular, but none came to mind; not even the simplest sentence. Moreover, I was wondering what sort of reception I would receive : whether I would be recognised by old friends, how many of them might have died in the meantime, how many of the little boys and girls with whom I used to spend many a happy hour playing games would still remember me now that they were adults. My German colleague had told the villagers of my impending return, so at least they knew I was coming. He told me that the farmers were all convinced that he was my son, even though he had tried to explain to them that we had never met before : all he knew of me and my work was through reading my book. When he informed them of my forthcoming return they kept repeating that they were not surprised since it was to be expected that a mother would visit her son even if he was only her classificatory son. Subsequently they told me that they had in fact met a number of my relatives: some brothers and sisters of mine and a few others whom they assumed to be my classificatory children. It soon emerged that they super-imposed on to researchers their own custom of expressing re-lationships in genealogical terms and regarded every research worker who visited their village after I left as my kin: my own generation they classified as my siblings and younger ones as my children. They recounted that at least seven or eight people had come to ask them questions the way I had done, but none had stayed for as long as I did. Unfortunately, on my return I could not actually live in the villages – it would have taken too much time and effort to arrange camping there – instead I stayed in one of Mandya's travellers' bungalows and commuted daily to Wan-gala or Dalena.

On my first day back in Mysore, when we were driving to Dalena, Mr Schönherr told me that a wedding was scheduled to take place that very day. The daughter of one of the headman's younger brothers was getting married. We arrived there just in time to observe the tying of the *tali*, a pendant on a necklace which, like the wedding ring in Western society, denotes a married woman. The welcome I received from Dalena villagers was indeed overwhelming. My fears of having completely for-gotten their vernacular were soon dispelled: as they surrounded me and many of them were chattering away at the same time I began to answer their questions and in turn put many to them.

The outward appearance of Dalena had not altered very much; a few of my old friends had died in the last fifteen years, but on the whole my first impressions were that things had con-tinued to develop along the lines I had already noticed earlier.

Typically, it was the leader of what I used to call the 'conserva-tive' faction of Dalena, to whom the villagers referred as chair-man in their vernacular, who welcomed me back and arranged my whole reception. He had lost his teeth, but was otherwise unchanged. The village headman put in only a fleeting appear-ance and welcomed me politely; he was too busy with his own affairs to pay much attention to my return. Some of the village A.K.s turned up to greet me but remained discreetly in the back-ground. It was obvious that they regarded it as the Peasants' prerogative to welcome me back. The Peasants treated me and my German colleague as guests of honour at the wedding and the subsequent feast which was an elaborate meal of rice and meat curry as well as various choice sweets.

I soon fell back into my old field work routine and in the evening of my first day spent back in Dalena I typed out a long and detailed account of the wedding I had been fortunate enough to observe. I noticed there and then that there had been a change in wedding practice among Peasants; whereas previously the groom's people met all expenditure, now it was the bride's family that paid it all.

On my second day back in South India I returned to Wangala. Somehow I had always felt closer to Wangala people than to those of Dalena. This may have been due to the fact that it was in Wangala that I started my field work; moreover, I stayed a full year in Wangala whereas in Dalena I only had about eight months. At any rate, after the warm reception I had in Dalena I began to expect big things from Wangala people. The warmth of their welcome exceeded even my highest expectations. The old headman, Chennamma, his distinguished-looking wife, Tugowda, the enterprising leader of what I used to call the 'progressive' faction and many other of my old friends who were now in their seventies, gathered round me and took it in turn to touch my toes and their eyes three times in succession as a sign of respect. Many young men now in their late teens or early twenties crowded round to shake hands with me. Karegowda, who was about four years old in 1954 and who was then my special favourite in the village, rushed up to me and we embraced in a way quite un-common among South Indian villagers. He kept muttering how much he had missed me throughout the years and how happy he was to see me again. Altogether, my return to Wangala and Dalena provided some of the most moving experiences I have ever had.

Wangala's appearance had altered considerably : there was now a new migrant labour section, electric street lights, a number of new and impressive-looking two-storey houses, more wells and many other outward changes. However, my first impressions of its social life, which were subsequently reinforced, were that nothing much had changed. The village A.K.s did not even put in an appearance on the day I returned. Only the following day the A.K. headman dared to approach me and request me to spend some time also in their section.

It did not take me long to re-establish *rapport* with my many village friends. This fact, together with the help Mr Schönherr offered me in my re-study, gave me right from the outset confidence in tackling it in spite of the short time I had available. He himself had been doing research in Dalena and Wangala for over one year; he had with him a team of Mysore graduate research assistants, three of whom he put at my disposal. Moreover, he had conducted a 100 per cent village census, details of which he promised to let me have as soon as his material was processed. Without at least some ready information on the total universe I felt I could not compile a meaningful sample, let alone a properly stratified random sample, which was necessary if I was to bring my numerical data up-to-date.

I began my systematic field work by working together with some of my best village informants through the contents of my earlier schedules checking how far they still applied and what alterations were required : some new things had to be added to my crop schedules as well as to my lists of the different items of household income and expenditure as well as property. Then, while I was waiting for my revised schedules to be printed, I arranged to have new sketch maps made for comparison with my earlier village maps. Both villages had grown considerably in the meantime. This time therefore it was a much bigger exercise; moreover, I was more pressed for time. Fortunately, I was able to contact the two research assistants with whom I had worked together in 1954–6. Both of them were now married with families of their own and were in regular urban employment. But they readily agreed to return to the villages with me and help once more in my study. Mr M. S. Sharma could come only for one day but Mr A. P. Suryanarayana joined me for two weeks. It was a thrilling experience for me and they assured me equally so for them, to be able to take up our joint research efforts after all these years. Our village friends also seemed pleased to see all the members of my old team working together once again. Mr Schönherr and his assistants also joined our map-making operation.

The new maps were not quite as useful in my work as the earlier ones had been, for this time I could not conduct a total village census and therefore I could not pinpoint particular households on the map. Nevertheless, it was a big help to have these sketch maps and locate housing of particular individuals on them. By comparing the 1955 maps with their 1970 counterparts it was possible to see the pattern of movement within the village and identify my earlier sample householders, some of whom had moved into new homes.

## (a)  *Sample*

Together with my assistants and many village friends it did not take us long to identify by far the greater proportion of my earlier sample households : 56 out of the 64 Wangala sample households and 38 out of 48 Dalena sample households. I then decided to confine my statistical enquiry to the examination of half the number of my 1955 sample families. We randomly selected 32 households of the Wangala sample, 2 of whom we failed to identify, which left us with a sample of 30 units. In order to learn more about the recently established migrant settlement I randomly selected two migrant households and included them in the sample. In Dalena we managed to track down all the 24 households we randomly selected from my earlier sample.

My 1955 samples of Wangala and Dalena were to a high degree representative of the whole villages. But 50 per cent of these earlier samples could not be regarded as representative of the same villages 15 years later. I could, of course, have randomly sampled the villages by selecting one household out of every fifth or tenth house in the village streets, but I decided that this would not be a satisfactory procedure either. I considered it more meaningful to re-examine the very same households, rather than to try and compile a truly random sample to represent features of the whole villages as such. My 1970 Wangala and Dalena samples do in fact represent about ten per cent of all households in these villages (32 out of 338 Wangala households and 24 out of 235 Dalena households). But the sample is hardly representative of the villages' composition as it is now.

## (b)  *Crop statistics*

As soon as my schedules were ready we began in Wangala to collect details of the inputs and outputs of crops among my sample farmers. The information we got is likely to be much less accurate than my earlier crop data. This time we only had a few days to do what we had previously done in many weeks. It was not possible for me to check the time farmers said they took over the different cultivation operations, nor could I personally observe the quantities harvested. As on the previous occasion, so now each sample farmer was asked for details of his inputs and outputs of each of the major crops for an area he actually cultivated. We tried our best to elicit truthful information from the farmers we questioned. Most of them were genuinely keen to discuss the cultivation of their crops; they appeared to think carefully before answering our questions so as to make sure their answers were correct. Usually interviews were conducted amid a crowd of villagers; if the informant diverged noticeably from facts there were at least one or two of his fellow villagers present who queried his statements.

I tried to cross-check output data for cane by copying the Mandya refinery records relating to Wangala cane growers, as well as by gathering information from the owners of Wangala's cane-crushers as to the quantities of cane my sample farmers had processed into jaggery (inedible brown sugar easily distilled into alcohol) during the last crop year. Therefore, the cane output details I collected are probably fairly accurate. Data on paddy and ragi output were far more difficult to check than for cane; I copied the paddy procurement list for Wangala and identified my sample farmers on it; I looked into their paddy sales to traders. By combining these totals with the details of their subsistence consumption of paddy, which I derived from their expenditure details, I tried to check the output data the farmer himself had given me. By and large there was remarkable consistency in my informants' crop data. Moreover, I compared my villagers' output totals per acre with the averages given in the Mysore Crops Surveys (B.E.S. 1966) and there was on the whole a surprisingly high coincidence. Unfortunately, these crop surveys do not investigate inputs, so I had no means of comparing my own data on crop inputs with those collected elsewhere in the region. Because of my various attempts to verify my sample farmers' information I do not think that the error in my 1970 basic data can be unduly high, though it must be expected that it is higher than was the case in 1955.

In computing averages of inputs and outputs of the different crops I proceeded in exactly the same way as I had done for my earlier material (see page 12). To make the data comparable for the two points in time I recalculated my 1955 totals on the basis of my 1970 sample. Therefore the 1955 crop details in tables 9 and 10 differ somewhat from the estimated sample averages I published earlier (1962:47 and 218). Since prices of inputs and outputs have risen considerably and it was difficult to establish the exact price rises for all the different inputs I have this time amplified my material by giving averages and frequency distributions not only in monetary but also by weight and volume (see tables 7, 8, 12, 13, 14, 15).

So as to put into a wider perspective my new crop data derived from a sample which was now fifteen years out of date I copied out the Wangala land register as well as Dalena wet landholdings in neighbouring villages. This clearly indicated how much more land had been irrigated in Wangala as well as how much of the village land belonged to residents and how much to outsiders. Furthermore, I copied out the refinery records relating to the sales of Wangala plantation land, which showed how much of this land was acquired by Wangala farmers, how much by neighbouring villages, and how much by urban landlords. For Dalena farmers the village dry land remained unchanged; all that has happened there is that they have acquired more wet land in neighbouring villages. Most of this wet land is situated in four neighbouring irrigated villages. To get fairly accurate details of all the wet land owned by Dalena farmers I needed to check the land registers of these four villages. This I did in 1955. Unfortunately, this time I was able to do it only for two of the four villages. In 1955 the Dalena-owned wet land in these two villages contributed about sixty per cent of all Dalena wet lands. Assuming that the distribution of Dalena wet lands over the four neighbouring villages has remained roughly the same, I estimated the total Dalena wet land holdings and tried to check this estimate by asking residents about details of wet land they had bought since I left the village. Although my Dalena wet land details are only estimated, I believe the figures fairly well represent the facts of the situation.

## (c) *Property data*

I attempted to bring my data on productive and non-productive property up-to-date by collecting details of what my sample households owned. However, I soon discovered that the pricing of the different old and new items of property presented too big a problem. It was relatively easy to establish the 1970 replacement value of all the articles owned, but this in itself would not have resulted in a meaningful comparison between the average values of property among sample households in 1955 and 1970. To do this required an investigation into the price change of each of the articles my village friends possessed. This, I am afraid, was too time-consuming a procedure. It is something I would have very much liked to do and still hope to accomplish some day soon, so as to show the rate of property accumulation by the different economic strata of villagers.

(d)   *Household budgets*

I did in fact collect one set of budgets for June 1970 from each of my sample households. Once more I carefully compiled a list of market prices for the different articles of village household expenditure. On the basis of my May 1955 price list I was able to calculate June 1970 price indices for the different items of expenditure. Moreover, by evaluating 1970 expenditure at 1955 prices I can throw into relief changes in the standard of living in real terms. However, this time it was not possible for me to collect budgets for more than one month in the year, nor was I able to check so carefully by observation the details given by informants. In the little time at my disposal I could not possibly collect all the data myself nor could I be present when each of my four assistants questioned informants. I therefore decided to concentrate on case studies rather than make the attempt to calculate the average household budget for a sample which in any case was not representative.

I selected one budget from each of the different economic strata in the villages: for Dalena I chose one Peasant magnate, one Peasant middle-farmer and one of the poor A.K.s; for Wangala I did the same but added one migrant to cover the full range of economic differentiation there. I used several criteria for selecting my cases from all the sample households for which I had collected budgets: first, I was personally present when one of my research assistants conducted the interview and posed myself some of the questions to elicit accurate details; moreover, I had notes amplifying the budget data; second, I wanted to illustrate particularly relevant developments; for Dalena I selected a Peasant farmer who had managed to get regular urban employment to show the part his wage income plays in his overall standard of living; for Wangala I chose a Peasant middle-farmer whose family had grown in size to indicate the strains and stresses resulting from population increase.

In presenting these case studies I am able to show the changes that have occurred during the last fifteen years in particular households. This seems to me much more meaningful than to gauge economic development on the basis of sample averages alone. I do not wish to imply here that I regard all survey data as useless or without meaning; quite the contrary, it is essential, particularly for special enquiries such as the rate of population growth or national income statistics. All I am trying to suggest is that case studies can supplement survey data, for they can play an important role in learning to understand the process of economic development at village level at least. Moreover, there is a greater chance that the basic material of case studies is much more accurate than that of a number of different units which are all part of a large sample. The availability of computers has made the processing of masses of data much more sophisticated, but it does not follow that the efficiency in the collection of basic data has increased likewise. The accuracy of processed data cannot be any greater than the accuracy of the basic data fed into the computer, however advanced the processing methodology employed. Admittedly, case material does not lend itself to such sophisticated statistical treatment, but at least there is a much greater chance that the basic details are accurate than is the case with large-scale surveys.

Many planners and economists are becoming aware of the difficulties involved in collecting accurate survey data of household income and expenditure; Dandekar, for instance, perceptively notes that 'the richer households, both in rural and urban areas, have become increasingly inaccessible to the N.S.S. investigators who are after all class III government servants. It thus seems perfectly possible that the consumer expenditure of the upper middle and the richer sections has been progressively underestimated, as the statistical evidence shows' (1970:37). By contrast I feel confident that the error in the basic data relating to even my village magnates' budgets is very small. As a complete outsider to the villages, not connected with the public service, but readily accepted by residents and aided by indigenous research assistants, I was in a much better position to elicit factual information than a government clerk. Moreover, by investigating the various socio-economic data of one and the same household from various angles it was possible to detect quickly inconsistencies in the information : for instance, I could readily query it if I discovered a great discrepancy between a household's food crop output and sales details on the one hand and subsistence consumption on the other. Such checking of internal consistencies in basic data is possible only in a small-scale enquiry, and is easiest with case studies.

## (e)   *Wedding budgets*

Unfortunately, I arrived in South India at the end of the village wedding season and therefore was able to observe only one Peasant wedding. I did try to collect details of wedding expenditure from men whose daughters or sons had got married during the 1970 season, but since I myself could observe only one wedding, and that on the very first day of my return to Dalena when I was not fully tuned again to South Indian village life, I am reluctant to present my data on wedding expenses in table form. I do use it however to illustrate how the new development of a dowry inflation among Peasants is affecting the poorer members of the society.

## (f)   *Qualitative data*

The shortness of my second trip also severely limited my chances of personally observing the many different social and political aspects of village life. There were no village council meetings I could attend, not a single death occurred and therefore there was no funeral for me to watch and so on. Thus I was compelled to rely mainly on long talks with various villagers when I had to listen carefully, sort out the relevant from the irrelevant and make a mental note of, and subsequently try to pursue further, any hint of changes in the socio-economic organisation of village life.

For instance, when one of my Dalena informants happened to mention that Chennu, the young man who already in 1955 worked in the Mandya refinery and had just then managed to become one of the accepted spirit mediums in the village, now lived in the refinery compound, I tracked Chennu down. We spent two evenings together when we sat till late at night and I encouraged him to tell me about his life and experiences since we had last met.

I also conducted structured interviews with the leading entre-preneurs in Dalena and Wangala, as well as with village political spokesmen : for instance, I spent two days with Wangala's A.K. headman and one day with his Dalena counterpart just listening to their various requests and complaints. Thus I tried as hard as I could to gain a full picture of the 1970 socio-economic system of Mysore villages and to detect and analyse the changes that had occurred since my first study there.

# PART ONE
# YESTERDAY

# 3 Mysore Villages in 1955

WANGALA and Dalena are situated in the *Maidan*, the plains of Mysore State. Both villages are in the vicinity of Mandya, a rapidly growing town at the centre of an irrigated region. Wangala is about four miles away on a secondary road; Dalena lies a few hundred yards off the major highway six miles out of Mandya on the way to Mysore. Both villages are multicaste with Peasants occupying a position of dominance (Srinivas, (b); 1955:18); in 1955 almost 90 per cent of the land owned by Wangala inhabitants belonged to Peasants, who made up 66 per cent of the village households (see table 2). In Dalena Peasants constituted 80 per cent of village households and owned as much as 98 per cent of the land (see table 3). In both villages the *panchayat*, or village council, had been composed of the hereditary elders of the 'major' Peasant lineages residing in the village; the *patel*, or village headman, was also a Peasant. Moreover, Peasants had important roles in village rituals. Dalena was in 1955 a slightly smaller village than Wangala. It had a population of 707 living in 153 households whereas Wangala had 958 people living in 192 households.

The layout of both villages was similar: the road first led to the caste settlement occupied mainly by Peasants interspersed with some Functionary[1] households. In the caste part of the villages were a number of temples of which the Marichowdi, dedicated to the village goddess Maramma and the centre of village political and social life, was the most important. The majority of houses in the caste streets were square in shape with walls of red mud and roofs of hand-made tiles. Only a few of the caste households lived in huts with thatched roofs. By contrast, the A.K. quarter, which both in Wangala and Dalena was set apart from the village caste households, was composed mainly of small mud huts with thatched roofs. Their houses, hardly big enough to accommodate a family, marked their settlements as the poorest section of the villages.

---

[1] Functionary households include the various craft and servicing castes such as the Blacksmith and Washerman.

Wangala and Dalena, situated so near each other, were in the same culture area and used to be almost identical in all aspects of their economic, political and social life. The turning point in their development came in the 1930s as a result of the introduction of canal irrigation, which created a regional economy in which Wangala and Dalena assumed distinct and complementary roles. The resulting differential development formed the topic of my 1954–56 research in South India. In the following pages I attempt to present a summary picture of my earlier findings so as to set the stage for an account of the changes that have occurred since my first study, and as a base for evaluating them.

Cultivated land in India falls into two major categories: dry and wet. Dry lands are those which depend solely on rainfall for their cultivation, whereas wet lands receive a supplementary water supply from rivers, canals, tanks or wells. In zones, such as the Mysore plains, with low annual rainfall, irrigation can yield substantial benefits to the farming population. Accordingly, the Government of Mysore considered a project for a dam across the Cauvery river to extend irrigation in the State. In 1911 construction began on a big dam at Caniambadi, 12 miles from Mysore City. The dam was later named 'Krishnarajasagar' after the ruling Raja of the day. Irrigation from the dam began to flow in 1931; by 1956 about 100,000 acres had been irrigated while there were plans for still further spreading of the canals. The extent of irrigation is determined by topographical factors. Wangala was fortunate; by 1939 irrigation reached village lands. By contrast Dalena land lies above the irrigation level and therefore remained dry.

The newly irrigated land facilitated the cultivation of cash crops, in particular sugar-cane, which in 1933 led to the establishment of a sugar refinery at Mandya, the heart of the irrigated region. This in turn was responsible for Mandya's subsequent rapid expansion; from being a small market town prior to 1931 with no more than 6,000 inhabitants, its population increased to 21,000 by 1951.

The advent of irrigation in Wangala prior to the outbreak of war in 1939 enabled farmers to venture into cash cropping. Previously their land had been mainly dry: only one-eighth of the cultivable area was irrigated from a village tank, and many a year the tank failed to provide sufficient water to irrigate even this limited area. Paddy had been the major crop grown on tank-irrigated lands. Sugar-cane was rare and grown only for making jaggery, which is handled in the form of big cubes of inedible brown sugar. Two millets, ragi (*eleusine corocana*) and jowar (*sorghum vulgare*), were the staple crops grown on village dry land. These provided the staple diet supplemented by home-grown vegetables, pulses, spices and some fruit. Sericulture yielded the only major source of cash income, but was not widely practised, because it required considerable skill, working capital and trading experience. Wangala's and Dalena's economies were then predominantly subsistence : the villages as a whole produced most of their own requirements and paid for their marginal imports mainly with the cash earned from sericulture. When silk prices dropped drastically during the world depression in the early 1930s even those few farmers who had practised sericulture now found it uneconomic and switched back to food crops.

## WANGALA

Fortunately for Wangala, irrigation came to the area just at the time villagers were losing their cash income from sericulture. The construction of canals and roads immediately offered a number of employment opportunities to Wangala men. Five of them became contractors for the Public Works Department and a considerable number also worked as daily labourers for contractors or directly for the Public Works Department. Once their land became irrigated they relinquished their outside work and returned to full-time farming. Their newly irrigated lands at the outset of the war enabled Wangala farmers to grow paddy on a larger scale and thus they could easily have supplied the black market which developed as a by-product of rationing. Yet none of the Wangala farmers was ever known to have been a black marketeer. They were all small landowners, *ryots*, whose first interest lay in their land provided it yielded a 'reasonable' living to their families. Irrigation made their lands more productive and also more remunerative and Wangala farmers displayed little interest or aptitude in exploiting the black market. The rich men of Wangala were always referred to as 'sugarcane-made-rich', never as black market profiteers, as were, for example, their counterparts in Dalena.

In the early years of its operation the management of the Mandya refinery faced an uphill struggle in convincing local farmers that the cultivation of sugar-cane would bring them prosperity. The staple dry crops of ragi and jowar and even paddy, a wet crop, are all half-yearly crops whereas sugar-cane takes 12 to 14 months to mature. The difference in the crop period and the considerably higher investment and working capital required for sugar-cane deterred farmers from venturing on its cultivation. The refinery, keen to secure regular supplies, introduced several measures to overcome farmers' resistance : it offered to buy the full cane crop grown on an area under contract at a price per ton fixed in advance; it allowed suppliers credit facilities for the purchase of fertiliser and gave cutting advances, all at 6 per cent interest per year instead of 12 per cent per year, the ruling rate in the area; it provided extensive agricultural advisory services and operated experimental sugar-cane farms where cultivators could get advice on the problems involved in growing sugar-cane.

The first sugar-cane planted on Wangala lands was grown by a shrewd absentee landlord, who lived in the nearby town. He was one of a number of urban speculators who had bought newly irrigated land, seeking a stake in the growing rural prosperity. When irrigation reached the villages some of the farmers were prepared to sell part of their land simply because land prices had practically doubled overnight. This appeared an attractive windfall profit to them. Little did they realise at the time that in years to come they would have to pay considerably higher prices if and when they wanted to repurchase their wet lands. By 1955 the price differential between dry and wet land was one to three; one acre of wet land sold for about Rs. 1,200.

These early land sales to outsiders from the town proved in the long run economically disadvantageous for those who did sell land. Yet for Wangala as a whole the enterprising urbanites served a useful function by inaugurating the cultivation of sugar-cane in the village. Two years later one Wangala farmer imitated the example and planted sugar-cane. He was then a young and enterprising man who had some ready cash, accumulated from sericulture. By 1955 he was one of the wealthiest farmers in Wangala. His successful venture led many other farmers to follow suit. In 1955 about 35 per cent of the 352 acres wet land owned by Wangala farmers was under sugar-cane. They would have preferred to cultivate more of it but failed to secure more contracted acres. They faced the monopsonistic position of the sugar factory; there were no other sales outlets except to process their cane into jaggery, which at current prices was not an attractive proposition. By the end of the 1940s the refinery had secured sufficient interest among surrounding villages to ensure adequate supplies to satisfy its crushing capacity. It then adopted a policy of distributing contracts over as many farm units as possible by offering each a maximum of two acres. This in turn encouraged joint families to partition their estates – in some cases this was a purely fictitious arrangement – so as to qualify for more contracts; this gave a further impetus to the decline of joint families in Wangala. In 1955 only 10 per cent of the total 192 households in Wangala contained more than the members of the elementary family and an occasional grandparent. The new opportunities to earn cash had induced young men to seek independence from the parental productive unit; they wanted to be able to work and save money for new equipment or such items as watches and bicycles, or to buy jewellery and costly saris for their wives.

The arrangement existing between the sugar refinery and its suppliers sheltered cane farmers from the hazards of operating in the wider economy. It enabled them to concentrate on cultivating their fields without having to worry about demand and prices for the crops they were producing. Even the twelve Wangala men who in 1955 were employed as farmhands on a large cane plantation, which the Mandya refinery had established on Wangala lands, were still predominantly farmers. Seven of them, who were Peasants and had land of their own, always tried to fit in their working time on the plantation so as to be able to cultivate their own holdings. Though for most of them their wages were higher than the cash income derived from their own land, they all regarded wage-earning as a means to make their own farming a viable enterprise, rather than as a line of future activity.

The increased productivity of wet land enabled farmers to grow cash crops and raised the level of their incomes at one stroke. Yet Wangala's remained a discrete and wholly agricultural economy. Wangala Peasants still needed the same services from their Functionaries. Accordingly, when the indigenous Blacksmith desired to sever his hereditary bonds with Peasant households, he was compelled to provide a substitute before the *panchayat* agreed to release him from his obligations. The traditional system of hereditary relationships between Wangala Peasants and their Functionaries, which involved fixed rewards in kind, still existed in 1955 side by side with the new cash economy. Similarly, the hereditary patron–client relationship between Peasant and A.K. households also persisted. Peasant farmers needed more labour for growing their cash crops – for instance the average labour requirement per acre of sugar-cane cultivated in 1955 was 178 men days and 30 women days; by contrast, the respective figures for jowar, one of the traditional dry land crops, were no more than 13 men and 12 women days. This additional labour could quite easily be secured from within the village. *Ryots* themselves worked harder and they also employed their Peasant debtors and their A.K. clients for more days per year for which they paid them a daily wage in cash. The introduction of more labour-consuming cash crops in Wangala therefore reinforced the traditional hereditary relationships which had existed between Peasant households and their A.K. dependents. In turn this reaffirmed the traditional social and ritual differentiation between Peasants and A.K.s. Consequently, none of the All-India anti-Untouchability policies and legislation had any impact in Wangala. This was highlighted in the drama incident which happened during my stay in the village.

The A.K.s were incited by a Mandya A.K. Congress Party politician to make their actor-king sit on a throne as part of their annual drama performance. This infringed the laws which govern the relationship between castes and A.K.s, as no A.K. may sit on a chair while his caste audience squats on the floor. The Peasant elders were incensed when they heard of their A.K.s' 'outrageous' intentions. They called a formal *panchayat* meeting to which the heads of all caste households in the village were invited. There a unanimous decision was taken to enforce a lock-out against all village A.K. client and daily labour. Since the incident occurred during a slack period in the agricultural year the lock-out was not immediately effective. The village A.K.s, supported by their urban sponsor, went to a lot of trouble and expense to stage the drama which, unfortunately for them, turned out to be a com-

plete disaster. Wangala Peasants had sent word round neighbouring villages asking castes to boycott the performance. Consequently, the audience consisted only of A.K.s from Wangala
and some neighbouring villages. The small audience made it
difficult for Wangala A.K.s to meet the drama expenses, particularly at a time when the lock-out prevented them from earning
any daily wages by working for Peasant farmers. The lock-out
continued for a few weeks after the performance. Finally, both
Peasant employers and A.K. labourers found the situation
economically untenable. A *panchayat* meeting deliberated the
matter and decided to impose a fine on all A.K. households. The
outside politician had disappeared from the scene and the village
A.K.s found they had no option but to pay the fine and accept
the *status quo ante*. The whole episode amounted to a political
action by economic dependents against their masters and employers. The Peasants however formed a united front against
their rebellious A.K.s and used economic sanctions in order to
reassert the traditional social relationship.

In relations with other castes Peasants usually put up a united
front, whereas intra-caste relations were riddled with tension. In
1955 Peasants were the decisively dominant caste in Wangala in
terms of numbers, wealth, political power and ritual performance
(Srinivas, 1969:10). In all aspects of their socio-political organisation great emphasis was placed on strict hereditary succession:
the *patel* was always succeeded by his eldest son; hereditary elders
of 'major' Peasant lineages composed the *panchayat*. This, at
least, was the way Wangala Peasants perceived their own political
system. Yet in practice it had considerable flexibility. This was
essential in a system in which office was inherited but potential
heirs might not have the qualities to fill a position of political
importance. Moreover, it was also necessary to accommodate
political expression of economic mobility. The hereditary system,
which was still firmly entrenched in Wangala in 1955, took
account of accidents of personality and leadership and economic
mobility in two different ways: first, a temporary division of
political authority could be made to resolve the problem created
by the inadequacy of a particular office holder. This was the case
during my stay in the village. The official headman was a weak
and ineffectual man. By contrast, his younger brother possessed
most of the qualities demanded by the office, and it was he in

fact who acted as headman, carrying out most of the functions the *patel* was generally expected to perform. The villagers referred to him as chairman, using the English word which has become part of local usage. Nevertheless, all villagers, including the chairman and his sons, agreed that the eldest son of the *patel* would become the next headman and he was already then referred to as 'small headman' (*chick patel*). The chairman's son accepted this arrangement without question and displayed no interest in competing for political office with his patrilateral cousin.

New political offices within the traditional system were created only when they were warranted by relative changes in economic status among Wangala Peasants; these offices in turn became hereditary. The concept of the 'major' lineages composing the *panchayat* provided flexibility in the otherwise rigid hereditary principle allocating political offices. The vague formulation of what qualified a lineage to rank as major allowed 'minor' lineages to claim majority status, provided their economic power warranted it. One of the Peasant elders, who in 1955 was one of the wealthiest men in the village, managed to get his lineage recognised as major.

Being an extremely able man himself he became one of the most important *panchayat* members. His opponents in the village talked of the days when the magnate's household was still classified as of 'no lineage', having only recently immigrated into the village, and they pointed to the fact that the magnate's lineage had no part in any of the village rituals. This was certainly so and caused considerable concern to the magnate and some of his friends who were in a similar position.

Ritual status was generally regarded in the village as the criterion of social status. Therefore, Peasants who had become economically dominant used their political influence to try and bring their ritual status into line with their economic position. They were opposed by men who were ritually more important but economically less successful; these men were naturally reluctant to part with their prerogatives in ritual matters.

The opposition between the more recently arrived but economically dominant lineages and the older-established but poorer lineages was thrown into relief by many intra-village disputes. There were within the limits of Wangala's traditional hereditary political system informal and loosely organised groups in mutual opposition to each other. These were the active political units which I referred to as factions, though the villagers themselves used the English term 'parties'. Membership of factions was on the basis of kinship; the units involved were lineages. A whole lineage jointly supported one or other of the factions, or it remained neutral. The hard core of one faction, which I called 'conservative', was made up of the two ritually most important, though poorer, lineages. The other, which I called the 'progressive' faction, was made up of two of the structurally younger but economically dominant lineages. This should not be taken to imply that lineages had uniform economic status; in fact lineages were internally highly differentiated. Nevertheless, for an economically successful Peasant to achieve social and in particular ritual status he had to act through the medium of his lineage. The progressive faction was under the leadership of three of the five magnates in the village in 1955; the magnate referred to above was one of them. These men tried to establish a balance between their economic, political and ritual status.

There were also a number of uncommitted smaller lineages. Two of these tended to side with the conservative faction on ritual matters, but vacillated on political issues according to expediency. These two lineages were economically dominant – they included the two remaining magnates – and by tradition they played an important role in the performance of village rituals.

The progressive faction tried to wedge their way into ritual roles by duplicating some of the village rituals and having their own men officiate there. This duplication of ceremonies created a number of new ritual offices which enabled the progressive faction to acquire ritual status although they did not hold any ritual office by hereditary rights. Their position had not been fully recognised by members of the conservative faction, nor by the neutral lineages, in 1955. Nevertheless, the economic dominance of the progressives added weight to their claim to ritual status.

The insistence on hereditary succession to socio-political office and status in Wangala continued unaffected by the new democratic legislation. The *Mysore Village Panchayat and District Board Act 1952*, a revolutionary piece of legislation, introduced universal adult franchise into village government and substituted, at least in a legal sense, elective for hereditary authority. I attended the first election in Wangala under the new Act. The concepts of majority rule and elected authority were so alien to the villagers that they displayed little interest in the election. Yet, the Revenue Inspector, who acted as Electoral Officer, was obliged to submit to his superiors a list of duly elected *panchayat* members. As a result of these two contradictory influences the election turned out to be nothing less than a farce; randomly mentioned names became the 'elected' representatives. To satisfy legislative provisions two Wangala A.K.s were literally forced to put their thumb print on the election form so as to signify their consent to becoming members of the newly 'elected' village *panchayat.* All Wangala villagers, as well as the Revenue Inspector, realised there and then that the 'new' *panchayat* would be simply a *de jure* body; no one was in any doubt that the traditional *panchayat* composed of hereditary Peasant lineage elders would continue to function and remain the *de facto* village council.

Wangala's social and political system continued to operate along customary lines hardly affected by the economic development which succeeded the introduction of canal irrigation. In my earlier report I argued that Wangala's traditional economic, social and political system had survived because of the unilinear nature of Wangala's economic growth – agriculture remained the dominant economic pursuit of villagers – and because of the flexibilities which operated within the limits of the traditional system. This I contrasted with the much more drastic changes that had taken place in the dry land village I studied.

## DALENA

Dalena remained a dry land enclave in the midst of an irrigated belt; the village land was actually traversed by a canal yet remained completely dry. Across the canal Dalena farmers could see immediately before their eyes the benefits resulting from irrigation and exactly what was involved in growing cash crops. This spurred some of them on to efforts leading to their own economic progress, and encouraged them to participate in the economic growth resulting from irrigation in the region.

As mentioned earlier, before canals were built in 1934, villages in the area around Dalena had largely subsistence economies. Uncertainty of rainfall and poor quality of soil restricted Dalena *ryots* to subsistence cultivation of dry crops on their own lands; small-scale sericulture and sheep-breeding provided the only village sources of cash income. In pre-irrigation days, the economy of Dalena was almost identical with that of Wangala. Irrigation upset the balance of these almost stagnant economies. To Wangala inhabitants irrigation brought one dominant opportunity: they were enabled to grow cash crops. To Dalena farmers irrigation presented no such single outstanding opportunity. Yet Dalena villagers, like Wangala people, referred to the advent of irrigation as the turning point in their history. Alternative economic opportunities which occurred in the new wet land region made dry land farming comparatively less advantageous to Dalena farmers. Consequently, they reached out into the wider economy; the village dry land continued to be cultivated, but mainly by female labour. This allowed men to take up other income-earning opportunities. Since they could not grow cash crops on their own village land, some of them purchased newly irrigated land in neighbouring villages, where they could then grow crops for sale. In 1956 as much as 73 per cent of Dalena's Peasant households owned and cultivated wet lands in the vicinity.

A fair number of Dalena *ryots* came to act regularly as contractors in building the canal network and the accompanying road system. Unlike their counterparts from villages whose land became irrigated, and who then returned to full-time farming, Dalena men provided a much more stable supply of labour for regional needs. Most of Dalena's poorest farmers and landless have worked at one time or other as labourers for contractors or for the Public Works Department directly. Their contact with the Administration made Dalena people realise the importance of education. Accordingly, a few sent their sons to secondary school in Mandya and two of these students subsequently secured jobs in the Mandya Administration. They worked in 1955 in the town's Agricultural Office and transmitted the latest techniques of farming to *ryots* in Dalena.

Dalena's *patel*, one of the village's most enterprising men, was thus encouraged to experiment with the Japanese method of paddy cultivation on wet land he had purchased in a neighbouring village; he succeeded in increasing the yield per acre fourfold and won the prize for the best paddy cultivation in the region in 1954. By contrast, Wangala *ryots*, who cultivated paddy on their own village wet land and had it transplanted by their hereditary dependent labourers whose rewards were fixed, did not manage to implement the more productive method of Japanese paddy cultivation.

As soon as Dalena men began to respond to the new opportunities which arose in the regional economic expansion, each new effort perpetuated the village's economic diversification. Dalena entrepreneurs, having been conditioned to operating in the wider economy, were thus quick to take to black market dealings when rationing and shortages during the war made these very profitable. A number of the wealthiest villagers in 1955 were supposed to have made their fortunes in this way. The black market in paddy and ragi induced Dalena's *patel* to establish a flour mill at a nearby rail junction, which was a roaring business during the war. His younger brother, Kempegowda, was keen also to profit from such enterprise and wanted to open a flour mill and cane-crusher in Dalena itself. To do so power had to be brought to the village. It took Kempegowda years before he managed to get the *panchayat* to agree to contribute two-thirds to the cost of installation while he himself paid the remainder. By the time Kempegowda got his mill and crusher into operation the black market was beginning to disappear. Yet he and the *patel*, as well as other enterprising Dalena men, remained alert to new profitable opportunities.

Dalena developed into a kind of servicing centre for neighbouring irrigated villages. Some Dalena men bought carts and bullocks and transported cane from nearby villages to Mandya's refinery at a daily hiring charge. Others again became cattle traders and/or middlemen in bullock sales.

These diversified activities have taken Dalena men outside the sphere of their own village economy and they established external links, frequently with complete strangers. Many of these ties, however, were fluid and activated only occasionally. At the same time there were a number of Dalena men who had relations with the wider economy more intensive and lasting than those of entrepreneurs and traders. In 1956 altogether twenty-six men (13 per cent of the male working population) went daily from Dalena to work in Mandya; most of them worked as labourers in the sugar factory; others were clerks, orderlies or drivers. Twenty of these commuters were Peasants, five belonged to Functionary castes and only one was an A.K.

Their regular employment took them out of the everyday life of the village and knitted them into town life. Yet the commuters were by no means a homogeneous group. They were differentiated among themselves according to certain principles of social organisation; some of these stemmed from their common residence in the village, such as caste and kinship, whereas others, for instance occupational differentiation, derived from participation in the wider economy. However, the principles upon which a man acted as a member of a group often overlapped. For instance, the common interests of factory workers cut across village caste differentiation when sugar factory workers all came out on strike. On the other hand, in certain social situations caste differentiation operated also in the town and cut across occupational differentiation. The general manager of the refinery belonged to the same caste as most of the labourers from Dalena. Peasants from Dalena soon realised that they could utilise caste loyalties to try and secure jobs in the town.

All Dalena Peasant commuters also held some land in the village, and often also wet land in the vicinity. In order to ensure the successful cultivation of their own lands they took days off work periodically; for instance, for ploughing or harvesting. Every commuter, while pleased to work in the town, wanted to become a rich farmer and regarded his job simply as a means to accumulate money to buy land. This preoccupation with farming prevented them from looking for advancement in their industrial careers. They were thus neither good farmers, because they could not always tend their fields when needed, nor were they good urban workers, because they did not feel committed to employment and often stayed away from work. The contradictory pull of village and town on commuters from Dalena accounted for much of the inconsistency in their behaviour. They wanted to become full-time farmers and at the same time live like townsmen. This inconsistency in their behaviour undermined the village system by subjecting it to the impact of new urban values. At the same time the traditional social organisation was reinforced by the commuters' attempt to translate urban income into social status in the village in terms of customary values.

The multifarious economic changes which had occurred in Dalena as a result of the advent of irrigation in the region were reflected in changes in the village's social and political system. Dalena Peasants used to have the same hereditary relationship with their A.K. dependents that still existed in Wangala, but by 1955 it had completely disappeared in Dalena. Peasants then had ceased to give their A.K. clients any annual rewards. As soon as they entered the wider economy as contractors, owners of wet land outside their own village and so on, they began to regard the hereditary labour relations with their A.K. clients as inefficient and the annual rewards in kind as an unnecessary burden from their point of view. The low labour requirements of Dalena's dry land economy at the time the regional economy began to expand facilitated the radical changes which took place in intra-village labour relations. Dalena employers of labour outside their own village wanted to be free to engage whomsoever they saw fit and have work done according to their own instructions. The establishment of new and purely contractual economic relations with labour outside their own village encouraged and enabled Dalena farmers to introduce innovations in agriculture. By contrast, the rigid labour relations which still persisted in Wangala were the dominant factor in preventing the introduction there of improved methods of cultivating traditional crops.

Dalena Peasant masters severed the hereditary relationship with their A.K. clients because they saw it as an unnecessary economic burden. In extending their economic relations over a wider area, intra-village labour relations became less intense and lost their customary attributes. Instead, competition entered into intra-village economic relations. Dalena A.K.s had no option but to accept the Peasants' decision to discontinue their customary relationships. For them it meant losing the assurance of at least a minimum of subsistence; they were forced to seek income wherever they could. Being A.K.s they were at a disadvantage in the labour market where particularly regional urban employment remained largely the prerogative of the dominant Peasant caste. Only one A.K. from Dalena had by 1955 managed to secure urban employment; he worked as an orderly in the Engineering department at Mandya. His less fortunate fellow A.K.s in the village were envious of his success. They had to try and scrape a living by working as casual labourers in nearby villages. In the mid-1950s, the growing regional economy provided at least some opportunities for Dalena A.K.s to earn some money by casual labour. Yet they had lost the security of a minimum subsistence and had to compete for employment outside their home village.

The disappearance of the economic aspect of the hereditary relationship between Peasants and A.K.s also led to the disappearance of the ritual aspect. Previously, for instance, the A.K. client carried the torch ahead of the funeral procession of his master's household; in 1956 when there was a death in a Peasant household they still sent for the A.K., asking him to perform his customary ritual obligation, but now he no longer heeded their request. On one occasion, when a Peasant came to fetch the A.K. but could not enter the house because this would have polluted him, the A.K. refused to answer the call. Subsequently, he explained to me that he had done so simply because he saw no reason why he should do anything for a Peasant who did nothing for him. In contrast to Wangala, Dalena Peasants could no longer use economic sanctions against their village A.K.s to insist on their ritual subordination : Peasant masters no longer gave their A.K. clients annual rewards, so the A.K.s ceased to perform many of their customary ritual functions.

Dalena's economic diversification and integration into the wider economy thus seriously undermined the persistence of the hereditary principle of social organisation. It affected village political organisation similarly. The broadening of the economic horizon also broadened the villagers' political horizons. Unlike Wangala, where nobody read papers and only few were aware of the wider State system, Dalena men were acutely conscious of, and interested in, discussing wider political issues. Dalena commuters were members of Trade Unions; as factory workers they not only participated in a strike but also became familiar with the principle of elected authority and majority decisions. This facilitated the implementation of the 1952 Mysore village government legislation. The first election under the new Act took place before I moved into Dalena. It resulted in an elected *panchayat* membership :[1] five councillors were hereditary Peasant lineage

[1] In Dalena one A.K. was made to fill the seat reserved on the council for Scheduled Castes. He had no intentions of attending *panchayat* meetings nor would Peasants have allowed him to do so had he attempted to participate. His membership of the elected Dalena council remained fictitious.

elders, the remaining four were not elders but important men in their own right. Three of the four men were magnates, and the fourth was an intelligent and able arbitrator. *Panchayat* members were still thought to represent 'major' lineages in the village; the nine elected members did in fact represent eight lineages, but the individual councillor was no longer necessarily a hereditary lineage elder. In Dalena personal ability and drive rather than the size of the ancestral estate or the number of heirs with whom it must be shared had become the effective determinant of economic status. Accordingly, political office came to be associated with personal qualifications rather than ascribed position.

In Dalena as in Wangala, there were two opposing factions with a floating support oscillating between the two. In Dalena, too, lineage was an important principle of faction organisation, for factions became operative on occasions such as weddings when the ritual unity of the lineage was stressed. Faction differences in Dalena were more rigid than in Wangala. Wangala's progressives were all still full-time farmers just like the conservatives. Whenever there was a drought, or a cattle or crop disease, all villagers were equally affected and they all joined efforts to avert the disaster. By contrast, in Dalena there were far fewer occasions which affected all villagers jointly and thereby served to unite them. Consequently, sectional interests outweighed joint interests. Dalena's progressives were still farmers, but the major part of their income originated from activities carried on outside their own village. The village headman, who was the leader of Dalena's progressives, was an outstanding innovator who ran commercial and industrial businesses. Through their regular contacts with the wider economy, Dalena's progressives had learnt to manipulate the wider political system by calling on caste loyalty or using bribery. By contrast with Wangala, Dalena's progressives did not seek ritual status in the village. Their faction represented a new element in village organisation; a breakaway section which undermined the traditional unity of the village. To the headman the village ceremonies were no longer of great importance; he was much more interested in the wider political and social system, in which his economic interests had come to be vested.

The hereditary principle of social organisation appeared to be compatible only with a closely integrated society, in which economic, political and ritual relations were concentrated within the boundaries of the village. Once the range of these relations was extended beyond the limits of the particular society, the dependence on fellow-villagers diminished and the personal character in the indigenous relationships gave way to an impersonal one. This had happened in Dalena, where participation in the regional economy had increased economic mobility. Dalena's radical economic change, its integration into the regional economy, undermined the very principles on which its society had been organised; the absence of such economic change allowed the hereditary principle to continue largely unchallenged in Wangala.

Fifteen years have passed since my first study in these two South Indian villages. In succeeding chapters I examine the new economic opportunities and the resulting changes that have occurred in the intervening period.

# 4 New Economic Opportunities

ECONOMIC expansion in under-developed rural communities is normally the result of an interaction between external stimulus and internal response. There are few, if any, village economies where economic growth has been internally generated. Usually new opportunities for villagers are either the result of conscious planning by State or other external authorities or they are the by-product of private enterprise activities in the wider economy. Rural residents may face one dominant, or a combination of different, types of new economic opportunity. The whole community or a section thereof may respond positively to some new chance while rejecting or neglecting others for no obvious rational reason discernible by outsiders. It is therefore essential to examine the total range of new opportunities which come within reach of villagers to be able to analyse the regularities, if there are any, in their response.

For the period prior to 1955 I have already outlined how positively Wangala people responded to the introduction of irrigation whereas they seemed to ignore other opportunities such as those offered by the presence of a black market. Dalena villagers did not face just one dominant new chance in the form of irrigation and different people took up different activities: many bought wet land in neighbouring villages, some set up crop processing plants, others became cattle traders or operated in the black market, and again others became wage earners. Here I want to bring the study up-to-date by discussing the further opportunities which have arisen in Mandya District in the intervening years.

The economic expansion of Mandya region, which had started as a result of the introduction of canal irrigation, has continued at an increasing pace. The irrigation network has been further extended: by 1970 120,000 acres were directly irrigated from canals and a further 100,000 are estimated to receive indirect irrigation by diverting water from major canals through narrow channels. Cane has remained the major cash crop grown on wet land. The extension of irrigation has enabled farmers to plant larger acreages with cane. Increased cane output has not been matched by an appropriate growth in crushing capacity in the Mandya region. Since the sugar content of cane quickly deteriorates if it is not processed soon after harvest, there was an increasing demand for more small-scale cane-crushing facilities to convert cane into jaggery, inedible brown sugar, which is readily distilled into alcohol. The demand for these village cane-crushers was boosted by the soaring jaggery prices which followed the extension of prohibition over the whole of Mysore State and other parts of India in the early 1960s.

The authorities realised Mandya District's overall economic potential and consequently it was included in 1962 in the all-India Intensive Agricultural District Programme (I.A.D.P.). 'This programme aims at, among other things, maximisation of production by providing facilities such as supplies of improved seeds, fertilisers, agricultural credit and technical know-how and marketing to all the participating farmers and also at providing opportunities to the officers concerned to get training and experience' (M.S.G., 1967:149).

The growing wealth in the rural hinterland resulting from increased productivity encouraged a faster rate of urban expansion, offering more and more commercial and employment opportunities. Lastly, but also most important for villagers in the area, were the improved schooling facilities provided.

The further opportunities which came within reach of Wangala and Dalena after 1955 fall roughly into four categories: first, expert advice and help in improving the cultivation of customary crops; second, demand for small-scale cane-crushing facilities, boosted by rapidly rising jaggery prices; third, regional expansion with its concomitant opportunities; and fourth, improved education. I discuss these four different types of economic opportunities under the headings : 1) Agricultural Productivity, 2) Cane versus Jaggery, 3) Regional Growth, 4) Education.

## AGRICULTURAL PRODUCTIVITY

I have already discussed the impact of canal irrigation on farming in South India. It increased considerably the productivity of land

and facilitated the growing of cash crops. It raised the level of incomes and the standard of living. Most farmers soon began to appreciate the advantages of having a reasonably reliable source of water for their lands. 'Keeping in view that soil types in the area are largely non-moisture retentive, rainfall only meagre and rate of crops-transpiration losses quite high, irrigation is a very critical factor in raising a good crop in the district' (M.F.A.C., 1970:574).

For those whose lands received irrigation this was a great improvement over their previous dependence on uncertain and scarce rainfall. Canal irrigation has considerably reduced the risk in cultivating crops, but it has not eliminated it altogether. In years such as 1950 and 1953 or again in 1966 when the monsoon failed so completely that the Cauveri river could not supply the Krishnarajasagar dam with sufficient water, the canals provided very little irrigation or ran altogether dry. Such occasions reminded farmers of the great benefits they were deriving from irrigation during the years when their lands received full supplies of water from canals. Moreover, these recurring failures of canal irrigation have been an important consideration in making Peasant farmers prepared to continue their hereditary labour relationships with their village A.K.s (see p. 139). The increase in productivity per acre of irrigated land was reflected in rising wet land prices.

The obvious advantages to be derived from wet land cultivation made not only villagers, but also urbanites from regional towns, keen to purchase irrigated land. The pressures of demand for a limited supply of land coming on to the market resulted in rises of land prices which far exceeded those of general consumer goods prices in the same period. The records of the Sub-Registrar's office, Mandya, where all land sales have to be registered, show that in 1958 4.08 wet acres changed hands in Wangala at an average price of Rs. 1,325 per acre; this price had risen by 1968 to Rs. 6,445 per acre for the 8.61 acres sold in that year, and to Rs. 7,095 for altogether 6.33 acres sold in 1971. Thus Wangala wet land prices increased by about 330 per cent between 1958 and 1971. Significantly in the irrigated villages near Dalena, wet land prices are even higher than in Wangala; in 1971 in Indavalu altogether 2.56 wet acres were sold at an average price of Rs. 8,007 per acre and in Yeleyur

0.17 acre was sold for Rs. 2,000, amounting to a price of Rs. 12,000 per acre. Indavalu and Yeleyur are both villages with land strategically placed along the main Mysore State highway, and even dry land there demands premium prices : in 1971 five different dry plots ranging in size from 0.10 to 0.50 acre were sold in Indavalu at an average price of Rs. 5,000 per acre; in the same year in Yeleyur two plots, one 0.17 acre and another 0.30 acre, were sold at an average price of Rs. 2,100 per acre. It is likely that these small plots of dry land were bought for other than agricultural purposes : probably to put up cane-crushers or cafés or other such business enterprises. In Wangala too dry land prices have risen considerably from an average price per dry acre of Rs. 176 in 1958 to Rs. 985 in 1971, but these sales were for agricultural purposes and therefore reflect the lower productivity of dry as compared with wet land.

Inflation in land prices made investment in land, particularly wet land, a profitable proposition which attracted urban speculators. Such speculative demand gave land prices a further push upwards in a way which the urbanites had anticipated but which impaired the villagers capacity to compete with the wealthier and more knowledgeable townsmen. This trend is illustrated by the pattern of purchases of Wangala factory farm land when it was auctioned in the late 1960s.

The management of the Mandya refinery had come to regard their own plantations as uneconomic enterprises; it was cheaper to purchase cane grown by individual farmers than to grow plantation cane. Consequently, factory farm land began to be auctioned off. By 1970 all Wangala factory farm land had been sold to individual buyers. The bidding at the land auctions was so brisk that prices rocketed to previously unknown heights – one acre of irrigated land sold for up to Rs. 20,889. This made it difficult for many Wangala farmers to acquire some of this land, though they had cherished hopes of being able to do so. No more than 18 per cent of the 170 acres of Wangala factory plantation land was bought by sixteen resident farmers; 59 per cent was purchased by urban buyers and the remainder was acquired by farmers from nearby villages. Urban buyers bought on an average more than three acres each, whereas village farmers bought less than two acres each. The average price per acre paid by urban buyers was about Rs. 3,500; Wangala farmers paid an average of Rs. 6,500 and other villagers Rs. 11,350. This quite considerable difference in the average price paid per acre may be related to the situation and/or fertility of the soil, but it certainly also reflects the fact that townsmen are shrewder buyers at auctions than are villagers.

The average price per acre paid altogether for Wangala plantation land was considerably lower than that raised for factory plantations elsewhere. The refinery report for 1968–9 states that during the year a further 589 acres of land was sold for an aggregate amount of Rs. 4,437,212 (M.S.C., 1969:6). The average of Rs. 7,500 per acre is almost Rs. 2,000 higher than that paid for Wangala plantation land. It is difficult to analyse the reasons for these differences in per acre prices without reliable data on the variation in site and fertility. Productivity of land is certainly an important factor in determining per acre prices, but other factors such as pressure of demand also play a decisive part. These high prices for wet land certainly throw into relief the great demand for irrigated acreage.

In order to meet the rapidly growing demand and increase available wet land supplies, Mysore Engineering Authorities tried to push ahead as fast as they could with the extension of canal irrigation. Wangala benefited considerably from this extension of the canal network which has taken place since 1955. Some of the villagers' dry land became irrigated; furthermore, land that was classified formerly as government waste became wet and consequently cultivable. At the same time part of the village tank land was drained so that it too can now be cultivated. Altogether the total irrigated acreage in Wangala increased by 60 per cent to 830 acres since 1955; the wet acreage owned and cultivated by resident farmers has grown by almost 80 per cent to 630 acres in the same period (see table 1).

The bulk of the 85 acres government waste which have been irrigated has been acquired by Wangala Peasants. This in spite of the land rules which lay down that 50 per cent of the land available for disposal in any village shall be granted to persons belonging to Scheduled Castes and Scheduled Tribes (M.L.G.R., 1969:1057). *The Mysore Land Grant Rules, 1969* set out the government rates for selling this land to Scheduled Castes: the price of one wet hectare must be less than Rs. 2,500 but more than Rs. 500. Thus the maximum price of Rs. 1,000 for one wet

TABLE 1

OWNERSHIP AND TYPE OF WANGALA VILLAGE LANDS

| | Villagers | | | | Outsiders | | | | Government | | | | Total | | | |
|---|---|---|---|---|---|---|---|---|---|---|---|---|---|---|---|---|
| | 1955 | | 1970 | | 1955 | | 1970 | | 1955 | | 1970 | | 1955 | | 1970 | |
| | Acres | % | Acres | % | Acres | % | Acres | % | Acres | % | Acres | % | Acres | % | Acres | % |
| Irrigated | 352 | 68 | 630 | 76 | 165 | 32 | 200 | 24 | — | — | — | — | 517 | 100 | 830 | 100 |
| Dry | 249 | 60 | 180 | 78 | 166 | 40 | 50 | 22 | — | — | — | — | 415 | 100 | 230 | 100 |
| Waste for grazing | — | — | — | — | — | — | — | — | 542 | 100 | 457 | 100 | 542 | 100 | 457 | 100 |
| House sites, paths, etc. | 42 | 65 | 42 | 65 | — | — | — | — | 23 | 35 | 23 | 35 | 65 | 100 | 65 | 100 |
| Tanks and ponds | — | — | — | — | — | — | — | — | 118 | 100 | 75 | 100 | 118 | 100 | 75 | 100 |
| Total | 643 | 39 | 852 | 52 | 331 | 20 | 250 | 15 | 683 | 41 | 555 | 33 | 1657 | 100 | 1657 | 100 |

*Source:* Village land records.

acre government land is well below the market rate of Rs. 7,095. As we shall see, Wangala A.K.s had great difficulties in raising sufficient finance to enable them to buy even this reasonably priced government wet land. Consequently, the total A.K. landholding in Wangala has increased by only 11 per cent to 48 acres, of which only 28 acres are irrigated. This land has to suffice for all 44 Wangala A.K. households. Peasant-owned land, on the other hand, has increased by 37 per cent to 732 acres, of which 590 acres are irrigated (see table 2). The average wet land holding per A.K. household is 0.60 acre and per Peasant household 2.50 acres. Wangala Peasants have thus gained considerably from the extension of the canal network while A.K.s have hardly benefited at all. The proportion of Wangala wet land owned by outsiders has slightly decreased from 32 per cent to 24 per cent. However, here it must be remembered that in 1955 almost three-quarters of the 165 wet acres externally owned was land owned and worked by the Mandya refinery; by contrast in 1970 all of the 200 wet acres were owned by various different individuals residing outside the village but farming in Wangala. Almost 60 per cent of this externally owned land is held by townsfolk, mostly living in Mandya. The remaining 80 wet acres, i.e. 40 per cent, are owned and cultivated by Peasant farmers residing in nearby villages.

Dalena Peasants have also increased their wet acreage; since 1956 they have bought approximately 100 wet acres in neighbouring villages. In these land purchases they had to compete with men from Mandya who are keen to invest in wet land, as well as with farmers from other surrounding villages. As already mentioned, wet land prices in the vicinity of Dalena are higher than in Wangala because Dalena lies on the fringe of the irrigated belt, while Wangala is situated right in the centre. The prohibitive wet land prices make it impossible for Dalena A.K.s even to consider buying such land. The number of Dalena A.K. households has increased by 40 per cent to 21 since 1956; while their landholding has decreased by one acre to only 15 dry acres. During the same period Peasant landholding has altogether increased by about 15 per cent to 815 acres, of which about 30 per cent is wet land (see table 3).

Village A.K.s appear not to have been able to take advantage to any sizeable extent of irrigation. Dalena Peasant farmers are bravely struggling to try and participate in wet crop cultivation

TABLE 2

WANGALA POPULATION AND LANDHOLDING BY CASTE

| Caste | Households | | | | Landholding* | | | |
|---|---|---|---|---|---|---|---|---|
| | 1955† | | 1970‡ | | 1955† | | 1970§ | |
| | No. | % | No. | % | Acre | % | Acre | % |
| Lingayat Priest (Saivite) | 3 | 2 | 3 | 1 | 9 | 1 | 10 | 1 |
| Peasant | 128 | 66 | 228 | 68 | 532 | 89 | 732 | 92 |
| Functionary (Resident) | 19 | 10 | 25 | 7 | 15 | 3 | 20 | 2 |
| Functionary (Migrant) | 0 | 0 | 11 | 4 | 0 | 0 | 0 | 0 |
| Muslim | 2 | 1 | 2 | — | 2 | — | 0 | 0 |
| A.K. | 28 | 15 | 44 | 13 | 43 | 7 | 48 | 5 |
| Vodda | 7 | 3 | 23 | 7 | 0 | 0 | 0 | 0 |
| Miscellaneous | 5 | 3 | 2 | — | 0 | 0 | 0 | 0 |
| Total | 192 | 100 | 338 | 100 | 601 | 100 | 810 | 100 |
| Total population | 958 | 100 | 1603 | 100 | | | | |

* Totals do not include land in neighbouring villages owned by Wangala residents.

Source: † Own census 1955.
‡ Schönherr, 1972:35.
§ Village land records.

TABLE 3

DALENA POPULATION AND LANDHOLDING BY CASTE

| | Households | | | | Landholding* | | | |
| | 1955† | | 1970‡ | | 1956† | | 1970§ | |
| Caste | No. | % | No. | % | Acre | % | Acre | % |
|---|---|---|---|---|---|---|---|---|
| Lingayat Priest (Saivite) | 1 | | 0 | 0 | 0 | 0 | 0 | 0 |
| Peasant | 122 | 80 | 196 | 83 | 715 | 98 | 815 | 98 |
| Functionary (Resident) | 11 | 7 | 7 | 3 | 4 | — | 5 | — |
| Functionary (Migrant) | 4 | 2 | 8 | 4 | 0 | 0 | 0 | 0 |
| A.K. | 15 | 10 | 21 | 9 | 16 | 2 | 15 | 2 |
| Vodda | 0 | 0 | 3 | 1 | 0 | 0 | 0 | 0 |
| Total | 153 | 100 | 235 | 100 | 735 | 100 | 835 | 100 |
| Total population | 707 | 100 | 1072 | 100 | | | | |

* Totals include land Dalena farmers own outside their village.

*Source:* † Own census.
‡ Schönherr, 1972:35.
§ Estimate (see p. 25).

in spite of the fact that all of their own village land is still dry. A few Dalena men have purchased costly diesel pump sets to try and irrigate their own land in this fashion. In spite of all their efforts Dalena villagers have not been able to add sufficient land to their property to counterbalance the increase in population: the average landholding per resident Dalena household was 4.90 acres in 1956, of which 17 per cent was wet land; by 1970 it had fallen by 26 per cent to 3.70 acres, of which 25 per cent is wet land. Wangala farmers have been much more fortunate in this respect; the number of resident households has increased by 57 per cent to 302 since 1955 : in the same period total wet landholding in Wangala has almost doubled. Consequently, the average Wangala wet landholding by resident households has increased from 1.70 to 2.00 acres. In addition, Wangala Peasant farmers probably own at least another 50 wet acres in neighbouring villages. This increases the average wet landholding per resident household to about 2.25 acres. Peasant farmers in Wangala and the other irrigated villages in the region were thus obviously in the best position to benefit from the network of canals.

Irrigation attracted outsiders to acquire land and try and cultivate it in the most profitable way. The arrival of these outsiders in Wangala helped to introduce up-to-date cultivation techniques, while at the same time strengthening the influence and jurisdiction of Wangala's traditional hereditary *panchayat*.

The case of Ramakrishna from Mandya illustrates this point. He purchased three acres of Wangala wet lands in 1963 from an ex-serviceman. Prior to 1958 the Government had allocated 200 acres of Wangala lands to ex-servicemen, many of whom never even attempted to cultivate it. Ramakrishna proudly relates that he was the first farmer in Wangala ever to use a tractor to plough virgin land. He hired it from an Agricultural Research and Training station about 6 miles north-west of Mandya and paid Rs. 12 per acre. Nowadays, a number of Wangala farmers use tractors for ploughing and bulldozers for levelling their lands; about 60 acres have been levelled by bulldozers which can be hired from the Mandya Community Development Block office at a cost of Rs. 62 per hour.[1] The charge for hiring a tractor from

---

[1] The bulldozers thus hired have 90 h.p.

this office is Rs. 25 per acre.[1] There are also private owners of bulldozers and tractors in the area, who let their machines for a charge considerably higher than that asked by the official agency. A wealthy Peasant farmer living near Wangala charges as much as Rs. 40 per acre for the use of his tractor. This has given one Wangala progressive magnate the idea of buying a tractor and letting it to fellow villagers. He was still toying with the idea when I left South India in 1970.

Ramakrishna, the outsider, has thus been an important innovator in Wangala agriculture. He planted two acres of cane and one acre of paddy. He bragged that his one acre of paddy produces two crops per year : the more productive *hain* crop sown in July yields about 30 *pallas* and the less productive *kar* crop yields roughly 15 *pallas*. These yields are considerably higher than those obtained by Wangala resident farmers. Ramakrishna explained that this was due to the fact that he employed the most up-to-date cultivation techniques recommended by agricultural officers; he plants the recommended variety of seeds; he applies fertiliser to his nursery as well as to his paddy fields; his paddy is transplanted according to the Japanese method of cultivation and is regularly weeded. He employs migrant coolie labourers, some of whom reside in Wangala; others he recruits himself in Mandya. He never employs any Wangala resident A.K. because, as he says, they are too set in their ways and routine of working. 'It is practically impossible to tell any of them a new way of doing a task he is used to perform in customary fashion – they will never learn !' By contrast, he claimed that the migrant labourers quickly pick up new methods and apply them efficiently, thereby reducing costs of labour. To make his point he referred to the many Wangala farmers who, having realised the local A.K.s' resistance to changed cultivation methods, are now also employing migrant labourers.

Ramakrishna is a Peasant like the majority of Wangala's population; he therefore fits in reasonably well with village customs. He used to be a refinery employee, but has recently retired. He comes regularly to Wangala on his bicycle whenever he wants to keep an eye on his crops. Many a time he finds that water that should have irrigated his own fields has been diverted to neigh-

---

[1] The tractors hired have either 20 h.p. and 37 h.p. and take two to three hours to plough one acre.

bouring lands. On such occasions he immediately contacts some of the hereditary elders of major lineages; they hold a meeting at which his complaint is discussed and the defendant either warned not to be so greedy again or ordered to pay compensation to Ramakrishna. The latter related an incident when one Wangala Peasant who owned land neighbouring his own accused him of having diverted water from the plaintiff's land to his own. He argued his innocence in front of the lineage elders, but they did not believe him and instead accepted the plaintiff's word. Ramakrishna was fined Rs. 12, Rs. 10 of which he paid over to the plaintiff and the remainder to the *panchayat* fund. He explained that he had considered taking the case to the Mandya courts but had decided that this would not be a wise move on his part. In the longer term he thought it was better to abide by village customs and place himself under *panchayat* jurisdiction rather than involve external authorities in intra-village matters. By subjecting himself to the jurisdiction of Wangala's hereditary lineage elders he added new support to this traditional body of men and reaffirmed their authority and power in the village.

While irrigation thus buttressed Wangala's traditional political system, it also subjected the village to many novel influences. Shortly after I left South India in 1956 Dalena and Wangala were included in the Mandya Community Development Block. This meant that a *gramasevak* or village level worker began to visit villagers regularly once or twice a month. The *gramasevak*'s main job is to promote agricultural production by advising farmers on improved methods of cultivation and encouraging them to adopt more efficient ways of farming. Wangala farmers have adopted some of the improved strains of paddy and ragi seeds, which the *gramasevak* recommended to them some years ago. Wangala's chairman did not seem altogether very impressed with the *gramasevak*'s activities. He said disparagingly : 'All the *gramasevak* has done for us is to show us better seeds; his infrequent visits are now more social calls than to offer advice and help!' This is how the work of Community Development appears to a farmer in one of the villages in the all-India Intensive Agricultural District Programme. Villagers do not view the State's varied efforts to help farmers as part of a co-ordinated scheme, but regard different agencies as independent and competing entities. They praise one and criticise the other, depending on what advantage each offers. The *gramasevak*'s usefulness has been overtaken, at least in the eyes of Wangala farmers, by that of the village co-operatives. The co-operative movement in Mandya district received a boost when the region became included in the Intensive Agricultural District Programme at the beginning of 1962.

In each of the States composing the Union of India one district has been selected for this programme, usually the district with the highest economic potential. 'The programme on the whole aimed at immediate gain in agricultural production by (i) providing all inputs of production; (ii) demonstrating the most effective ways of increasing food production by the application of technical know-how' (B.E.S., 1970:62). A unique feature of this scheme is that all the production requisites such as seeds, fertilisers, chemicals and improved implements are made available through a single agency, namely the service co-operative institutions (M.S.G., 1967:143).

The Mandya District Co-operative Central Bank Limited started functioning in October 1953 in Mandya town to serve as a banking centre for all affiliated co-operative institutions in the district. The promotion of economic welfare of the cultivating class, by providing them with prompt finance through service co-operatives, is also one of its objectives. In the economic development of the Mandya district the co-operative movement has played an important part. By the end of 1965 all the 1,339 villages in the district had been covered by co-operative institutions. During 1965–6, there were 394 primary agricultural credit societies in Mandya district covering 98 per cent of the villages. So far as co-operatives are concerned, an important feature of the Intensive Agricultural District Programme is the quick disposal of loan applications of members and the timely supply of fertilisers and other necessary materials for increasing agricultural production (M.S.G., 1967:201).

Farmers must be shareholders in their local co-operative before they qualify for a loan. The usual price of one share is Rs. 25, and the amount of the loan is directly related to the number of shares. Since the 'introduction of crop loan system, the cultivators are getting their credit requirements according to the scale of finance fixed for each crop. Up to Rs. 1,000 loans are issued on personal surety basis and over and above this limit, on the mortgage of landed property. Normally the time lag between making an application and receiving the loan ranges from 15 to 45 days' (M.F.A.C., 1970:583). Co-operative credit is enabling farmers to buy seeds and fertiliser without worrying about how to finance these purchases until their crops mature. However, co-operative credit, like so many other types of external aid offered to cultivators, helps the wealthiest most and the poorest least. Many smallholders do not even have sufficient money to buy a single share in their village co-operative society. The poorer farmers who manage to become shareholders are limited in the amount they can borrow by the small number of shares they own and by the size of their landholding. In Mandya District 'while there was a general increase in the amount of credit taken in 1967–68 compared to the preceding year for almost all categories of farms, credit availed of by very small farmers from co-operatives shrank from Rs. 93 to Rs. 52 per hectare. This development called for special consideration to the problem of weaker sections of the farm population' (M.F.A.C., 1970:587).

State agencies as a whole and the Package Programme in particular have devoted considerable amounts of money and effort to promote agricultural development in Mandya District. During the year 1970–1 public expenditure on agricultural development per head in Mandya District was more than three times that in the neighbouring Mysore District: in the former it was Rs. 1.60 while in the latter only Rs. 0.50.[1]

As I have outlined here villagers in Mandya District have been very fortunate in the last decade. They have been offered many new facilities to help them improve their agricultural output: the network of canals has been extended to provide irrigation for a larger acreage; a *gramasevak* visited them regularly and advised them on new improved seeds and the most efficient application of fertiliser; they can hire bulldozers and tractors from the Community Development Block Office at well below market rates, and they can obtain working capital in the form of loans from their village co-operatives.

[1] Personal communication from the Director of Agriculture, Mysore, dated 29.12.1971. I am trying to collect the necessary data to enable me to make a cost-benefit analysis of the Package Programme in Mandya district.

## CANE VERSUS JAGGERY

Cane growers in South India have the option of supplying their cane to a refinery where it is purified into white sugar or of processing it into jaggery for sale as brown sugar. Except for the rare occasion described in my earlier study (1962:56), it used to be much more profitable for cane-growers to supply their cane to refineries. One ton of sugar-cane yields roughly one quintal (100 kgs) of jaggery and costs about Rs. 12 to process. Unless the price of one quintal of jaggery exceeds that of one ton of cane by more than Rs. 12 it is less profitable for growers to process their cane into jaggery than to supply it to their local refinery. The refinery had for years already pursued a policy whereby it tried to distribute its cane-growing contracts over as many farmers as possible. As long as contracts were made in terms of acreage, it was possible for growers to sell more or less cane than was produced on the contracted acreage. This enabled them, within limits, to arrange their cane sales to their own best advantage. The refinery management could therefore never be sure what supplies it could expect. This was an untenable situation and in 1957 contracts were changed from an acreage to a tonnage basis. This prevented growers from overfulfilling their contracts, but did not stop them from undersupplying as they still could, if they so wished, plead failure of their crop.

The increasing wet acreage in the Mandya region resulted in a growing extension of cane cultivation which, however, was not matched by an increased crushing capacity. The Mandya Sugar Factory can crush a maximum per year of about 500,000 tons, which is the total product of approximately 11,000 acres. In Mandya *taluk* alone, however, there were 15,417 acres under cane in 1964–5 (M.S.G., 1967:129). Thus the factory could not possibly process all the cane grown in the region. The result was a growing demand for the services of village cane-crushers to produce jaggery. In turn this encouraged village entrepreneurs to set up such cane processing facilities.

Beregowda, one of Wangala's progressive magnates of earlier days, had been taking his own cane, over and above what he could sell to the refinery, to his friend's cane-crusher in a village about five miles away, where it was processed. He saw there how much money could be made out of operating a cane-crusher with attached rice mill, and considered starting such a venture in his home village. In spite of discouragement from his local friends he decided to go ahead. He complains that he received no help from anyone in Wangala and had to organise everything himself : he had to arrange for electricity to be brought to the village; he had to purchase machinery and engage a contractor in Mandya to come to Wangala to build the shelter for his crusher and mill and to instal it all. To bring electricity to Wangala cost Beregowda Rs. 2,000; for the machinery and shelter he had to pay Rs. 25,000; moreover, he spent Rs. 500 on getting a licence and another Rs. 500 on miscellaneous expenses. The total expenditure for his cane-crusher and flour mill thus amounted to Rs. 28,000. He had saved Rs. 8,000 and the rest he borrowed from money-lenders in other villages at 12 per cent interest per year. In 1960 Beregowda was ready to start operating his new enterprise. The Minister for Power and Electricity was invited for the occasion and with due ceremony opened the new venture and inaugurated electricity in Wangala. As soon as Beregowda had arranged for power supplies to reach the village, the *panchayat* seemed quite pleased to be able to share in the new facility by having street lights set up in the caste quarters. Subsequently, some Peasants decided to instal electricity in their own homes. This last development has had a considerable impact on social life in Wangala; villagers sit up later and school children can do their homework at night, and so on. Beregowda's business innovation thus had much more far-reaching effects on life in Wangala than he himself or any of his fellow villagers anticipated.

The first months of operating the new enterprise were quite profitable for Beregowda and proved to him and some of his friends that he had been right to go ahead with it. He had been shrewd enough to woo away one of the experienced labourers who worked at the cane-crusher which had inspired him to start his own. By offering the man a higher wage than he had been getting he managed to make him come to Wangala and operate the new crusher there. Thus he avoided many of the teething troubles the new enterprise would have otherwise suffered. The crusher allowed cane-growers from the village and the vicinity to have their cane processed locally without having to incur transport costs in carting their cane elsewhere. Beregowda's cane-crusher can process a maximum of nine tons a day. During the first year of operation it worked almost continuously. In 1960 Wangala growers cultivated 282 acres of cane which at an average output of 45 tons per acre yielded 12,690 tons of cane. Of this no more than 4,280 tons was grown under contract to the refinery; much of the remainder was processed by Beregowda. Wholesalers touring the area soon heard of the new crusher and it was not long before lorries began to visit his plant.

TABLE 4

JAGGERY PRICES AND ACREAGE SOWN UNDER PADDY AND CANE IN WANGALA FROM 1960 TO 1969

|  | *Jaggery**<br>*price per 100 kgs*<br>*Rs.* | *Sugar-cane†*<br>*acres* | *Paddy†*<br>*acres* |
|---|---|---|---|
| 1960 | 59.70 | 282 | 386 |
| 1961 | 55.63 | ? | ? |
| 1962 | 58.99 | ? | ? |
| 1963 | 104.96 | 291 | 501 |
| 1964 | 107.88 | 451 | 372 |
| 1965 | 70.83 | 364 | 265 |
| 1966 | 84.87 | 90‡ | 277 |
| 1967 | 152.17 | 305 | 391 |
| 1968 | 185.52 | 354 | 410 |
| 1969 | 74.35 | ? | ? |

*Source:* * Chief Marketing Department, Bangalore (personal communication).
† Village Crop Records.
‡ Irrigation failed in 1966; this accounts for the exceptionally small cane acreage.

? Data not available.

In 1963, about two years after Wangala's first cane-crusher had been opened, jaggery prices soared to unprecedented heights: from Rs. 58.99 the price increased to Rs. 104.96 per quintal of jaggery (see table 4). This big price jump reflected the extension of prohibition throughout the whole of Mysore State in 1962, as well as the stricter enforcement of the prohibition of liquor sales throughout the rest of India. Jaggery lends itself well to illegal distilling and became a highly-desired and highly-priced commodity in people's attempts to circumvent the law. Intermediaries in these illicit transactions toured sugar-cane growing areas and offered premium prices for jaggery. Wangala farmers responded by extending their acreage under cane : in 1963 they had planted altogether 291 acres of cane; the following year they extended the acreage by over half to 451 acres. They not only planted larger areas under cane but they also underfulfilled their contracts with the factory. Jaggery prices remained much more attractive than those of sugar-cane for a number of years; in 1963 and 1964 it was almost twice as remunerative for farmers to process their cane into jaggery and sell it as such than to supply it directly to the refinery.

The greater comparative advantage which jaggery offered over cane sales had important consequences for the Mandya refinery. In 1966 it incurred a deficit before tax of Rs. 2,144.00; this was the first time since 1954 that the factory operated 'in the red'. The losses incurred in 1951 and 1954 were solely due to failures in canal irrigation, whereas the more recent deficit was largely the result of competition from jaggery. The refinery closed down altogether in 1967; drought conditions in the previous year adversely affected cane cultivation. Farmers preferred to sell the little cane they could produce at premium prices in the form of jaggery rather than supply it to the refinery. Though the refinery re-opened in 1968, it continued to make losses. Table 5 shows a clear inverse relationship between the price of jaggery and the quantity of cane purchased by Mandya refinery. Its 36th Annual Report for 1968–9 states explicitly that production of sugar fell short of estimate by nearly 15,000 tons, due to the factory having been deprived of a third of the contracted cane, which was diverted for manufacture of jaggery in the early part of the year (M.S.C., 1969:4). The factory had actually to shut down from July 1968 to January 1969 for want of cane. In 1967 Wangala farmers had contracted to supply 5,305 tons to the refinery, of which they delivered no more than 2,782, i.e. about 50 per cent; the following year they contracted to supply 6,125 tons, of which they delivered 5,303 tons, i.e. about 80 per cent.

The refinery's losses were the village cane-crushers' gains. High jaggery prices increased the demand for village cane processing facilities. The number of power-driven cane-crushers in Mysore

State increased from 2,830 in 1961 to 6,342 in 1966 (B.E.S., 1969:37). Dalena's enterprising headman established a cane-crusher and a flour mill at a strategic road junction along the major Mysore highway. At the same time his younger brother decided to move his machinery from Dalena to a site on the main road. Similarly, Wangala farmers became keen to participate in the jaggery boom. This encouraged other village Peasants to emulate Beregowda's example. By 1965 three more crushers had been established in Wangala and their number further increased to eight by 1969. Unfortunately, for some of these new Peasant entrepreneurs, by that time the Mysore Government had decided to remove prohibition once more from most parts of the State. These legislative steps resulted almost immediately in a severe fall

TABLE 5

CANE VERSUS JAGGERY

| | Price | | Mandya refinery | |
| | Sugar cane*<br>Rs. per ton | Jaggery†<br>Rs. per 100 kgs | Quantity of*<br>Sugar cane<br>Processed tons | Net profit‡<br>before tax<br>Rs. (100,000) |
|---|---|---|---|---|
| 1960 | 48.60 | 59.70 | 316,100 | 2,710 |
| 1961 | 46.60 | 55.63 | 400,812 | 2,007 |
| 1962 | 44.10 | 58.99 | 381,053 | 1,210 |
| 1963 | 45.00 | 104.96 | 255,760 | 157 |
| 1964 | 51.40 | 107.88 | 198,087 | 1,268 |
| 1965 | 56.80 | 70.83 | 368,050 | 668 |
| 1966 | 53.60 | 84.87 | 310,102 | —2,144 |
| 1967 | 59.60 | 152.17 | —§ | —3,595 |
| 1968 | 110.00 | 185.52 | 38,963 | —3,227 |
| 1969 | 100.00 | 74.35 | 242,261 | 6,519 |
| 1970 | 80.00** | 55.00** | ? | ? |

*Source:* * M.S.C. 1969:35.
     † Chief Marketing Department, Bangalore (personal communication).
     ‡ M.S.C. 1969:34.
     § Irrigation failed in 1966 and the refinery closed down the following year.
   ** Village informants.
    ? Data not available.

in jaggery prices. Consequently, selling cane to the refinery instead of processing it into jaggery has again become comparatively more attractive to cane-growers in the Mandya region. Farmers, who underfulfilled their contracts with the refinery while jaggery prices were high, are once more struggling to secure contracts. The cane and jaggery prices ruling during 1969 and 1970 (see table 5) induced farmers to try and keep down to a minimum the cane they sell in the form of jaggery. This in turn is responsible for village cane-crushers standing idle for many months in the year. In many instances this means an outright loss to owners. The honeymoon with cane-crushers is over now, at least for the time being: for many a local entrepreneur it was over almost before it started.

## REGIONAL DEVELOPMENT

The extension of canal irrigation, the Package Programme and the jaggery price boom in Mandya district have injected further growth into an already expanding economy. The overall regional development is reflected in a rapid urban expansion. The urban population of Mandya district increased by 22 per cent between 1951 and 1961 and by as much as 59 per cent in the last decade, while the rural population increase has been no more than 20 per cent in the earlier and 24 per cent in the later period. Mandya town had a population of 6,000 in 1931, 11,000 in 1941, 21,000 in 1951, 33,000 in 1961 and about 55,000 in 1971. The town has now more than nine times the population it had forty years ago.

During my earlier stay in South India the refinery constituted the only large-scale industrial firm in Mandya. It is still the outstanding landmark in Mandya town and the single biggest employer: it now has 2,200 workers on its payroll. Since then a number of other factories have been started in the area. The extension of irrigation and the resulting increase in sugar-cane output necessitated the establishment of another refinery. Accordingly, one was started in 1956 at Pandavapura, which is suitably situated about fourteen miles from Mandya on the main Bangalore to Mysore railway. The Pandavapura refinery is a co-operative enterprise. It is managed by a Board of Directors with an elected chairman. Twelve of the fifteen Board members are elected and the remaining three are nominated by Government and the Industrial Finance Corporation. A capital of Rs. 3,350,000 has been invested in the factory, out of which an amount of Rs. 1,770,600 was contributed by the cane-growers and another Rs. 1,500,000 by the State Government. The rest of the capital was borrowed from co-operative institutions and patrons (M.S.G., 1967:165). The Pandavapura refinery is considerably smaller than its Mandya counterpart : its employees number only 620 and its daily crushing capacity is 800 tons as compared with Mandya's 2,000 tons. It ;pays slightly higher prices for cane than are offered at Mandya and does not insist on processing only cane grown under contract. In fact a few Wangala cane-growers take some of their cane to Pandavapura, in spite of the twenty-mile distance and consequently greater cost of transport involved.

Another new factory, the Mysore Acetate and Chemicals Co., was in 1963 incorporated as a public company under the Companies Act. This factory is situated near the refinery, for its major raw material is one of the by-products of processing cane. The objects of the company are to manufacture, buy, sell, import from or export to any part of the world, cellulose, triacetate, and so on, as well as all kinds of materials used in the film, plastic and rayon industries, and to manufacture all kinds of chemicals and alkalis with their derivatives and by-products (M.S.G., 1967:172). The enterprise has thus a very wide scope and consequently great promise of continued expansion and success.

Another by-product of sugar production led to the establishment of the Mandya National Paper Mills in 1962. Bagasse, the fibrous residue resulting from the crushing of sugar-cane, is successfully used there as raw material for paper-making. This seems a remarkable success in view of the many attempts that have been made to produce from bagasse a fibre suitable for paper-making. Hitherto the processes had been too costly or did not produce an entirely satisfactory paper (*Encyclopaedia Britannica*, 1961 : II/918). The paper mill is situated near the Krishnarajasagar dam where adequate land, water, housing and community facilities are available.

The mineral poverty of Mandya district necessitates industrial development which utilises the available agricultural raw material.

Sugar-cane is one and paddy another. The production of paddy in the district has been increasing steadily year by year : 104,893 tons of rice were produced in 1960–1, 121,684 tons in 1962–3 and 131,106 tons in 1964–5 (M.S.G., 1967:173). These figures indicate the importance of paddy in the district's economy. Mandya region in fact is one of the procurement areas in India where the farmers with larger paddy holdings are compelled to sell to the authorities 450 lb. paddy per acre paddy grown at a fixed price which is well below the open market rate. In 1969 12,000 tons of paddy was the levy demanded for Mandya district, of which all but 300 tons was realised. The Central Authorities arrange for redistribution of these procured quantities of paddy to food deficient areas in India.

Rice milling is the most widespread of all small industries in Mandya district. The conversion rate from paddy to rice is thus an important factor to be considered in the region. The Ford Foundation deputed a team of experts to investigate rice milling; the team suggested that there is ample scope for obtaining increased output of rice from paddy by adopting a combination of steps involving control of moisture, safe storage of paddy and rice, parboiling of paddy and providing modern processing equipment. Consequently a decision was taken by the Central Government to establish modern rice milling units in each of six Package Programme areas, of which Mandya district was one.

The Ryots' Agricultural Produce Co-operative Marketing Society Ltd, Mandya, has taken up this project; it arranged for the purchase and import of Japanese machinery and began the rice milling operation in 1965. The combined efforts of efficient processing and proper storage have increased by about 10 per cent the outturn of rice from paddy (M.S.G., 1967:174).

To meet the demand in the district for agricultural implements, which resulted from the implementation of the Package Programme, an implements factory was started in Mandya town in 1966. The Mysore Sugar Company, Mandya, has a large workshop of its own where many of the factory's necessary metallic components, such as brace bearings, pump impellers, pistons and shafts, are manufactured.

These various new factories are responsible for a considerable increase in Mandya's wage earning population. Men and women now come from near and far in search of work. Many small landowners from the Mandya vicinity have been attracted to employment in the town and commute daily to work from their village homes. Dalena's wage earners provide a good example of such village commuters. The continuously growing influx of people into Mandya creates further economic opportunities : new houses are being built; more shops, cafés and other amenities are opening up to meet the increasing requirements of the growing population. In 1956 there was only one picture house in Mandya, now there are four. In a regional economy where the population has a high marginal propensity to consume, as is the case in Mandya district, the multiplier effect is considerable. The weekly fair in Mandya attracts growing numbers of sellers and buyers from a widening area. Altogether Mandya gives the impression of a busy town where crowds throng through choked bazaar streets.

## EDUCATION

Universal and compulsory free primary education has long been accepted as one of the main educational policies in Mysore State. A regulation of 1913 provided for an element of compulsion in selected centres. Compulsion was restricted to the ages from seven to eleven. The regulation also prohibited the employment of children of the compulsory age. In the year 1926 the whole question was reviewed and compulsory education was deferred for the time being. Since Independence, Indian Authorities have placed great emphasis on education. One of the most important educational programmes included in the Third Five-Year Plan was the expansion and improvement of primary education with a view to making it universal, free and compulsory. In line with the Union Government's educational policies the Mysore State legislature passed in 1961 the *Compulsory Primary Education Act*. This Act provides for the establishment of primary schools within a walking distance of one mile from the home of every child in the State and makes every parent responsible for sending his children to a recognised school. The *Mysore State Gazeteer For Mandya District* relates that in 1965–6 the primary school district enrolment for all eligible boys was 95 per cent and for girls 93 per cent (M.S.G., 1967:397). However, no account is given of the regularity of school attendances by these children.

Until 1954 a pupil having completed four years primary

education could go on to four years of middle school, which was termed the lower secondary education. In 1955 the duration of primary education was extended to eight years. After the formation of the new Mysore State in 1956 attempts were made to standardise the educational pattern throughout the State. Accordingly the State's primary and secondary stages of education were reorganised and an eight-year course of primary education and a four-year course of higher education were introduced.

There were only two high schools in Mandya district in 1944 with a total pupil strength of 480; by 1966 there were fifty high schools with a total enrolment of 13,860 youngsters. As an incentive to students pursuing secondary education, scholarships are being offered to poor and deserving candidates. During 1964–5 and 1965–6, 120 middle school scholarships and 60 high school scholarships were awarded to Scheduled Caste candidates at Rs. 5 and Rs. 10 each per month respectively (M.S.G., 1967:443). It is difficult to see how a poor parent can afford to send his son for secondary education on such a limited grant. By working five full days as casual field labourer a young man can earn Rs. 10 plus five big meals of rice. This alternative opportunity is an important consideration to bear in mind when examining the high school attendance of village A.K. boys in Mandya district.

Commercial education is imparted in three types of institution, namely high schools, colleges and private commercial schools. The University of Mysore was established in 1916 but until 1948 there was no tertiary education institution in Mandya district. In that year the Intermediate College was established there. In 1962 the College was upgraded into a First Grade College and the first-year degree classes in B.A. and B.Sc. were opened with a strength of 56 students. The College provides courses at pre-university level in arts and science and at higher level in arts and social science subjects leading to a B.A. degree; and in physics, chemistry and mathematics leading to a B.Sc. degree. In 1966 the People's Education Society, Mandya, started a new College of Science in Mandya town, with physics, chemistry and mathematics as optional subjects. The same Society had started four years earlier a College of Engineering at Mandya, which offers courses in civil, mechanical and electrical engineering. Prior to this, the government had opened a Polytechnic at Krishnarajpet in 1960, with diploma courses in the same engineering subjects.

The increase in educational facilities in Mandya district has certainly been very substantial. It is interesting to note, though, that among all these various schools and colleges which have recently been established in Mandya there is not a single agricultural training institution. Mandya, it must be remembered, is the centre of a region whose economic expansion is based on increasing agricultural production. The State Education Authorities do not appear to attach any importance to teaching farmers the science of cultivating crops. During the Second Plan approval was given to introduce agriculture as an elective subject in only 33 out of a total of 778 high schools in Mysore State (B.E.S., 1970:163). The only real attempt made at directing learning to produce better trained villagers is in the form of 'basic education'. This emphasises that schooling must centre round some suitable basic craft, chosen with due regard to the occupation of the locality. It was decided that this system should be tried as an experimental measure in Mysore State : by 1965 52 junior basic schools with classes I to IV had been established in Mandya district, of which 17 were in Mandya *taluk* itself; not a single senior basic school had been started by then (M.S.G., 1967:398).

Villagers do not seem to attach much prestige to studying agriculture nor do the Authorities encourage them to do so. The University of Agricultural Sciences was established in Bangalore in 1965; the two agricultural colleges which used to be affiliated to Mysore and Karnatak Universities and the veterinary college are now under the jurisdiction of the Agricultural University. There is, however, not the same strong demand for student places at the Agricultural University as there is at medical and engineering colleges. In 1962 the Mysore Government issued an order for providing for reservation of 68 per cent of seats in medical and engineering colleges for backward classes (see p. 189) and Scheduled Castes and Tribes. The order listed 81 'backward' classes and 135 'more backward classes'. Since caste is the qualifying criterion for backwardness education even at universities re-emphasises caste differences. Similarly, the activities of the Social Welfare Department, though intended to help Scheduled Castes, in fact may harm their status : with a view to providing more educational facilities to the Scheduled Castes, welfare maintains 13 hostels in Mandya where needy Scheduled Caste students can get free board and lodging. Though this is a laudable exercise in one sense, it reinforces the caste barrier at the same time. In a society where caste membership rather than personal performance at school determines a student's chance of success, education cannot act as the powerful solvent of caste differentiation it might in other circumstances be able to do.

# PART TWO
# TODAY

# 5 Economic Development and Change

*THE VILLAGE SCENE IN 1970*

Both villages have changed considerably in appearance since 1955; Wangala much more so than Dalena (see sketch maps). On the outskirts of Wangala to the right of the road leading from Mandya to the village, there is now a quite sizeable Vodda[1] settlement of 23 households. The Vodda huts are so small that their inhabitants have to crawl inside through a narrow opening and can hardly stand up straight in the interior of their homes. These huts are poorly built with thatched roofs which often leak in rainy weather. The size and low standard of Vodda accommodation indicates that the majority of residents in this section do not consider themselves as permanently settled there (see plates 1 and 2). In fact most of them are migrant workers who stay in Wangala only as long as there is sufficient demand for labour in the village to keep them occupied and provided with at least a minimum subsistence income. None of their huts existed in 1955; nor were there then any two-storey houses or electricity in Wangala. All this is new. Now there are a number of very impressive big two-storey houses lining Mandya road as well as street lighting in the caste section of the village.

Wangala's *patel* built himself a spacious new house on the big square right opposite the disused Public Works Department bungalow, which had provided my quarters during my earlier stay, and now houses the village school. The *patel*'s younger brother, who used to be referred to as chairman, has now a brightly painted two-storey home to the west of Mandya road. A number of other important elders in the village have also established large new homes in this new part of the village residential area. These two-storey homes combine old and new features of village housing. In line with traditional arrangements there is a large room at the back, half of which is occupied by cattle;

---

[1] Vodda are a Stonecutter caste from Tamil Nadu State where they are not regarded as untouchable and therefore do not have to live in a separate section of villages. In Wangala they rank below the indigenous A.K. caste.

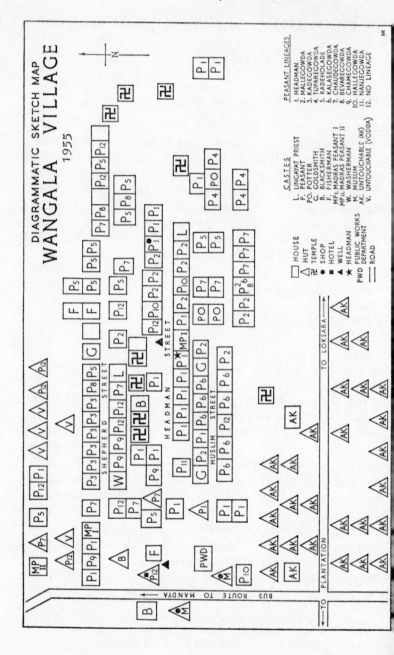

DIAGRAMMATIC SKETCH MAP
WANGALA VILLAGE
1955

HOUSE
△ HUT
卐 TEMPLE
● SHOP
■ HOTEL
▲ HEADMAN
PWD PUBLIC WORKS DEPARTMENT
ROAD

CASTES
L. LINGAYAT PRIEST
P. PEASANT
PO. POTTER
G. GOLDSMITH
B. BLACKSMITH
F. FISHERMAN
MPI. MADRAS PEASANT I
MPII. MADRAS PEASANT II
W. WASHERMAN
M. MUSLIM
AK. UNTOUCHABLE (AK)
V. UNTOUCHABLE (VODDA)

PEASANT LINEAGES
1. HEADMAN
2. MALLEGOWDA
3. KADEGOWDA
4. TUPAREGOWDA
5. KADEHOLADE
6. KALASEGOWDA
7. CHAUDEGOWDA
8. BEVAREGOWDA
9. CHAMEGOWDA
10. HALLEGOWDA
11. NANJEGOWDA
12. NO LINEAGE

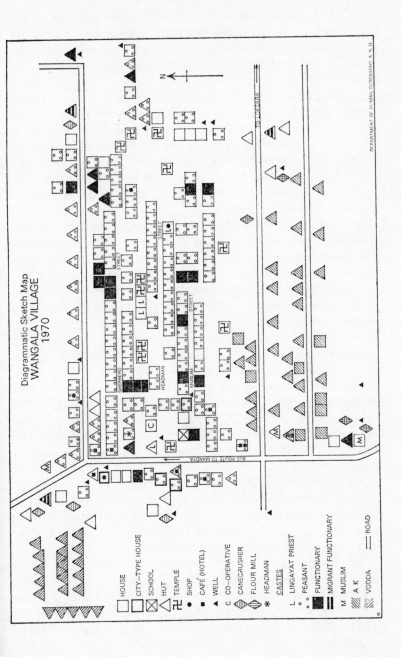

Diagrammatic Sketch Map
WANGALA VILLAGE
1970

HOUSE
CITY.-TYPE HOUSE
SCHOOL
HUT
TEMPLE
SHOP
CAFÉ (HOTEL)
WELL
CO-OPERATIVE
CANECRUSHER
FLOUR MILL
HEADMAN

CASTES
L LINGAYAT PRIEST
PEASANT
FUNCTIONARY
MIGRANT FUNCTIONARY
M MUSLIM
A K
VODDA

DEPARTMENT OF HUMAN GEOGRAPHY A.N.U.

animals are usually led in from the rear. The frontage of the house and its second storey represent housing innovations. By contrast with the old style terraced housing the new structures are fully detached and give a much more spacious impression than does the interior of the village.

Many of these elaborate new houses have their own well placed right outside. In 1955 there were only two caste wells in Wangala: one had been prepared by the village for residents, the other had originally been built by the Public Works Department for the use of the engineer who resided there, but was subsequently freely used by all caste households. Now there are seventeen caste wells in the village, of which fifteen are owned by individual households.

Along the main road passing through the village there are now five cafés which serve coffee and tea as well as light refreshments. For most parts of the day all of them have at least a few customers. These refreshment places are housed either in small huts built specifically for the purpose, or they operate in one or two rooms of house structures. The strategic position of Wangala's roadside has gained in importance during the last 15 years. This is illustrated by the fact that in 1956 there were only 4 buses passing the village daily; there are now 18. Buses have become the most popular means of transport. There is hardly anyone these days who attempts walking to Mandya from Wangala; some go by bicycle, others use bullock carts, but by far the majority of villagers travel by bus. During my earlier stay in the village I never once drove to or from Mandya without being stopped and asked for a lift by one of my village friends. In 1970 no one ever stopped me on the way and I never saw any Wangala villager walking between Mandya and his home village.

Power-driven cane-crushers are another innovation in Wangala. Four of the eight village cane-crushers are situated along the main road. One of these is beyond the village A.K. quarter; another four have been placed at the borders of the caste settlement.

The interior of Wangala has changed very little except for the introduction of street lighting. Here and there a new house has replaced an old structure. Yet the old crooked and bumpy village streets look still very much as they did in earlier years. The old Marichoudi temple has been given a facelift; it has been closed in and elaborately painted and decorated.

Altogether the caste section of the village clearly indicates a considerable increase in wealth; the big new two-storey houses, their own wells, street lighting, power cane-crushers, crowded cafés are all signs of a new affluence. In glaring contrast to this the A.K. section looks, if anything, even poorer and more dilapidated than it did 15 years ago. It has no street lights, although one of the Peasant-owned cane-crushers sandwiches the A.K. residential area between caste houses and therefore power lines pass over A.K. housing. Many village A.K.s are keen to have their streets also lit at night. However, they complain that they are not able to pay for the current let alone the installation charges. Fifty-nine of about 200 caste houses have electric lights; only one of the 44 A.K. households is equally fortunate. There is only one A.K. shop and one small café. The change in the very appearance of Wangala shows at a glance the increased economic differentiation that has taken place during the past fifteen years.

Dalena, too, shows obvious signs of increased prosperity, but again this is limited to the caste quarter of the village. Wangala's population has not only increased through natural growth but also as a result of immigration. By contrast, there has been little immigration into Dalena; in fact some young men have moved out of the village. Since 1956 nine men have emigrated, seven of whom were married and have taken their families with them. Dalena's population has increased by 51 per cent since 1955 whereas Wangala's has grown by as much as 67 per cent (see tables 2 and 3). Dalena's new homes are mainly situated at the northern side of the 'old part' of the village. They are bigger and more elaborate than the older ones, but, except for one, they are all single-storey. The first house on the road leading from the Mysore–Bangalore highway into the village is an impressive-looking new two-storey building: it houses the local school. Dalena already had electricity when I first stayed there : the caste quarters had street lights and three Peasant households had installed light in their own homes. Now there are 25 Peasant homes with current connections and ten have their own radios. Fifteen years ago there were no street lights in the A.K. quarter of Dalena, nor did any A.K. home have electricity. Nothing has changed in this respect, nor has any A.K. now got a more elaborate home; most of them still live in the same small dilapidated thatched huts. There used to be five caste wells and one A.K. well in

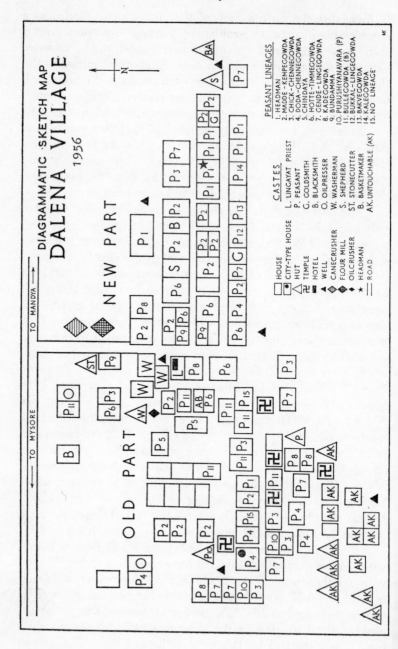

DIAGRAMMATIC SKETCH MAP
DALENA VILLAGE
1956

CASTES
L. LINGAYAT PRIEST
P. PEASANT
G. GOLDSMITH
B. BLACKSMITH
O. OILPRESSER
W. WASHERMAN
S. SHEPHERD
ST. STONECUTTER
B. BASKETMAKER
AK. UNTOUCHABLE (AK)

PEASANT LINEAGES
1. HEADMAN
2. MADDE – KEMPEGOWDA
3. CHICK – CHENNEGOWDA
4. DODA – CHENNEGOWDA
5. CHINDAYA
6. HOTTE – TIMMEGOWDA
7. CENDE – LINGEGOWDA
8. KADEGOWDA
9. BUNDAMMA
10. PURUSHYANAVARA (P)
11. BULLEGOWDA (B)
12. BUKKAL – LINGEGOWDA
13. BAKEGOWDA
14. KALEGOWDA
15. NO LINEAGE

HOUSE
CITY-TYPE HOUSE
HUT
TEMPLE
WELL
HOTEL
CANECRUSHER
FLOUR MILL
OILCRUSHER
HEADMAN
ROAD

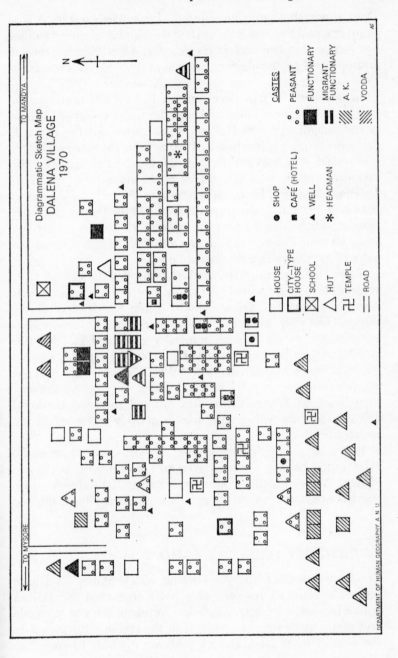

Diagrammatic Sketch Map
DALENA VILLAGE
1970

N

TO MANDYA
TO MYSORE

HOUSE

CITY-TYPE
HOUSE

SCHOOL

HUT

TEMPLE

ROAD

SHOP

CAFÉ (HOTEL)

WELL

HEADMAN

CASTES

PEASANT

FUNCTIONARY

MIGRANT
FUNCTIONARY

A. K.

VODDA

DEPARTMENT OF HUMAN GEOGRAPHY A N U

Dalena; now there are nine caste wells but still only one for A.K.s.
From one café and one store in 1956 the number of these facilities
has increased to five and six respectively. All of these are owned
and operated by members of castes and cater almost exclusively
for a caste clientele.

In line with its past development, Dalena has continued to
become increasingly integrated into the wider economy. I have
already mentioned that Dalena's *patel* opened a large rice mill
and cane-crusher a few hundred yards from the village. He still
has his old flour mill and shop at the nearby rail junction. His
younger brother, who was the first to start a cane-crusher in
Dalena, transferred his machinery also to the main road so as to
have it more strategically placed. Another of the Dalena magnates
bought a site in Mandya near the bus-stop. He has not yet decided
what he wants to do with his property. As Mandya grows the
value of such a strategic site rises rapidly.

Dalena entrepreneurs have thus continued to extend their
ventures outside their own village; by contrast Wangala's investment has remained almost wholly within the borders of the
village. The only exception to this general rule concerns Kinegowda, the *patel's* younger son, who graduated in 1964 (see
p. 226). At the beginning of 1970 he opened a fertiliser shop at
the outskirts of Mandya on the road to Wangala. Moreover, he
competed in the last *taluk* board elections. He is as yet the only
man living in Wangala who has invested in non-agricultural
assets outside the village and who is actively interested in the
wider polity.

Wangala's economic introversion and Dalena's entrepreneurial
extroversion become apparent even on a fleeting visit to the two
villages. Moreover, this is firmly reflected in the different socio-
political orientation which the population in these villages display.


## THE IMPORTANCE OF FARMING

Land has remained the pivot round which almost all village
economic activities revolve. This holds true even for Dalena
where farmers have been much less fortunate than in Wangala
and many other wet land villages in the region with respect to
the availability of land. Dalena lands are still only by-passed by

the canal without deriving any water from it. Already in my earlier study I noted that Dalena residents had practically exhausted the extent of cultivable land within the boundaries of their own village (1962:214). The population increase since then in a period when rainfall has been abnormally low has made matters worse. To increase agricultural output Dalena farmers have to acquire more land outside and/or increase the productivity of their village acreages. They have in fact tried both these possibilities; the former with greater success than the latter. First, they purchased about 100 more acres in neighbouring villages, of which approximately 20 per cent is dry land. Second, they attempted irrigating their dry land with the aid of pumps. Kempa, one of the most enterprising village Peasants, was the first who in 1965 decided to buy a diesel pump set to help him irrigate his six dry acres. He paid Rs. 3,000 for it out of his own savings; he explained that it would have been much too cumbersome a procedure to try and get a loan from the rural credit organisation: 'First you have to get the village accountant's certificate to show how much land you own, then you have to complete innumerable forms, etcetera; in my own case it was just not worth all the effort' he said.

Kempa claimed that irrigation enabled him to double crop his acres, producing an annual yield per acre of about 10 pallas ragi altogether, which just about trebled the productivity of his land. In spite of this obvious gain in yields, Kempa used his diesel pump for only three years and then sold it in Mandya for no more than half what he had initially paid for it. He complained that it had been much too costly to irrigate land with the aid of the diesel pump. In the meantime two other Dalena Peasants had followed Kempa's example and each bought such a diesel pump set. They too found operating costs prohibitive. Accordingly, they decided to rent their sets out to other farmers in Dalena and nearby villages at the rate of Rs. 5 per hour. This at least offered some compensation for the high cost of using the pumps on their own lands. While Kempa was telling me about his problems a crowd of farmers gathered. Many of them claimed that the British pump sets, which at present are the only ones available to them, are too big and clumsy for their purposes: some said they had heard of Japanese or German pumps which are much smaller and more efficient. They requested my help in securing the necessary import licences, which unfortunately I was unable to do. It is interesting to note here that Dalena farmers were aware of different makes of foreign-produced pumps.

The high running cost of diesel pumps is not the only obstacle Dalena farmers encounter in their attempts to bring water to their lands. Rama, one of the headman's younger brothers, who is also a keen entrepreneur, had bought six dry acres in a neighbouring village. The land bordered the canal. He arranged to have a well dug at a distance of about 100 feet from the canal – at least so he claims. To avoid the problem his fellow farmers had encountered with their diesel pumps he bought an electric pump set which altogether cost him Rs. 12,000 to instal. Rama bitterly complained that as soon as he was ready to start using his new pumping system, an Irrigation Overseer came along and told him not to proceed because the well was too near the canal and therefore illegally diverted canal water. He was still negotiating with the authorities while I was there and asked my intervention on his behalf, which I had to refuse. The case had not been finally settled by the time I left South India; since he is a brother of the headman, who has many contacts with influential officials in Mandya, Rama may yet be allowed to use his well to irrigate his land. In the meantime he feels bitter that his venture is being frustrated.

Kempa's and Rama's experiments with pump irrigation reveal the serious difficulties dry land farmers face in their attempts to keep pace with developments in an irrigated region. Purchases of land in neighbouring villages have helped somewhat in this respect. The additional land Dalena farmers have managed to acquire since 1955 has in terms of area not fully compensated for the population growth in the intervening years. Consequently, the average land per indigenous Dalena household has declined from 4.90 acres to 3.70 acres. However, the proportion of wet land has gone up: it was less than 20 per cent and is now approximately 25 per cent. Since the yield of wet land is considerably higher than that of dry land not only in monetary but also in real terms the appropriate weighting shows that the average landholding per Dalena household did not decline very much over the last 15 years. However, economic differentiation has considerably increased during this period as no more than seven of the richest Dalena Peasants purchased about 60 of the additional 100 acres acquired by villagers.

Dalena's dry land economy has continued to force farmers to participate in the regional expansion. Previously this pressure was felt most by the village entrepreneurs on the one hand, and the poorest on the other : the former did not want to be left behind by their counterparts in neighbouring irrigated villages, whereas the latter, having lost the protection of traditional hereditary labour relations with Peasant landowners in the village, were forced to supplement their meagre subsistence income by wages earned outside. During my earlier stay Dalena farmers cultivated altogether 549 dry acres, which yielded about 116,500 seers of millet for a total population of 707. One seer of millet weighs slightly more than 2 lb. and contains about 3,000 calories. Accordingly the *per capita* subsistence supply of millet amounted to approximately 340 lb. per year or 0.9 lb. per day, which provided 1,295 calories per day per head of Dalena's population in 1956. By contrast the daily *per capita* calories available in the form of home-grown millet has now fallen to 475. Two major factors are responsible for this drastic drop in dry land output per head : first, population has increased and second, unfavourable weather conditions during the last few years, especially abnormally low rainfall, played havoc with Dalena dry land farming. Many acres partially or even completely failed to produce crops for several successive seasons. This made Dalena farmers wary of investing labour and money in preparing their dry fields without much hope of getting due returns. Thus they reduced their millet cultivation from 549 acres to 460 acres which, due to lower yields, provided no more than 68,250 seers. Employing the same conversion rates as above, this total millet output provides only 475 calories a head daily, which is less than half the 1,035 calories each East Bengal refugee was given daily in the form of 300 grammes of rice just to keep him alive. Dalena's home-grown aggregate supply of basic food therefore falls a lot short of villagers' aggregate demand. This, probably more than anything else these days, accounts for the increasing number of Dalena villagers attempting to buy land outside and/or to earn profits or wages in the wider economy. It is their fundamental need to supplement their own millet output with basic food either grown on wet land or purchased with cash. The only alternative is to migrate, which villagers are reluctant to do as long as they own even small plots of land.

Dalena residents encounter great difficulties in their attempts to buy more wet land outside the village. Very little such land comes on the market and there is a big demand for it. Therefore land prices are booming. However, it is not merely a matter of raising the money, in itself quite a considerable problem; more important is the need for Dalena prospective land buyers to have a network of links in neighbouring villages. Without this they would not hear of land coming on to the market at all or would find out about it too late. Only those Dalena farmers who carefully cultivate their kinship and friendship ties outside their own village are successful in getting to know in good time about the rare occasions when wet land is offered for sale. Moreover, they have the necessary local contacts to help them approach the seller and can count on indigenous support in their quest to conclude the transaction. Thus Dalena farmers have to spend much time visiting neighbouring villages not just for social purposes but to remind their kin and friends of their keen interest in acquiring more land.

By contrast, Wangala farmers continue to be able to concentrate on activities within their own village. In my earlier study I noted that Wangala still had a large uncultivated area, therefore 'its agricultural economy may yet expand within its boundaries' (1962:214). This is precisely what has happened. Extension of canal irrigation has considerably increased the village's cultivable acreage. More important still, the proportion of wet land has increased from 60 per cent to 75 per cent. Thus population growth has resulted in a smaller decrease in the average landholding per indigenous household in Wangala than in Dalena; the decrease in Wangala is from 3.10 acres to 2.70 acres. This decline, however, was more than offset by the increase in average wet land holding per household from 1.70 acres to 2.00 acres. Moreover, average yields per acre have also increased. In spite of Wangala's population growth of almost 70 per cent during the last 15 years the *per capita* home-grown basic food supply has increased considerably. In 1955 Wangala farmers cultivated 320 acres of dry millet as well as 228 acres of paddy and 33 acres of wet ragi. The total output of millet amounted then to about 96,000 seers per year and that of paddy to 245,000. For the then village population of 958 this amounted to a daily *per capita* supply of 0.55 lb. millet and 0.80 lb. rice, which together provided 1,920 calories. By 1970 this comparative abundance of home-grown food had further increased: 83 acres under dry millet produced about 30,000 seers, 145 acres wet ragi another 169,790 seers and 410 acres paddy provided 615,000 seers. This total output meant daily *per capita* availability of staple village produce of approximately 0.70 lb. millet and 1.20 lb. rice, which together contain about 2,650 calories.

These average figures do not imply that this is the normal *per capita* consumption in Wangala; extremes of economic differentiation which I have already hinted at and which I discuss in detail in a later section (see p. 171), prevent this. Yet it is important to note here that Wangala's aggregate home-grown basic food supply exceeds village needs. Wangala has a surplus in staple food whereas Dalena has a deficiency. This is the glaring contrast between these two villages which accounts for much of the difference in the path of development that each has pursued.

## CROP PATTERN

The most important food crops still grown in the Mandya region are paddy and ragi; sugar-cane has remained the major cash crop. Wangala farmers now produce 75 per cent of their ragi on wet land. They rotate their wet crops: usually two crops of ragi follow three of cane. They have diversified their dry cultivation. They used to grow mainly ragi and jowar whereas now they have almost given up growing jowar – among my 29 sample farmers there was not a single one in 1970 who cultivated jowar whereas seven of them had done so in 1955. Instead they now produce more of vegetables for their subsistence needs. Prices of some spices, in particular of chillies, have risen much faster than those of staple food items. Therefore farmers aim at overall self-sufficiency in their household consumption. This is reflected in their different crop pattern: in 1955 Wangala farmers cultivated 116 acres of jowar, and only 12 acres of miscellaneous dry crops. By 1969 they had changed their cropping to only 20 acres jowar and as much as 133 acres of miscellaneous dry crops. Altogether the area under various food crops has increased by about 55 per cent since 1955 (see table 6).

TABLE 6

## DALENA AND WANGALA CROP PATTERN

| | Dalena | | | | Wangala | | | |
|---|---|---|---|---|---|---|---|---|
| | 1956 | | 1969 | | 1955 | | 1959 | |
| | Acres* | % | Acres† | % | Acres* | % | Acres‡ | % |
| Jowar | 177 | 24 | 180 | 20 | 116 | 16 | 20 | 2 |
| Ragi: | | | | | | | | |
| Dry | 372 | 51 | 230 | 29 | 204 | 28 | 63 | 6 |
| Irrigated | 0 | 0 | 50 | 6 | 33 | 4 | 145 | 13 |
| Paddy | 101 | 14 | 170 | 20 | 228 | 32 | 410 | 36 |
| Sugarcane | 24 | 3 | 35 | 5 | 129 | 18 | 354 | 31 |
| Miscellaneous: | | | | | | | | |
| Dry | 28 | 4 | 50 | 6 | 12 | 2 | 133 | 12 |
| Fallow: | | | | | | | | |
| Dry | 33 | 4 | 120 | 14 | 0 | 0 | 0 | 0 |
| Total | 735 | 100 | 835 | 100 | 722 | 100 | 1125 | 100 |

*Source:* * Own census.
† Estimate based on interviews.
‡ Village crop records.

Dalena farmers had already a greater variety of dry crops than their Wangala counterparts during my earlier study; richer Dalena Peasants have continued to diversify their dry cultivation, while poorer ones, without any or only little wet land, still produce mainly their staple dietary crops of ragi and jowar on their own dry lands.

As already mentioned, the dry yields have declined drastically in the Mandya region during the last few years due to abnormally low rainfalls. The majority of Dalena farmers, therefore, concentrated on producing as much as possible of their staple dietary crops instead of trying to diversify their output. Their attempt to make themselves self-sufficient in basic foods is shown in the fact that they grow paddy on about 80 per cent of their wet lands, in spite of their full awareness that cane is by far the more remunerative crop. In 1956 the position was very much the same in this respect. I then discussed the various reasons why Dalena farmers preferred to grow paddy (1962:217): their small and dispersed wet plots, the lower cash requirements for paddy cultivation and so on. These factors still operate. To them must be added another important one, namely the rapid rise in paddy prices over the years: while the retail price of paddy has almost trebled since 1956 the factor cane price has only doubled. Dalena's concern with food self-sufficiency reflects a rational attitude in a period of rapidly rising food prices. Informants did tell me, though, that like so many others in the area, some Dalena farmers had planted more cane while jaggery prices were booming. As soon as these prices dropped again they returned to growing paddy on the majority of their wet acres.

By contrast, Wangala farmers planted more cane and less paddy as soon as jaggery prices began to rise. In 1963 they planted 291 acres of cane and 501 acres of paddy on Wangala land. This was the year when jaggery prices soared to unprecedented heights. The following year there were 451 acres of cane and only 372 acres of paddy planted in the village. This clearly shows a quick response to price incentives. If we make allowance for one year's lag between changes in jaggery prices and acreages under cane, table 4 indicates a continuing positive reaction to price fluctuations. The year 1966, however, was an exception as rains failed even in the irrigation catchment area in Mysore so that canals could not supply sufficient water for cane cultivation. This accounts for the drastic decline in cane acreage during that year. As soon as canal water began to flow once more wet land farmers were again guided by jaggery price fluctuations in varying their cane acreages.

'It is often asserted that farm output in under-developed countries responds very little to movements in prices and costs. This lack of responsiveness is attributed to production being oriented primarily to subsistence and the bulk of the inputs being available within the producing units' (Gupta; 1965:1). Wangala farmers are no doubt still basically subsistence farmers; they supplement rather than substitute their own food production with cash crops. I suggest that in their case their self-sufficiency enables them to be sensitive to price fluctuations for the cash crops they can grow on their surplus wet land. Farmers with not enough or just sufficient land to meet their own basic food needs are not as flexible in their crop pattern as those who have surplus land. The different attitudes displayed by Wangala and Dalena to jaggery price movements reveal the importance of subsistence farming in price responsiveness. Dalena farmers had to make the choice whether to grow more cane for sale or to plant rice for their own subsistence need on their limited wet land in neighbouring villages; most of them decided in favour of rice. The wealthier Wangala farmers who did not have to choose between the two alternatives, but could plant both, were quick to respond to price incentives. Official reports on the area do not appear to take into consideration the impact of prices on crop pattern; *Modernising Indian Agriculture* notes that in Mandya District 'the proportionate share of ragi and rice in the cropping pattern decreased from 35 per cent and 27 per cent respectively to 29 per cent and 17 per cent in the period between 1962–3 and 1967–8. Meanwhile there was sizeable increase in the area under sugarcane' (M.F.A.C., 1969:572). No mention is made of concomitant rises in jaggery prices, which obviously influenced the crop pattern of farmers with more wet land than they needed to grow their own food.

*Sugar-cane* : The further extension of irrigation over Wangala land has enabled more farmers to cultivate cane : of the 28 sample households cultivating cane in 1970 no more than 20 had done so in 1955. Average yield per acre of cane has increased somewhat from 43.3 tons to 45.2 tons. The range of yields per

acre produced by sample cane farmers has widened from 24 to
56 tons in 1955 to between 19 to 80 tons in 1969 (see table 7).
There is a high positive correlation between years of experience
in cane farming on the one hand and yield per acre on the other.
The six sample farmers who in 1969 produced less than 40 tons
per acre have had only two or three cane crops, whereas the
others have planted cane for many more years.

TABLE 7

### DISTRIBUTION OF CANE YIELDS PER ACRE IN WANGALA SAMPLE HOUSEHOLDS

|  | *Number* | | *%* | |
| --- | --- | --- | --- | --- |
| *Tons* | *1955* | *1969* | *1955* | *1969* |
| 0 < 20 | 0 | 1 | 0 | 4 |
| 20 < 40 | 4 | 5 | 20 | 18 |
| 40 < 60 | 16 | 18 | 80 | 64 |
| 60 < 80 | 0 | 3 | 0 | 10 |
| 80 < 100 | 0 | 1 | 0 | 4 |
| Total No. of Households | 20 | 28 | 100 | 100 |
| Average Yield per Acre | *tons* 43.3 | 45.2 | | |

Similarly in Dalena more wet land owners now cultivate cane,
though the numbers were small among the sample households,
being only three in 1955 and four in 1969. There, too, the average cane yield per acre has increased from 44.3 tons to 49.3 tons
during the same period, and the range has widened from between
29 to 55 tons per acre to between 25 to 66 tons per acre (see
table 8). These output figures compare favourably with Mandya
District average yields of 41.5 tons in 1964–5 (B.E.S., 1966:63);
they are considerably higher than the 14 tons average yield in
1961–2 reported for Eastern Uttar Pradesh (Gupta, 1965:29).
Average inputs per acre of cane are also a lot higher in Mysore
villages than in Uttar Pradesh.

Table 8

## DISTRIBUTION OF CANE YIELDS PER ACRE IN DALENA SAMPLE HOUSEHOLDS

|  | Number | | % | |
| --- | --- | --- | --- | --- |
| *Tons* | *1956* | *1969* | *1956* | *1969* |
| 0 < 20 | 0 | 0 | 0 | 0 |
| 20 < 40 | 1 | 1 | 33 | 25 |
| 40 < 60 | 2 | 2 | 67 | 50 |
| 60 < 80 | 0 | 1 | 0 | 25 |
| Total No. of Households | 3 | 4 | 100 | 100 |
| Average Yield per Acre | *tons* 44.3 | 49.3 | | |

Farmers rarely try to evaluate their subsistence inputs. To them the difference between gross yields and cash expenditure represents the most important aspect of return. The proportion of cash inputs per average cane acre cultivated in Wangala has declined from 44 per cent of output to 26 per cent. In Dalena it has fallen somewhat less, from 56 per cent to 46 per cent. In both villages there has been a shift from cash to subsistence inputs : in Wangala the percentage of subsistence inputs has increased from 36 per cent to 51 per cent (see table 9) and in Dalena from 36 per cent to 44 per cent (see table 10).

More farmers use their own cattle for ploughing these days. In 1955, 53 per cent of Wangala and 37 per cent of Dalena households had at least one pair of bullocks; the respective percentages had increased to 65 and 45 by 1970. During this period the price of cattle fodder almost trebled. Consequently, farmers now try to provide their animals with home-produced fodder rather than purchase it. These changes in farm management are reflected in a considerable increase in subsistence overheads: cattle maintenance constitutes the bulk of this cost item.

The greater farm self-sufficiency in animal power resulted in less cattle being hired. In 1955–6 all the charges for hired equipment involved the rent of bullock teams for ploughing and other

TABLE 9

WANGALA: COST, OUTPUT AND INCOME PER ACRE – ESTIMATED AVERAGE

| | Cane | | | | Paddy | | | | Wet Ragi | | | | Dry Ragi | | | | Jowar | |
| | 1955 | | 1969 | | 1955 | | 1969 | | 1955 | | 1969 | | 1955 | | 1969 | | 1955 | |
| | Rs. | % | Rs. | % | Rs. | % | Rs. | % | Rs. | % | Rs. | % | Rs. | % | Rs. | % | Rs. | % |
|---|---|---|---|---|---|---|---|---|---|---|---|---|---|---|---|---|---|---|
| **Cost:** | | | | | | | | | | | | | | | | | | |
| a. Subsistence Labour | 123 | 13 | 190 | 9 | 73 | 24 | 126 | 15 | 52 | 24 | 138 | 23 | 26 | 19 | 42 | 15 | 22 | 28 |
| b. Hired Labour | 119 | 12 | 199 | 10 | 65 | 22 | 159 | 19 | 20 | 9 | 136 | 23 | 33 | 24 | 42 | 15 | 3 | 4 |
| c. Subsistence: Seeds and Fertiliser | 126 | 13 | 555 | 28 | 53 | 18 | 127 | 15 | 69 | 33 | 134 | 22 | 46 | 34 | 98 | 35 | 19 | 24 |
| d. Cash: Seeds and Fertiliser | 369 | 38 | 583 | 29 | 23 | 8 | 214 | 25 | 5 | 2 | 64 | 10 | 4 | 3 | 18 | 6 | — | 2 |
| e. Hired Equipment | 53 | 6 | 68 | 3 | 17 | 6 | 8 | 1 | 18 | 9 | 4 | 1 | 3 | 2 | 7 | 2 | — | 3 |
| f. Subsistence: Overhead Expenses | 96 | 10 | 276 | 14 | 32 | 11 | 139 | 16 | 22 | 10 | 77 | 13 | 15 | 11 | 38 | 14 | 20 | 25 |
| g. Cash: Overhead Expenses | 64 | 7 | 113 | 6 | 21 | 7 | 57 | 7 | 13 | 6 | 32 | 6 | 8 | 6 | 24 | 9 | 12 | 15 |
| h. Tax | 14 | 1 | 27 | 1 | 14 | 4 | 19 | 2 | 14 | 7 | 11 | 2 | 1 | 1 | 10 | 4 | 1 | 1 |
| i. Total Cost | 964 | 100 | 2011 | 100 | 298 | 100 | 849 | 100 | 213 | 100 | 596 | 100 | 136 | 100 | 279 | 100 | 79 | 100 |
| j. Subsistence Cost (a + c + f) | 345 | 36 | 1021 | 51 | 158 | 53 | 393 | 46 | 143 | 67 | 349 | 59 | 87 | 64 | 179 | 64 | 61 | 77 |
| k. Cash Cost (b + d + e + g + h) | 619 | 64 | 990 | 49 | 140 | 47 | 456 | 54 | 70 | 33 | 247 | 41 | 49 | 36 | 100 | 36 | 18 | 23 |
| l. Output | 1413 | 100 | 3708 | 100 | 294 | 100 | 1064 | 100 | 418 | 100 | 605 | 100 | 205 | 100 | 188 | 100 | 106 | 100 |
| k. Cash Cost (b + d + e + g + h) | 619 | 44 | 990 | 26 | 140 | 48 | 456 | 43 | 70 | 17 | 247 | 41 | 49 | 24 | 100 | 53 | 18 | 17 |
| m. Income: Farm Wages and Profits (l − k) | 794 | 56 | 2718 | 74 | 154 | 52 | 608 | 57 | 348 | 83 | 358 | 59 | 156 | 76 | 88 | 47 | 88 | 83 |

*Today*

## TABLE 10

COST, OUTPUT AND INCOME PER ACRE CULTIVATED BY DALENA FARMERS* – ESTIMATED AVERAGE

| | Cane | | | | Paddy | | | | Dry Ragi | | | | Pump Irrigated Ragi | | Jowar | | | |
|---|---|---|---|---|---|---|---|---|---|---|---|---|---|---|---|---|---|---|
| | 1956 | | 1969 | | 1956 | | 1969 | | 1956 | | 1969 | | 1969 | | 1956 | | 1969 | |
| | Rs. | % | Rs. | % | Rs. | % | Rs. | % | Rs. | % | Rs. | % | Rs. | % | Rs. | % | Rs. | % |
| **Cost:** | | | | | | | | | | | | | | | | | | |
| a. Subsistence Labour | 256 | 17 | 103 | 3 | 145 | 37 | 81 | 8 | 39 | 33 | 35 | 18 | 75 | 15 | 20 | 37 | 56 | 28 |
| b. Hired Labour | 325 | 22 | 450 | 13 | 64 | 16 | 182 | 18 | 20 | 17 | 9 | 4 | 53 | 11 | 8 | 15 | 17 | 8 |
| c. Subsistence: Seeds and Fertiliser | 196 | 13 | 415 | 12 | 61 | 16 | 112 | 11 | 32 | 27 | 49 | 25 | 42 | 8 | 3 | 5 | 16 | 8 |
| d. Cash: Seeds and Fertiliser | 480 | 33 | 976 | 29 | 40 | 10 | 193 | 19 | — | — | 6 | 3 | 12 | 3 | — | — | — | — |
| e. Hired Equipment | 82 | 6 | 73 | 2 | 10 | 3 | 6 | 1 | 2 | 1 | 2 | 1 | 3 | 1 | — | — | 1 | 1 |
| f. Subsistence: Overhead Expenses | 73 | 5 | 982 | 29 | 32 | 8 | 198 | 20 | 15 | 13 | — | — | 94 | 19 | 13 | 24 | 26 | 13 |
| g. Cash: Overhead Expenses | 48 | 3 | 367 | 11 | 22 | 6 | 214 | 21 | 9 | 8 | 89 | 44 | 203 | 41 | 8 | 15 | 73 | 37 |
| h. Tax | 14 | 1 | 27 | 1 | 14 | 4 | 19 | 2 | 2 | 1 | 10 | 5 | 11 | 2 | 2 | 4 | 10 | 5 |
| i. Total Cost | 1474 | 100 | 3393 | 100 | 388 | 100 | 1005 | 100 | 119 | 100 | 200 | 100 | 493 | 100 | 54 | 100 | 199 | 100 |
| j. Subsistence Cost (a + c + f) | 525 | 36 | 1500 | 44 | 238 | 61 | 391 | 39 | 86 | 72 | 85 | 42 | 210 | 43 | 36 | 67 | 99 | 50 |
| k. Cash Cost (b + d + e + g + h) | 949 | 64 | 1893 | 56 | 150 | 39 | 614 | 61 | 33 | 28 | 115 | 58 | 283 | 57 | 18 | 33 | 100 | 50 |
| l. Output | 1701 | 100 | 4090 | 100 | 382 | 100 | 1260 | 100 | 93 | 100 | 162 | 100 | 350 | 100 | 56 | 100 | 178 | 100 |
| k. Cash Cost (b + d + e + g + h) | 949 | 56 | 1893 | 46 | 150 | 39 | 614 | 49 | 33 | 36 | 115 | 71 | 283 | 81 | 18 | 32 | 100 | 56 |
| m. Income: (Farm Wages and Profits) (l − k) | 752 | 44 | 2197 | 54 | 232 | 61 | 646 | 51 | 60 | 64 | 47 | 29 | 67 | 19 | 38 | 68 | 78 | 44 |

* Dalena farmers cultivate cane and paddy on wet land in neighbouring villages.

operations; in 1970 the greater proportion of this average cost item represented expenditure on hiring bulldozers and tractors. The comparatively small average charge for hiring equipment per acre of cane indicates that mechanisation of agriculture is still in its infancy both in Dalena and Wangala. Only three of the twenty-eight Wangala sample cane farmers and no more than one of the four from Dalena used any large mechanical equipment.

Average labour input per acre of cane has fallen in Dalena from 328 days to 290 days and in Wangala from 208 to 190 (see table 11). This reduction in labour requirements is only partly due to increased mechanisation; more important is the fact that experienced cane farmers have learned to rationalise their cane cultivation. In Dalena there has been a considerable substitution of hired for subsistence labour: in 1956 only 56 per cent of average labour input per acre of cane was hired, now this percentage has increased to 82 per cent. Dalena cane farmers find it more efficient to act in a supervisory capacity and engage more casual labour instead of their own household members walking miles to their fields in neighbouring villages and then performing labouring jobs themselves. This accounts for the 10 per cent reduction in average labour day inputs Dalena cane farmers have achieved over the years. Moreover, they now employ more female workers than they used to do to reduce costs of labour. Females are paid only half the rate of males per day.

Cane, however, is still the most demanding village produce not only in terms of labour but even more so in regard to other inputs. It is also the most remunerative crop, but unlike others produced in the villages it is grown purely for cash and does not lend itself readily to subsistence consumption. Cane can be consumed only after it has been processed into jaggery and then no more than small quantities can be used by a household.

*Food crops*: Paddy and ragi are the major food crops grown on village wet land. Wangala's average yields per acre of paddy have increased by almost 50 per cent from 10.8 pallas to 15.0 pallas. The range of yields per acre has widened: the lowest is still 8 pallas while the highest has increased from 16 to 24 pallas (see table 12). In Dalena, too, the average paddy yield per acre has gone up from 16.1 pallas to 18.6 pallas, yet there the range has narrowed: 12 pallas is still the lowest yield while the highest has

TABLE 11

## WANGALA'S CROP LABOUR REQUIREMENTS
(estimated average labour days per crop acre)

| | 1955 | | | | | | 1969 | | | | | |
|---|---|---|---|---|---|---|---|---|---|---|---|---|
| | Male | | Female | | Total | | Male | | Female | | Total | |
| | No. | % | No. | % | No. | % | No. | % | No. | % | No. | % |
| Jowar | 12 | 50 | 12 | 50 | 24 | 100 | 37 | 77 | 11 | 23 | 48 | 100* |
| Ragi: | | | | | | | | | | | | |
| Dry | 23 | 43 | 30 | 57 | 53 | 100 | 37 | 77 | 11 | 23 | 48 | 100 |
| Irrigated | 28 | 48 | 30 | 52 | 58 | 100 | 111 | 80 | 27 | 20 | 138 | 100 |
| Paddy | 97 | 78 | 28 | 22 | 125 | 100 | 114 | 79 | 30 | 21 | 144 | 100 |
| Sugar-cane | 178 | 86 | 30 | 14 | 208 | 100 | 159 | 84 | 31 | 16 | 190 | 100 |
| Miscellaneous | — | — | 45 | 100 | 45 | 100 | 37 | 77 | 11 | 23 | 48 | 100* |

* I am assuming here that average labour requirements for jowar and miscellaneous crops equal those per acre of dry ragi.

come down from 36 to 26 pallas (see table 13). Farmers claim
that this increase in average yields resulted from the improved
variety of seeds the *gramasevak* introduced accompanied by an
increased application of manure and fertiliser. Average yields per
paddy acre in Wangala and Dalena are slightly less than the
19.5 pallas recorded for Mandya District for 1964-5 (B.E.S.,
1966:57).

In Mandya district there has as yet been no equally successful
improved variety of paddy seeds that could compare with the
revolutionary dwarf variety of wheat. The Taichung-65 paddy
variety has been tried but its 'popularity in irrigated tracts as a
single crop has limited scope because the marginal increase in
yield is not often attractive when compared with local varieties
which are fine to medium in quality and fetch higher prices with
relatively low cost of cultivation' (M.F.A.C., 1970:582). Most
Wangala and Dalena paddy growers use the I.R.8 variety of
seeds; some plant Taichung-65, while others still continue to use
their traditional varieties. All farmers in the two villages now
know that the improved varieties of seed can increase yields of
paddy per acre, but they also know that more inputs are required
to ensure increased productivity per unit of land. Farmers with
less than two wet acres often cannot raise the necessary working
capital to provide the additional inputs and therefore are virtually
forced to continue their customary paddy cultivation (see table 12).

Average labour inputs per paddy acre have increased in Wangala from 125 to 144 days, and in Dalena from 135 to 151. As
with their cane cultivation so with paddy Dalena farmers have
substituted hired for household labour and engaged more females
to reduce cash expenditure on casual labour. Wangala farmers,
too, now pay cash for a greater proportion of their labour inputs
on paddy fields. It is interesting to note here that Wangala and
Dalena farmers have rationalised their labour inputs only with
cane, their cash crop. By contrast they now invest more labour
days in their subsistence crops than they did in 1955.

There has hardly been any mechanisation in paddy cultivation,
but there has been an increase in the application of fertiliser. The
resulting rise in yields has increased the carrying capacity per
paddy acre; i.e. the number of individuals for which it can supply
a daily intake of about 1,500 calories has risen from three to four
in Wangala and from four to five in Dalena. Therefore the

TABLE 12

DISTRIBUTION OF RAGI AND PADDY YIELDS IN WANGALA SAMPLE HOUSEHOLDS

| Palla | per acre of wet ragi | | | | per acre of paddy | | | |
| | Number | | % | | Number | | % | |
| | 1965 | 1969 | 1965 | 1969 | 1955 | 1969 | 1955 | 1969 |
|---|---|---|---|---|---|---|---|---|
| 0 < 5 | 0 | 0 | 0 | 0 | 0 | 0 | 0 | 0 |
| 5 < 10 | 1 | 8 | 50 | 40 | 6 | 3 | 32 | 11 |
| 10 < 15 | 1 | 6 | 50 | 30 | 12 | 9 | 63 | 35 |
| 15 < 20 | 0 | 6 | 0 | 30 | 1 | 7 | 5 | 27 |
| 20 < 25 | 0 | 0 | 0 | 0 | 0 | 7 | 0 | 27 |
| Total No. of Households | 2 | 20 | 100 | 100 | 19 | 26 | 100 | 100 |
| Average yield per acre | *palla* 8.8 | 11.7 | | | *palla* 10.8 | 15.0 | | |

minimum wet area required to provide rice for the average household of five is one acre in the case of Dalena and one and a quarter acres in Wangala. The average wet land owned per household is 2.1 acres in Wangala whereas in Dalena it is less than one acre. Therefore many Dalena farmers are forced to turn to other sources of income outside agriculture to enable them to supplement their subsistence output with food purchased for cash (see table 13).

TABLE 13

### DISTRIBUTION OF PADDY YIELD PER ACRE IN DALENA SAMPLE HOUSEHOLDS

| | per acre of paddy | | | |
| | Number | | % | |
| Palla | 1956 | 1969 | 1956 | 1969 |
| --- | --- | --- | --- | --- |
| 0 < 5 | 0 | 0 | 0 | 0 |
| 5 < 10 | 0 | 0 | 0 | 0 |
| 10 < 15 | 6 | 2 | 46 | 14 |
| 15 < 20 | 6 | 5 | 46 | 36 |
| > 20 | 1 | 7 | 8 | 50 |
| Total No. of Households | 13 | 14 | 100 | 100 |
| | *palla* | | | |
| Average Yield per acre | 16.1 | 18.6 | | |

Ragi is the second most important food crop grown on wet land. Wangala farmers use it now extensively as crop rotation on cane land. Dalena farmers do not grow any ragi on their wet lands outside their own village. As already mentioned, a few Dalena farmers have attempted to irrigate some of their dry land with pumps and to grow ragi on it. Average yields per acre of wet ragi in Wangala are almost four times those in Dalena, yet in the latter case wet ragi acres produce considerably more subsidiary crops than in the former. This accounts for the fact that in monetary terms the average output per acre of wet ragi in Wangala is less than might first have been expected and not quite double that in Dalena. In Wangala in 1955 only 40 per cent of the average output per wet ragi acre was ragi itself : the remainder was made up of fodder and subsidiary crops. Now this proportion has fallen to less than 10 per cent. Wangala farmers nowadays prefer to use the more amply available paddy hay as fodder.

Average labour inputs per wet ragi acre in Wangala have more than doubled since 1955. This considerable increase is largely due to the fact that ragi is nowadays grown in crop rotation with sugar-cane, which necessitates labour-intensive removal of cane roots before the ground can be prepared for ragi. The range of labour days employed to cultivate one acre of wet ragi varies from 48 to 299 among the 20 sample farmers; only two of them used more than 200 labour days. These were two young men who were cultivating wet ragi for the first time after three crops of cane on their land. Each explained that he had been anxious to ensure that this crop rotation should yield the expected results and therefore put more labour into his wet ragi cultivation than into tending his other fields. These two young farmers felt slightly embarrassed when on separate occasions they gave details of the number of labour days they had employed for the various ragi cultivation activities. Each assured me that in future years he would be more sparing with his labour. They stressed the extraordinary nature of their cases and wanted me to exclude their details of cultivation from my calculations of wet ragi input and output among my sample households. I did not do so because I suspect that each year, at least for some years to come, there will be some farmers in Wangala who cultivate wet ragi for the first time after cane and who, like my friends, in their anxiety to assure good yields will similarly overinvest in labour.

Average labour inputs per pump-irrigated ragi acre in Dalena amount altogether to 66 days : 50 male and 16 female. It is the most male labour-intensive crop grown on Dalena village land. Moreover, it is also the most cash demanding of all the village crops. This comparatively high proportion of cash to total cultivation expenditure is due to the high cost of pump irrigation which is reflected in the cash overhead expenses. If subsistence inputs are evaluated at market rates and included as part of cultivation costs, all dry land crops produced in Dalena and Wangala involve deficits. However, the evaluation of subsistence inputs is not a realistic consideration for South Indian *ryots*. The market could not possibly absorb all their subsistence inputs and therefore does not really represent an alternative opportunity. Farmers are mainly concerned with yields per acre in real terms and how much cash is required to produce their crops. Average cash cost per pump-irrigated acre in Dalena takes up as much as 81 per cent of output and the amount exceeds double the average cash cost Dalena farmers need to cultivate dry ragi or jowar. This accounts for the small number of Dalena farmers who use pump irrigation and explains why Kempa gave it up on his land.

Dalena dry ragi yields have been severely affected by the low rainfall in recent years. This appears to be representative of dry land cultivation in the region. In this connection *Modernising Indian Agriculture* states with reference to Mandya district that 'large areas have been eroded to such an extent that no top soil has been left and exposure to barren subsoil and rocks has taken place. Crop failure would be a normal feature in such terrain, especially in years of irregular and insufficient rainfall' (M.F.A.C., 1970:575). Average yields per acre of dry ragi in Dalena have fallen from 2.4 pallas per acre to 0.75 pallas (see table 14). This helps to explain the fact that of my 21 sample households in 1970 only six managed to produce dry ragi while two attempted to do so but failed, whereas 18 of them had been reasonably successful in 1956. It also accounts for the decline in the total Dalena acreage under dry ragi from 370 to 230 acres. Jowar appears to be a somewhat more resistant crop than dry ragi; average yields per acre have slightly increased from 1.5 pallas to 1.8 pallas per acre. This is mirrored in a shift of emphasis from ragi to jowar cultivation in Dalena. More than half of my 1970 Dalena sample households cultivated jowar whereas only one-third of them had done so in 1956. The village acreage under jowar increased slightly from 177 to an estimated 180 acres. Jowar, however, is only of marginal importance to households' basic food consumption and therefore many Dalena farms still persevere in trying to grow dry ragi.

In Wangala the acreage under jowar has fallen from 116 to 20 and none of my 30 sample householders in 1970 cultivated jowar while 16 of them had done so in 1955. Average yields per acre dry ragi in Wangala have increased by 50 per cent from 2.4 pallas to 3.6 pallas (see table 15). In monetary terms dry ragi has become an even less remunerative crop than it was in 1955. This

TABLE 14

DISTRIBUTION OF RAGI AND JOWAR YIELDS IN DALENA SAMPLE HOUSEHOLDS

| Palla | per acre of dry ragi | | | | per acre of jowar | | | | per acre of wet ragi | |
| | Number | | % | | Number | | % | | Number | % |
| | 1956 | 1969 | 1956 | 1969 | 1956 | 1969 | 1956 | 1969 | 1969 | 1969 |
|---|---|---|---|---|---|---|---|---|---|---|
| 0 < 2 | 5 | 6 | 28 | 100 | 5 | 6 | 71 | 50 | 0 | 0 |
| 2 < 4 | 11 | 0 | 61 | 0 | 2 | 4 | 29 | 34 | 5 | 100 |
| 4 < 6 | 2 | 0 | 11 | 0 | 0 | 1 | 0 | 8 | 0 | 0 |
| 6 < 8 | 0 | 0 | 0 | 0 | 0 | 1 | 0 | 8 | 0 | 0 |
| Total No. of Households | 18 | 6 | 100 | 100 | 7 | 12 | 100 | 100 | 5 | 100 |
| Average Yield per acre | *palla* 2.4 | 0.75 | | | *palla* 1.5 | 1.8 | | | *palla* 3.03 | |

is due to the fact that previously Wangala farmers derived much more in terms of subsidiary output from their ragi acreages than they do now.

TABLE 15

DISTRIBUTION OF RAGI AND JOWAR YIELDS IN
WANGALA SAMPLE HOUSEHOLDS

| | *per acre of* dry ragi | | | | *per acre of* jowar* | |
| | Number | | % | | Number | % |
| Palla | 1955 | 1970 | 1955 | 1970 | 1955 | 1955 |
|---|---|---|---|---|---|---|
| 0 < 2 | 1 | 1 | 17 | 14 | 10 | 63 |
| 2 < 4 | 5 | 1 | 83 | 14 | 5 | 31 |
| 4 < 6 | 0 | 5 | 0 | 72 | 1 | 6 |
| Total No. of Households | 6 | 7 | 100 | 100 | 16 | 100 |
| Average Yield per acre | *palla* 2.4 | 3.6 | | | *palla* 1.6 | |

\* None of the sample farmers cultivated jowar in 1969.

The crop pattern in Dalena and Wangala clearly indicates that villagers give subsistence farming first priority. There is not a single wet land owner in either of these villages who has specialised in growing cane to the exclusion of food crops. By concentrating on cane Wangala farmers could with the farm wages and profits from one acre purchase more than twice the total produce of one acre of paddy, yet no one does this. This must not be regarded as irrational farmers' behaviour but rather as a reflection of the high risk discount rate they place on giving up their self-sufficiency. When food prices are rising rapidly, as they have been doing during the last fifteen years (see table 20) and while in drought years paddy may be hard to come by, it is not surprising that farmers regard substituting subsistence crops by cash crops as too risky a proposition.

Wangala and Dalena farmers are all small owner-occupiers: Wangala's largest holding consists of no more than 20 wet and 5 dry acres and Dalena's of 10 wet and 5 dry acres. In this respect the villages are representative of Mandya district where in 1968 over 86 per cent of operational holdings were owner-operated (M.F.A.C., 1970:571) and where the average size of holdings has declined from 8.65 acres to 7.90 acres between 1963 and 1968 (M.F.A.C., 1970:587). Rosen remarks that 'Peasants with holdings of 15 acres or more market a much higher proportion of their total output than do farmers with smaller holdings who are much more subsistence-minded and whose crop sales are in large part due to economic pressures' (1966:166). Though this is true it should be noted here that even the bigger landholders are subsistence-minded in as much as they produce subsistence crops, only they have more land surplus to their subsistence needs which they can devote to cash crops than have smallholders. Wangala farmers displayed considerable price-sensitivity in respect of cane, a crop they cannot readily consume themselves. Moreover, they were more cost-conscious with their cash crops than with their subsistence production. This emerges clearly from their tendency to rationalise labour inputs for cane but not so for subsistence crops.

The same farmer seems to employ different criteria in allocating resources to his various agricultural activities : maximum yield in real terms per acre is his main consideration in subsistence production whereas maximisation of farm wages and profits per acre decide his cash cropping.

## RURAL CO-OPERATIVE SOCIETIES

Wangala and Dalena farmers are all *ryots*, of whom only a few are sufficiently wealthy to be able to finance increased inputs in agriculture without going into debt. The efficient provision of rural credit has been receiving official attention for a long time. One solution to this problem was suggested in the form of village co-operative societies. Accordingly a publicity campaign enrolled the support of villagers in Mandya district.

Wangala joins with four smaller neighbouring villages in one co-operative society, which was started in 1960 and now has altogether about 500 members. In 1970 Wangala had 244 co-operators, of whom 222 are Peasants, 12 are A.K.s and the remaining 10 belong to the resident Functionary castes. The small house which now provides office and meeting place for the society was originally built by the Public Works Department to house the servant of one of the irrigation engineers who lived in the village at the time the canals were being built. During my earlier stay in Wangala it was occupied by the sister of a man employed as irrigation overseer by the Public Works Department. When she vacated the house on the marriage of her daughter, the *panchayat* decided to adopt the property for public purposes. It has been the co-operative office ever since. When I went there to talk to the Society's paid secretary he proudly showed me the books he was keeping. From these it emerged that the 244 Wangala co-operators had a total share capital of Rs. 39,000; by July 1970 the Society had granted total credits amounting to Rs. 1,033,250.

For the year 1971, 195 Wangala farmers have taken loans from the co-operative society to a total value of Rs. 173,200, making an average loan of about Rs. 880 per borrower. The total sum of outstanding debts owed by 124 farmers was Rs. 112,279.

These overall totals of co-operative loans granted, though indicating the order of co-operative loan transactions in Wangala, do not reveal the different amounts loaned by individual farmers. Wealthy Wangala Peasants who have comparatively large landholdings manage to borrow big amounts ranging up to Rs. 3,000, while a large number of poorer farmers could only secure small loans of Rs. 100 or Rs. 200. The richer Peasants are therefore in a much better position to buy large quantities of fertiliser on credit and thereby ensure a good harvest than are the poorer farmers. The richer a man, the more credit-worthy he becomes. The richest therefore can easily get loans from the co-operative society at the official rate of interest of six per cent per year, which is just half the rate private money-lenders charge. Poorer farmers are still often driven to take loans from money-lenders, particularly if they need money for other than cultivation purposes, and therefore are at the mercy of these usurers. As already mentioned, the amount of money a member can borrow from the Society is limited by the number of his shares and the size of his landholding. Moreover, the Society is directed by a Board of wealthy landowners, who have a vested interest in restricting credits to the poorest farmers.

Wangala farmers readily saw the benefits to be derived from participating in the co-operative movement and therefore keep it a going concern. In this instance they are prepared to work together with four neighbouring villages, whereas they have opted out of the Group *Panchayat* because, they say, they want to be bosses in their own village and do not want councillors from other villages poking their noses into what is strictly Wangala business (see p. 176). Wangala villagers are not altogether opposed to participating in institutions introduced from outside; however, a positive response depends on their appreciating that it offers them benefits.

Dalena's co-operative society was far less successful. It was started in 1960 with a share capital of about Rs. 4,000, but soon began to run into difficulties; shareholders failed to repay their loans. Dalena co-operators did not only buy farm inputs on credit and much of the crops failed due to drought; they also borrowed money for activities other than agricultural where they could not expect seasonal returns. A number of villagers used the Society's short-term loans for longer term investments. This caused the collapse of Dalena's Society. By 1970 it had ceased functioning altogether. Its share capital was held in trust by the Mandya District Co-operative Society and it still had Rs. 12,000 outstanding debts. Some of the wealthier Dalena farmers have made repeated attempts to revive their Society but so far without much success.

The diversified economic interests of Dalena's population make it difficult for a rural co-operative society to function successfully in the village. By contrast, Wangala's more uniform farming activities ensure the continued existence of an institution specifically aimed at promoting agriculture. *Modernising Indian Agriculture* remarks in this context with reference to Mandya district that 'the performance of co-operatives in irrigated areas was better compared to those in dry areas, where recovery of loans was not satisfactory on account of chronic failure of rains and consequently of crops' (M.F.A.C., 1970:583).

## VILLAGE BUSINESS VENTURES

The increased wealth in the Mandya region which resulted from canal irrigation is now reflected in a growing number of business ventures in the rural hinterland. Most of the bigger villages in the area have several cafés (*hotelu*), shops (*angadi*), cane-crushers (*alémané*) and rice mills (*battad girni*); some also have specialised cattle traders (*dalali*). A period of rapid agricultural growth in small developing economies is usually followed by the establishment of processing and service facilities. I have found a similar pattern of development in a New Guinea society with a culture entirely different from that of South Indian villages (1968:45).

In 1955 there was only a single small café in Wangala, housed in a thatched-roof hut specially erected for the purpose. Nowadays there are five caste cafés strung along the main Mandya road, one more is in the interior of the village and one operates in the A.K. section : five of the six caste cafés are run by recent immigrants to Wangala; two are Lingayats and the rest are Peasants. Kempegowda's case is typical of a Wangala café. He comes from a place about five miles away where he has two acres of dry land and where he started a café, but without much success. He began to look around for alternative villages in which to run a café. During this period he visited Wangala frequently because his sister was married to a Peasant in the village and his younger brother married the daughter of a Wangala Peasant. On his visits he saw how frequently Wangala villagers travelled to Mandya and learnt how much time they spent in town cafés. This gave him the idea that a café in Wangala might be a profitable proposition. He moved to Wangala about three years ago when there were no more than three refreshment places in the village. Utilising links his brother-in-law had in the village, he managed to rent an old house from one of the Peasants who had built himself a new one. He pays Rs. 15 rent per month and lives there with his wife and six children. He uses one room as a kitchen and another one and the verandah to accommodate his clients. His total investment was no more than Rs. 20 for cups and plates and Rs. 10 for benches and one table. His average daily turnover is about Rs. 25, made up by selling 150 cups of tea and coffee at Rs. 0.10 each and light refreshments for Rs. 10; the raw food required for preparing all this costs Rs. 10 and the fuel, electricity and rent amount to another Rs. 7 per day. Kempegowda's business profit and his and his wife's wages per day amount to approximately Rs. 8, which is more than double what the two of them could earn in a day working as agricultural labourers. Kempegowda is thus considerably better off running his own café than working on the land. Moreover, he feels that he is more in command of his own destiny by preparing refreshments for sale than he would be if he worked as an agricultural labourer or even if he found employment in the nearby town. He proudly told me that by being a *good* cook he had managed to establish a reputation for himself for preparing excellent *idly* (a light refreshment, made of rice flour, which is widely consumed in South India) and good coffee and tea. In this way he has succeeded in building up a reasonably profitable business. He returns to his home village from time to time to cultivate the two acres of dry land he still has there. With the Rs. 220 which Kempegowda nets out of his café business every month and his subsistence output, he manages reasonably well. The only other income-earning alternative open to him would be rural wage labour, which is less remunerative and much harder to come by than running a café. Kempegowda explained that to keep a café is no easy job either : he is always at the beck and call of his customers, he has to keep a fire going all the time so as to be able to prepare hot drinks at a moment's notice and he has to get cups and plates washed quickly. Yet he stressed over and over again how pleased he was that he had managed to establish this café in Wangala rather than have to rely on uncertain casual labour for his income.

Village cafés are places where men meet fellow villagers as well as outsiders and where news is passed on and gossip exchanged. It is generally regarded as wrong for village women to sit down in a café and take drink and/or food there; by doing so they would imply that they were too lazy to prepare this for themselves. I never saw a single village woman in any of the many cafés I visited during my stay in the Mandya region. None of the cafés sell on credit; payment is always cash down. This is essential in businesses where a high proportion of the clientele is from outside. Kempegowda estimates that less than 50 per cent of his income is derived from intra-village customers, the rest are men who pass through Wangala on the way to or from Mandya.

Kempegowda's is probably the busiest café in Wangala. There is only one other of the six caste cafés in the village which gets anywhere near as much business as his does. This one is situated almost opposite Kempegowda's to the west of the main road. Its proprietor started the first café in the village. During my earlier stay there he ran it in a little hut near the Public Works Department well, where there is now a Shiva shrine. His new café has a thatched roof like the old one but is much bigger and provides much more verandah space for customers to sit and take their refreshments. This café frequently gets the overflow if Kempegowda's across the road is already full up. The fact that one and the same man still operates a café after fifteen years indicates that it must be a reasonably remunerative business. The two cafés between them sell about 300 cups per day. The remaining four caste cafés, which are less frequented, serve daily altogether probably another 350 cups. Five hundred of these 650 cups served daily in Wangala are probably consumed by indigenous villagers. As there are approximately 330 adult caste males resident in Wangala their daily *per capita* consumption of drinks in cafés amounts to one and a half cups. Some villagers regularly take three or four cups daily in the local café, which means that they spend at least a couple of hours each day chatting there.

In a society such as Wangala, where the literacy rate is still very low and newspapers and letters reach the village only on rare occasions, gossip provides an essential channel of communication. There are thirty-four radios in the village, but rarely are the broadcasts of immediate interest to Wangala listeners; they are interested in local gossip about forthcoming marriages or some neighbourhood quarrel or scandal. Some, however, do listen keenly to programmes relating to agricultural activities, such as advice when to plant what crop and so on.

Villagers had been conditioned to visiting cafés on their visits to Mandya, where there is a great number of small restaurants catering for the casual visitor to the town who wants a place where he can meet his friends and acquaintances and gossip with them or discuss problems over a cup of coffee. Villagers learned in the town to appreciate the facilities cafés provide. Greater rural wealth resulted in a rapid growth in the number of cafés in villages and this enables farmers to partake of the pleasures of a chat in a café while enjoying a hot drink even within the borders of their own village.

Each caste café has usually a set of cups specifically kept for A.K. customers. When an A.K. wants to buy a drink at any of Wangala's caste cafés he remains out of doors and the cup is passed to him, he hands over the money in return and leaves the cup outside the entrance to the café after he has finished his drink. There is one café in Wangala's A.K. section. Unlike caste cafés it is off the road and only serves hot drinks at odd times during the day. It is housed in a tiny thatched hut typical of village A.K. housing. Unless one knows that drinks can be obtained there one walks past without noticing it. I myself passed the hut several times – it was closed on each occasion – and I was not aware that it operated as a café until this was pointed out to me. My A.K. friends explained that the café had very little business. Most of them are too poor to treat themselves to the luxuries of coffee or tea and those few who do want to buy themselves drinks prefer to go to the caste cafés, although there they have to remain outdoors. They explained this preference on the basis that the A.K. café keeper was so poor that he could not afford to store much coffee or tea at any one time. He therefore has to make his stocks go a long way and puts less coffee or tea into a cup than is done in the caste café, which makes it less palatable. On an average there are no more than 20 cups served weekly in this A.K. café and this includes drinks served to visiting A.K.s from other villages. The low level of A.K. income deters the majority of them from 'wasting' their precious cash on visits to a café.

The greater number of cafés in villages is one visible sign of increased caste wealth, that of shops another. In 1955 there were three shops in Wangala, two run by Muslims who have since left; now there are six caste-run stores, four of which are part of new houses built along the main road.

The *patel*'s younger brother, called chairman, had decided before he ever embarked on building his new two-storey house by the roadside that he would have a store there. Accordingly, a suitable little room at the front of it formed part of the original house plan. Now in his early sixties, he runs the shop himself. He sits behind the counter and serves his customers personally. He opens seven days per week about five hours per day – from about 9.30 a.m. to midday and from 4.30 p.m. to 7 p.m., the times of the day when most housewives are preparing meals and when many of them find that they have need of certain spices or similar necessities in their cooking. The chairman refuses to sell on credit; frequently he insists on being handed, or at least shown, the appropriate cash before he starts weighing the item demanded. He explained that many times mothers send their children to get things from the shop without giving them the necessary money to pay. The chairman had firmly decided before he started his retailing activities never to sell on credit and he has kept to it.

Credit sales have become the rare exception in Wangala's shops, whereas formerly they used to be the general rule. The chairman attributed the change to the greater amount of cash villagers have these days. As long as cash was extremely scarce Peasants were reluctant to run shops simply because they knew they would be subjected to demands for credit, which they felt they could hardly refuse. Nowadays, there is the general feeling that each caste household in the village has more than sufficient cash income to meet basic requirements. Improved economic conditions have resulted in a relaxation of mutual aid requirements. This seems to have encouraged indigenous Peasants to open shops in the village and has removed the necessity for outsiders, such as Muslims, to keep shops in Wangala. All of Wangala's six caste shops are owned by indigenes.

The village shops stock mainly household requirements, such as staple grains, spices, cooking and heating oil, as well as sundries like country cigarettes, cigarettes, matches and areca nuts with betel leaves. Their stocks of any one item are never very big and are usually particularly low just before the weekly fair in Mandya, when most shopkeepers travel to Mandya to replenish their depleted supplies. The chairman is typical in this respect: every Wednesday he goes by bus to Mandya, where he buys goods worth about Rs. 90 from one or two wholesalers in Mandya, where he gets 20 per cent discount off retail prices. He spends another Rs. 10 on goods purchased at the fair and takes his supplies back with him to Wangala by bus. He sells his stock during the week for Rs. 140 while he himself pays no more than Rs. 100 for it. He does not think of charging for his labour in looking after his store and calculates that he makes about Rs. 40 weekly profits. However, he had to invest Rs. 300 in setting up his shop by acquiring a scale and having shelves put up; moreover, it costs him about Rs. 2 per week for electricity to keep his shop lit up in the evenings and he foregoes rent of Rs. 5 which he could get if he let his premises. Therefore, his net business profits and wages amount to approximately Rs. 28 per week, which is only 20 per cent of his turnover and hardly a very high reward for the business acumen required of a retailer and the risk he runs. The chairman is aware of the fact that other business ventures such as cane-crushers and cafés are much more profitable than retailing, but he explained that he lacked the necessary finance to invest in a costly capital asset such as a cane-crusher, while on the other hand he knew he could not run a café. 'I know that I could make a lot more money by running a café, but I could not possibly undertake the sort of work involved : washing dishes and cooking all day. This is no job for me !'

Almost all the customers in Wangala shops are indigenous to the village. It happens only rarely that outsiders passing through the village stop to buy country cigarettes or matches. The monthly turnover of Wangala's six caste shops amounts roughly to Rs. 3,500 for an estimated number of consumption units of 1,130. The monthly local cash purchases per consumption unit amount to no more than Rs. 3, which constitute about 25 per cent of Peasant middle-farmers' cash expenditure and less than 10 per cent of magnates'. Therefore in their role as buyers Wangala villagers have many links with the wider economy. Each indigeneous household is dependent for the majority of its cash purchases on trips to Mandya or occasionally even to Mysore or Bangalore. Villagers are shrewd customers; before buying they examine prices of a great many sellers and try to get the best deal by strong bargaining. By contrast with the buying pattern at the town fair or bazaars there is no bargaining at village shops. Wangala people explain that part of the fun of going to Mandya is the lengthy bargaining process even over the smallest purchases, but this is, they stress, possible only in an impersonal relationship between buyer and seller. It is unthinkable to them to start bargaining for a lower price for their small purchases with any of their fellow villagers acting as retailer.

There is only one A.K. shop in Wangala, which is run by the same man who operates the café. Like the café it opens only spasmodically and has a negligible turnover. Unlike the caste shops in the village, the A.K. one cannot refuse credit to his fellow residents of whose difficulties in making ends meet he is well aware. Therefore, periodically when his stocks run out and he has no funds to replenish them he has a hard time trying to call in his loans.

In Dalena, as in Wangala and most other villages in the area, the number of cafés and shops is bigger now than it used to be; in 1956 Dalena had one café and one shop, now there are five cafés and six shops. Trade in these cafés and shops, however, is a lot less than in Wangala; for most times during the day they are empty. They are fairly busy only in the evenings when men return home from their daily activities which take them outside the village. Moreover, as Dalena does not lie on one of the radial roads out of Mandya, but is situated a few hundred yards off the major highway, outsiders rarely pass through the village unless they have come for the specific purpose of visiting someone there. In Dalena's A.K. section there is neither a café nor a shop. Residents there are too few and too poor to warrant such facilities. The two Dalena A.K.s who managed to secure permanent employment are both working outside the village and one of them has actually moved to Mandya. The remaining A.K. households have a hard time trying to meet their basic subsistence requirements let alone spend money on luxuries such as drinking coffee or tea.

Dalena men have established a reputation in the region for being expert cattle traders. Frequently farmers from neighbouring irrigated villages go there to buy or sell cattle. One day when I sat talking to some of my friends in Dalena a party of four Wangala Peasants arrived, wanting to purchase a strong pair of bullocks. One Dalena man immediately invited the visitors to come to one of the local cafés, where he treated all of us to coffee and where the negotiations were conducted in an informal atmosphere. The Wangala farmers spent almost four hours in Dalena, during which they were shown two pairs of bullocks and treated to three coffees each. They carefully examined the bullocks and then argued over the price of the pair they were interested in acquiring. The Dalena seller asked Rs. 1,800 and the Wangala buyer offered Rs. 1,600. The deal was finally clinched at Rs. 1,700. The vendor had bought the bullocks two weeks previously at a nearby village for Rs. 1,450. He thus made a profit of Rs. 250 on the transaction, having had to keep the pair for no more than two weeks. This is a handsome amount: i.e. 17 per cent gain on his initial outlay. However, the seller was lucky on this occasion in finding a buyer so quickly. On other occasions he and other Dalena men who buy cattle for resale may have to wait many months before they manage to find a buyer; if and when they do, their profit is not always as high as it was in the case I myself witnessed and they have the expense of feeding the cattle in the meantime.

The customary type of middle-man in cattle trading (*dalali*) seems to have disappeared altogether in Dalena, though it still exists in Wangala. According to tradition each village in the area had its few men who were known to act as intermediaries in cattle transactions. Many of these *dalalis* had come to their office by hereditary succession. Their function was to bring buyers and sellers together, to narrow the gap between the price asked by the latter and that offered by the former. A *dalali*'s fee was very small, no more than Rs. 2 irrespective of the value of the transaction he mediated. The sale and purchase of cattle represents a very important economic transaction and has therefore always been the subject of keen haggling even among fellow villagers. *Dalalis* act as intermediaries in all sales between inhabitants of the same village; these mediating activities enable the two parties to a sale to continue social relations after they have faced each other as bitter opponents in the process of bargaining. *Dalalis* act in the role of the 'stranger' (Frankenberg, 1957:18) and are essential in avoiding the disruption in personal relations likely to result from the opposition between a buyer and a seller. In Wangala, where intra-village relations have continued to be strong, *dalalis* still operate in the customary way. By contrast, in Dalena, where the increasing range of social relations has reduced the intensity of intra-village links, *dalalis* have become cattle traders in the modern context of impersonal cash transactions.

The impartial intermediary in a cattle sale has given way to a self-interested dealer. The Dalena Peasant whose sale of bullocks I observed used to be a *dalali* of the traditional type. In this capacity he learned all about the cattle trade : the features in bullocks which make them into valuable beasts, price fluctuations and trends, sources of demand and supply, and so on. This expertise encouraged and enabled him to branch out into cattle trading as a business proposition. Profits from such transactions now form the major part of his annual cash income. There are at least a dozen Dalena Peasants who are skilled and reasonably successful cattle dealers, though each operates on a small scale only.

In Wangala and in Dalena there are some men who have shown quick and positive response to new economic opportunities not only in services but also in processing. For instance, when jaggery prices were booming and consequently demand for village cane-crushing facilities increased to unprecedented proportions some Wangala Peasants quickly tried to emulate Beregowda's example and set up cane-crushers : by 1965 four more had been opened in the village, three more had started operating by 1968. During the earlier period of the jaggery boom all of Wangala's five cane-crushers were operating at full capacity for about eight or nine months in the year. The annual net profits these processing plants earned amounted to approximately Rs. 6,000 each. Cost of labour constituted about 45 per cent of total expenditure. This labour is paid on a contract basis. The cane-crusher proprietor arranges with one experienced operative to process cane into jaggery at the rate of Rs. 12 per 1,000 cubes. The number of labourers actually working on the job depends on the efficiency of the contractor : the fewer helpers he employs the higher his own reward. Neither the contractors nor the owners of cane-crushers whom I questioned admitted that there is a general rule deciding the contractor's own share in the takings. Yet when I enquired into the specific distributions of contract money received in a number of instances it emerged that in most cases the contractor keeps two shares of the money for himself : one for his managerial function and the other for his own labour. If one contractor engaged seven helpers to process 3,000 pieces of jaggery in a day, he himself kept Rs. 8 of the Rs. 36 he received and each of his co-labourers got Rs. 4. The daily wage a man can earn by helping to process cane is thus almost double the rate for casual agricultural labour. However, it is much more difficult to get work in a cane-crusher than it is to do casual labouring for which the over-all demand is greater. Most of the men working at Wangala cane-crushers were migrants, who had acquired the necessary know-how at similar plants in other villages. At a later stage I discuss how the migrants affected Wangala labour; at this point in the argument I am mainly concerned with the entrepreneurial aspect of these new business ventures.

The overhead expenditure of village cane-crushers is made up

of an interest charge on the investment of Rs. 28,000, depreciation
of the building and machinery as well as a minimum electricity
charge of Rs. 60 per month. These liabilities are so high that it
is necessary for a cane-crusher to operate at least four months in
a year to break even. The greater the tonnage of cane processed
the greater the net profit : by operating eight months in the year
Beregowda's cane-crusher produces Rs. 6,240 profits, about 25
per cent of total takings (see table 16).

As long as jaggery prices were booming and demand for village
cane-crushers was high all Wangala plants were working at
almost full capacity. With a daily cane processing capacity of
nine tons a crusher can process about 1,000 tons in four months.
This quantity of cane is produced on approximately 25 acres.
Therefore, Wangala's eight cane-crushers now depend altogether
on processing the product of about 200 acres to enable them just
to cover their costs. This is a considerable acreage under cane for
village conditions : it represents approximately two-thirds of
Wangala's area under cane. There is of course the possibility of
cane-growers from neighbouring villages using Wangala crushing plants; however, it is unlikely that outsiders will make up
more than a small proportion of cane-crushing business in Wangala. Indigenous farmers undoubtedly are the main customers.

Since 1968 jaggery prices have slumped, which makes farmers
once more struggle to secure contracts with the refinery for the
maximum tonnage possible. Farmers now want to keep to a minimum the quantity of cane they process into jaggery and sell as
such. This in turn results in a drastic fall in demand for village
cane-crushers and means a net loss to many of their owners.
Four of Wangala's eight cane-crushers incorporate a rice mill.
The cost involved to instal this additional machinery was not
great, neither are these mills yielding much profit, if any. Wangala mills depend for business solely on their village clientele.
There is not enough indigenous demand to keep the village mills
busy.

Wangala's eight cane-crushers now constitute an over-invest-
ment and each of the proprietors complains bitterly about his
losses. Yet ownership of cane-crushers is not merely an economic
proposition, but a criterion for prestige. Each proprietor proudly
showed me his plant, which I duly admired. Yet some of these
village entrepreneurs are so disappointed by the failure of their

TABLE 16

ESTIMATED WANGALA ANNUAL CANE-CRUSHER ACCOUNT

| INCOME | Four months operations Rs. | Six months operations Rs. | Eight months operations Rs. | EXPENDITURE | Four months operations Rs. | Six months operations Rs. | Eight months operations Rs. |
|---|---|---|---|---|---|---|---|
| Cane processing | 12,600 | 18,900 | 25,200 | Labour (Rs. 36 per day) | 4,320 | 6,480 | 8,640 |
| | | | | Electricity | 1,080 | 1,260 | 1,560 |
| | | | | Fuel | 1,200 | 1,800 | 2,400 |
| | | | | Interest (Rs. 28,000 @ 12%) | 3,360 | 3,360 | 3,360 |
| | | | | Depreciation (Rs. 25,000 @ 10%) | 2,500 | 2,500 | 2,500 |
| | | | | Maintenance | 120 | 200 | 300 |
| | | | | Miscellaneous | 20 | 150 | 200 |
| | | | | Profits | 0 | 3,150 | 6,240 |
| Total | 12,600 | 18,900 | 25,200 | Total | 12,600 | 18,900 | 25,200 |

first ventures that they are discouraged from looking around for alternative opportunities, whereas others keenly seek new investment outlets.

For instance, Beregowda, the man who introduced power-driven cane processing in Wangala, is now considering converting his plant into an oil mill. He knows the owner of such an oil plant in Mysore and had visited it several times to investigate its possibilities for his own village. In 1970 he himself experimentally planted a crop of peanuts on his Wangala lands so as to find out the yield per acre and to establish if growing oil crops could successfully compete against producing sugar-cane. If he can show that the various oil crops can provide farm returns that compare favourably with those derived from sugar-cane then he intends introducing these crops while at the same time adapting his cane-crusher to act also as oilpress. Beregowda discussed all this with me in great detail. He wanted my advice on what I considered profitable ventures for him and some of his fellow villagers. In view of the considerable increase in traffic between villages and Mandya as well as Mysore I suggested he might consider acquiring a large truck. He gave this careful thought, but then replied that he did not think he could successfully compete with urban transport businesses.

In a similar discussion, Nanjegowda of Dalena immediately took up the idea of providing transport facilities. By contrast with Wangala's outstanding entrepreneur, the Dalena young man did not seem to be afraid of competing in the wider economy. Furthermore, he asked me to try and get him details of investment and operation costs of machinery to produce refined sugar on a small scale; he was seriously considering setting up in competition with the large sugar refineries in Mandya and Pandavapura. He had himself already unsuccessfully tried to obtain the cost details in Bangalore and even in Madras which he now expected me to supply.

Dalena entrepreneurs have already had experience of competing in the wider economy. The headman started his first flour mill by a nearby rail junction at the beginning of the last war. His son related that this first business venture proved so successful that they decided to open another such flour mill, this time together with a cane-crusher, right on the major highway so as to attract road transport, to have paddy and cane processed at their plants. The headman bought this strategic site for Rs. 1,500 in 1960. He then had a fine building erected and the necessary machinery installed. Altogether he spent about Rs. 70,000 on these various items. He only had about Rs. 15,000 ready cash at the time and borrowed the rest from a number of *ryots*. His monthly mill profits amount to about Rs. 840 (see table 17). He managed to repay his debt of Rs. 55,000 within about five years. His mill has become a landmark on the road from Mandya to Mysore; he has even installed a telephone in his office.

TABLE 17

### ESTIMATED DALENA MONTHLY FLOUR MILL ACCOUNT

| Income | Rs. | Expenditure | Rs. |
|---|---|---|---|
| Flourmilling (45 quintals per day @ Rs. 2 per quintal) | 2,430 | Labour | 350 |
| | | Electricity | 150 |
| | | Interest (Rs. 70,000 @ 12%) | 700 |
| | | Depreciation (Rs. 70,000 @ 5%) | 290 |
| | | Maintenance | 50 |
| | | Miscellaneous | 50 |
| | | Profits | 840 |
| Total | 2,430 | | 2,430 |

Both Wangala and Dalena entrepreneurs have thus branched out into providing services and processing facilities; they have opened cafés and shops, act as cattle traders and are operating cane-crushers and rice mills. The big difference, though, between the two villages in this respect is that Wangala's entrepreneurial activities are chiefly operated with a view to providing facilities for fellow villagers, whereas Dalena's business activities are largely directed at outsiders. This development is in line with Wangala's continued inward-looking concentration on the one hand and Dalena's further integration in the wider economy on the other.

## VILLAGE FUNCTIONARIES

Dalena's and Wangala's populations still include a number of Functionary caste residents, some of whom are migrants only temporarily in the village. Only three of the seven Functionary households in Dalena still pursue their traditional occupation: one Washerman, one Barber and one Blacksmith. The others work as factory or agricultural labourers.

By contrast, Wangala's more flourishing rural economy sustains a greater number of Functionary caste men who still follow their traditional crafts. Some of them continue to have hereditary relationships with indigenous Peasants and receive fixed annual rewards in kind disregarding the quantity and quality of work they perform. Two Washerman families are still washing the Peasants' dirty clothes for which they get the customary rewards. The Blacksmith, who by 1955 had already taken over the hereditary role of Wangala's indigenous Blacksmith, continues to repair farmers' wooden ploughs and other traditional equipment and gets paid in kind. The Blacksmith who was thus replaced still makes and repairs iron ploughs and other tools on a purely cash basis. He kindly allowed me to copy the book in which he records in detail his income and expenditure. From this it emerges that his gross income for the six months from January to June 1970 was Rs. 1,073.25, giving him an approximate average monthly net income of about Rs. 130 just from his craft activities. Besides this he cultivates two acres dry and one acre wet land. In terms of income he now ranks among the centre stratum of Wangala's middle-farmers. He managed to raise his economic status simply on the basis of his own initiative. None of the other indigenous Functionary households displayed anything like the drive shown by this one Blacksmith.

The Potters and Goldsmiths have more or less surrendered their craft occupations because of serious competition from outside. The Potters have completely given up making clay pots. Village households now prefer to use brass, aluminium or stainless steel vessels. Village pottery craft is therefore dying out. Yet some of the young Goldsmiths in Wangala are still highly skilled in their craft, having served their apprenticeship with their own fathers. One of them made by hand for me a silver necklace and pendant which are superbly finished. He and some of his fellow caste men are real artists. They would like to spend all their time making jewellery and bitterly complain that there just is not enough work for them to keep them going even for a few weeks in the year. They have to supplement the meagre income from their craft activities by cultivating their small plots of land and working as casual agricultural labourers.

Extension of irrigation, which increased demand for labour, has not only attracted migrant Voddas to Wangala but also a number of Functionary caste households. Some of them have settled more or less permanently on the outskirts of the village residential area. One Pigbreeder and one Salt-trader household have each built a small pigshed and make their living by breeding pigs which they sell in the village or in the wider region. Other Functionary households have settled in Wangala and depend for their income solely on casual agricultural labour. These are land-less Functionaries who left their home villages because there just was no livelihood for them there. Demand for their specific craft has either declined, as is the case with Goldsmiths, or it has disappeared altogether, as with village Potters; alternatively, increasing numbers in certain crafts created an oversupply of Functionaries in relation to fixed or only slowly growing demand; Washermen are a case in point.

The fate of Functionaries in Dalena and Wangala illustrates the decline in village crafts. Except for the very few who continue their hereditary relationships with the landowners in the village or the rare craft entrepreneur like the Blacksmith, Functionaries increasingly have to give up their traditional craft occupation and turn to other income-earning activities. Those Functionaries who are fortunate enough to own at least some land tend to remain in their villages and try to supplement their farm income by working as casual labourers for larger landowners. The landless Functionaries usually seem to have no other option but to join the mass of migrants in search of work.

## WAGE LABOUR

The economic expansion of the Mandya region has brought in its wake an increased demand for urban as well as for rural labour. This in turn has attracted a growing influx of migrants from other parts of Mysore as well as from neighbouring States. The streets of Mandya town throng with men and women many of whom just walk around in search of work. Frequently farmers from the rural hinterland use the facilities of urban cafés to engage some of these migrants to come to their villages to perform certain tasks on their lands. Though demand for various types of labour has increased, supply still outstrips it.

Urban growth (see p. 69) has provided an increasing number of more regular industrial employment opportunities. It appears that the regionally dominant Peasant caste exerts prior claims to these new jobs. A large number of these more permanent Mandya workers are Peasant farmers who live in surrounding villages. Their estates are too small to keep them fully occupied or provided with at least a minimum of subsistence. They therefore seek to supplement their meagre farm income by earning an urban wage. Dalena offers a good example to illustrate this point.

Dalena land is still dry; irrigation and resulting indigenous economic growth has passed the village by. Many Dalena Peasants acquired wet land in neighbouring villages. Their need to have local workers on the spot there and the limited labour demand for dry cultivation led soon after the arrival of the canals to the disappearance of the traditional hereditary labour relationships which had previously existed between Peasant farmers and indigenous A.K. households.

I estimated that in 1956 32 men working 300 days in the year should have been able to cope with all the work necessary to cultivate Dalena dry lands. However, as agricultural labour requirements are highly seasonal, particularly in dry areas, and men have other jobs to do besides cultivating their fields, I made a 100 per cent allowance for these factors. Even then 64 of the 199 men of working age could easily perform all the jobs within the village. Accordingly, Dalena's male labour force could then have been deemed more than 65 per cent under-employed within the boundaries of its home economy (1962:226). As already mentioned, some Dalena farmers now try to irrigate their dry land with the aid of pumps. Altogether about 50 acres of ragi are cultivated in this way. This wet ragi requires more than double the male labour input needed for dry ragi. Moreover, the increased population and the abnormally low rainfall during the past few years appears to be responsible for a greater number of male labour days worked even on dry crops. Although the Dalena dry acreage cultivated in 1969 was about 10 per cent less than in 1956, the total number of male days spent on cultivation have increased by about 50 per cent from 9,940 to 14,646.

The size of the male working population has also increased by about 50 per cent to 300 men in this period. Household members perform about 75 per cent of the male cultivating tasks. It is therefore possible that the increase in village under-employment may have induced farmers to spend more days cultivating their dry land by working less hard or fewer hours per day. The total male labour input of 14,646 days may therefore represent an exaggeration of labour day requirements. However, even if we assume that it is realistic, about 50 men each working 300 days per year would suffice. Then, if we double this number to allow for various contingencies, as for the earlier estimate, the total number of men required to meet all intra-village labour require-ments is no more than one hundred. This means that Dalena's whole labour force is under-employed to the extent of 66 per cent of its capacity within the village. This fact, together with the low productivity of dry land which cannot provide any more than even the bare minimum of staple crops for the growing popula-tion (see p. 89), has made outside work a dire necessity for many Dalena residents.

The number of Dalena men in regular employment outside has increased from 26 to 41 : 33 of these workers are Peasants, five are Washermen, one is an Oilpresser and two are A.K.s. All 33 Peasant workers own some land in Dalena; for them wages represent a necessary supplement to their small subsistence out-put. The Functionaries and A.K.s are all landless and depend solely on wages for their livelihood. Three of the Washermen, one A.K. and five Peasants have left Dalena and taken up resi-dence near their place of work. Seven of these nine emigrants were already married and have taken their families with them. In spite of the fact that some of these Peasant wage earners have by now been in regular employment outside the village for about 20 years – a few of them have even lived in towns for as long as ten years – they still regard themselves as villagers and look upon their urban employment as only a temporary phase in their lives.

All the Peasant wage earners have still got some dry land in Dalena; some of them have even bought wet land in neighbour-ing villages. All these men are keen to maintain their stake in the rural economy. The case of Chennu (Epstein, 1962:302), a Peasant worker who had become a spirit medium prior to 1956, illustrates the activities, attitudes and interests of Dalena men in urban employment, as well as the contradictory pulls to which these men are subjected.

Chennu is now a man getting on for forty; he started work in the sugar refinery as an unskilled labourer when he was 17 and commuted to work. His job in Mandya took him out of the village for most of his time. On the one hand he enjoyed becoming part of a wider community with a wider horizon : already in 1956 he sported a bicycle, a golden watch and went about dressed in spotless white shirt and *dhoti*; on the other, he resented being left out of village society, which may have led him to become a medium. As such he was expected to lead an exemplary life. During my earlier stay in Dalena, Chennu regretfully admitted that as a factory worker he could not avoid taking food in town cafés. Therefore, he found it impossible to be a strict vegetarian like the other village spirit mediums. However, at the time he vowed celibacy. When I met him again in 1970 he was married and had four children. Seemingly to make up for this lapse in his behaviour he had become a vegetarian. He related that through his contact with Peasant workers in the factory he managed in 1960 to have his marriage arranged to a Peasant girl from Mysore city. She had already reached maturity and therefore her parents were keen to marry her off to an outsider. He brought his young wife to live with him in Dalena, but having been used to a large city like Mysore she could not get accustomed to life in a village. In 1966 he had the opportunity of renting a house in Mandya at the refinery compound and under pressure from his wife he arranged their move to the town. Chennu and his family now live in one of the small factory-built and factory-owned houses for which they pay Rs. 2 rent per month. The walls of their small sitting-room are decorated all over with images of deities in silver and brass as well as large photographs of various Hindu gods. Chennu now works on the weighbridge and receives Rs. 142 monthly pay besides which he is likely to receive bribes from farmers delivering their cane who are keen to get it weighed without having to wait too long in the queue of carts.

Chennu and his family are always neatly dressed and give the appearance that they now feel firmly committed to urban life and work. This, however, is not so. In fact Chennu is still very much village oriented. He has three acres of dry land in Dalena; moreover he bought in 1958, before he got married, half an acre of wet land for Rs. 750 in a village near Dalena. His younger brother, who still lives in Dalena, cultivates all of Chennu's lands. He grows paddy on the wet land and gives Chennu half the product while keeping the rest. Chennu also receives half of the yield from his Dalena dry land. In return he subsidises his younger brother's cash needs and gives him money whenever the latter has to buy something in the town. Chennu and his brother do not have a joint estate – they partitioned their paternal property after the death of their father. They do not even live in the same village any more. Yet there exists a give and take between their two households which is reminiscent of joint families.[1]

Chennu visits Dalena at least once weekly and takes his family there for all the festivals and village feasts. Intra-village disputes and rivalries still occupy his mind. Although he works and lives outside the village he still struggles for recognition and prestige within it. He is not at all interested in making his mark in the many associations which operate in the town. He is a member of the local trade union but does not aspire to office within it; he displays no interest in the different political parties which are active in towns and which woo support from factory workers. His main ambition is to move back to Dalena and become one of the recognised magnates there. To this end he is trying to save up money so that he can buy more wet land. While he sees his own future in terms of a triumphant return to Dalena he wants his two sons to have good schooling and, if they have the necessary abilities, to go on to university. He does not see as conflicting the ambitions he has for himself and those he cherishes for his sons. He dreams of building for his family a modern city-type home in Dalena with all the amenities of urban living: electricity, running water, flush toilet, and so on.

On his frequent visits to Dalena he listens to all the gossip; he is a firm opponent of the chairman who still heads Dalena's conservative faction and accuses him of unfair dealings and self-interested manipulations (see p. 185). At the same time, Chennu is jealous of the *patel*'s success as an entrepreneur and therefore does not support his progressive faction either. He sees himself as

---

[1] I discuss this new type of what I call 'share family' in a later section (see p. 207).

the future leader of a 'new progressive movement' in Dalena composed of younger men who are familiar with the modern ways and seek to introduce them into village life. He points out that though he now lives in the town and dresses like a townsman, he still observes the dietary restrictions applying to village spirit mediums; he is a vegetarian and does not take cooked food in cafés, etc. He explains that this is the sort of fusion of urban and village life he has in mind.

Chennu's case is typical of those Dalena Peasants who work outside the village but yet have some lands : they are all still village oriented and regard their outside employment as a means to an end rather than an end in itself.

By contrast, Yeera the A.K., who already in 1956 worked as orderly in the Engineering department in Mandya, and who has since been promoted to some lowly clerical job, seems to have cut his ties completely with Dalena. He has moved with his wife and children to Mandya and now feels committed to life in the town. He hardly ever goes back to visit Dalena and displays no interest whatsoever in village affairs. He explained that there was nothing to attract him back there : he has no land there, never had any, and his Dalena fellow A.K.s are envious of his success and therefore do not show much warmth on the rare occasions he does visit the village. His brother still lives there, but he has no contact with him; neither one recognises a claim on the other. Yeera does not appear to feel any bond with his fellow A.K.s either in the village or in the town. He identifies himself with the Peasants and shares their judgement of his own caste people. He talks disparagingly about their laziness, apathy and dirtiness in precisely the same way that Peasants talk about their local A.K.s. In justification he points to himself as an example : how he managed to get on in the world by sheer hard work and by reliably carrying out his superiors' orders. He blandly ignores the fact that a good deal of his own 'success' was due to good luck. The contempt with which he regards his fellow A.K.s prevents him from acting as a bridge for his less fortunate village kin in helping them get urban employment. Unlike Peasants in his position, he does not appeal to other A.K.s' caste loyalty in the town nor does he encourage his fellow caste men to act in this way either. He stressed that he refuses to take food in village A.K. homes because, as he himself said, 'they are too dirty'.

However, in a society where inter-eating habits highlight the hierarchical organisation of castes, his refusal to dine with his fellow castemen must be seen as an attempt to raise his social status above theirs.

In a situation where jobs are scarce and largely monopolised by members of the dominant caste, an A.K. has to be lucky to get urban employment. Admittedly, once he has managed to secure a job his subsequent development is largely due to his own performance. However, there are several Scheduled and other landless castes who would be only too happy to work diligently if they were given the opportunity. But regular jobs are hard to come by even in the expanding economy of the Mandya region. Only two Dalena A.K.s have succeeded in getting regular wage employment, and both work as public servants. This is significant because a 1958 Mysore Government order reserved tentatively for Scheduled Castes and Tribes 18 per cent of public service appointments (G.A.D., 1962:72). Three years later this policy had not yet been successfully implemented: of the 94,266 Mysore public servants in 1961 only seven per cent, i.e. 6,647, belonged to Scheduled Castes and Tribes (G.A.D., 1962:17). *The Scheduled Castes and Scheduled Tribes Appointments Committee Report* from which this data is taken recommended that the educational level of these communities had to be raised to enable more of them to take advantage of public service employment opportunities (G.A.D., 1962:25). 'In fact up to now in government white collar jobs the actual percentage of ex-untouchables employed has fallen far short of the quotas. In 1963 they were only one to seven per cent filled. Government spokesmen say they cannot fill the quotas because there are too few qualified applicants' (Isaacs, 1964:107).

To join Class IV of the public service, which includes orderlies and peons, however, does not seem to require a particularly high level of education. Many village A.K.s could fill such jobs efficiently but only very, very few succeeded in securing this type of employment. In 1961 no more than 10 per cent of the 22,158 Class IV Mysore public service jobs were in fact held by Scheduled Castes and Tribes (G.A.D., 1962:17). It was recommended that as much as half the Class IV posts should be reserved for these Castes and Tribes (G.A.D., 1962:25). I have been unable to establish whether these recommendations have been accepted by the State Government and, if so, whether they are supposed already to have been implemented. Judging by what I heard from many village A.K.s about their unsuccessful attempts to secure regular employment little, if any, change seems to have taken place as yet in this respect.

Jobs in industry are even harder to get for the local A.K. 'Employment in private business firms in India is still heavily determined by regional, caste and family connections' (Isaacs, 1964:93) and Dalena A.K.s have none of these in Mandya enterprises. The only type of regular urban employment more readily available to Dalena A.K.s is as domestic servants to some of Mandya's money-lenders. In such instances the money-lender either employs his debtor in his own home or places him in the home of a relative or friend; whatever the arrangement the pay rarely amounts to more than Rs. 10 or Rs. 12 per month. The A.K. has little option but to accept the chance to reduce his debt burden and at the same time to ensure further credit from the money-lender.

As already mentioned, total A.K. landholding in Dalena has decreased by one acre though the number of their households has risen by 40 per cent to a total of twenty-one. Population increase has reduced their average holding per household from 1.60 dry acres to 0.72 acre during the past fifteen years. No A.K. owns any wet land outside the village. They are therefore increasingly dependent on wages for meeting their basic needs. Only a few of them are employed by Peasants from their own village. Dalena farmers have come to rely to a declining extent on the output from their village dry lands : their wet land cultivation in neighbouring villagers offers greater comparative advantages. They therefore do not want to engage more labour within Dalena. This is reflected in the decline in the number of households with contract servants : in 1956 eight Peasants had such contract arrangement, nowadays there are only four.

Dalena A.K.s are forced to look for employment outside their village. Their small landholdings anchor them in the village unless they find regular income earning opportunities elsewhere. In the meantime they wander around neighbouring villages or Mandya town in search of employment. Dalena A.K.s envy their fellows in Wangala the hereditary labour relationships the latter still enjoy with Peasant farmers in the village. They themselves have no longer such minimum protection; they have to compete for employment in the wider economy where supply of labour is plentiful and where the odds are heavily weighted against them.

In 1956 rural labourers received a slightly higher daily wage in Dalena than in Wangala. This can be explained by linking rates of casual rural labour to the higher daily wage the Public Works Department and other non-agricultural employers were paying in the area. The higher wage rate Dalena labourers were earning also implied some competition for labour between farmers and non-agricultural employers at least at certain crucial periods in the year. The natural increase in population in the area as well as the growing number of migrant labourers from other parts of Mysore and neighbouring States has swelled the labour force to such an extent that there are nowadays always people competing for jobs. This has removed the comparative advantage Dalena labourers enjoyed by getting higher wage rates than Wangala workers received.

The abundance of workers seeking rural employment and their lack of bargaining power explains why rural pay rates have risen considerably slower than industrial wages. 'Faced with the alternative of starvation labourers succumb to the instinct of survival and accept whatever is offered them, whether equitable or not. Attempts have been made to ensure for them the minimum subsistence wage by means of legislation such as the Agricultural Minimum Wages Act of 1948. . . . Workers in the organised sector, such as the industrial workers, have been able to secure the minimum wages not because there is a legislation but because these workers have improved their bargaining power by resorting to collective bargaining. This is not possible in the unorganised sector where a small amount of irregular and intermittent employment is enveloped in a mass of unemployment and under-employment' (Dandekar, 1970:73).

'Mysore and Kerala have also appointed special staff for the implementation of minimum wages in agriculture but unfortunately it was not enforced by the States' (D.S.W., 1969:132). Consequently, while consumer prices have almost trebled, the daily rural cash pay for Dalena men has increased by only 33 per cent from Rs. 1.50 in 1956 to Rs. 2 in 1970, that for Wangala men has gone up by 60 per cent from Rs. 1.25 to Rs. 2. In the same period the monthly wage of an unskilled worker in the

Mandya refinery has risen by as much as 152 per cent from Rs. 46 to Rs. 116 (see table 18). 'The disparity between agricultural and non-agricultural average income is obviously tied to the urban–rural differential as cause and as consequence and both are linked intimately with regional inequalities and with the ethnic composition of town and country. The latter, of course, are products of the social stratification that excludes certain ethnic or caste groups from the more highly paid, urban positions in industry, commerce and administration, and that restricts certain low status groups to the countryside' (Myrdal, 1968:579).

TABLE 18

CASH WAGES

|  | 1955 Rs. | 1970 Rs. | 1970 Index 1955 = 100 |
|---|---|---|---|
| Wangala: |  |  |  |
| Daily male | 1.25 | 2.00 | 160 |
| Daily female | 0.50 | 1.00 | 200 |
| Dalena: |  |  |  |
| Daily male | 1.50 | 2.00 | 133 |
| Daily female | 0.62 | 1.00 | 161 |
| Mandya: |  |  |  |
| Monthly unskilled | 46.00 | 116.00 | 252 |

Regional expansion affected Wangala's labour situation differently from Dalena's. The increase in Wangala's cultivable acreages accompanied by extension of canal irrigation has resulted in almost doubling paddy acreages and trebling the area under cane.

Wangala farmers appreciate that cultivation of even a small acreage of wet land yields a greater return to labour than alternative earning activities elsewhere. This emerges clearly from the following account.

The refinery cane plantation on Wangala's lands used to employ a number of villagers. When it closed down labourers were given the option of employment at Mandya's refinery; of the 20 labourers indigenous to Wangala, all of whom were caste men, only one, a young and newly married Peasant, accepted this offer. He lives together with his parents and younger, as yet unmarried, brother. Their joint household has no more than one and a half acres wet and one acre dry land. His labour is therefore not needed to farm their estate. He is now working as watchman in the Mandya refinery and commutes daily from the village. It is likely that his relationship with his father and brother will develop into a 'share family' (see p. 207).

All the other Wangala plantation labourers decided to turn down the offer of urban employment and became full-time farmers instead. Boma, for instance, is one of this group of men. He was employed on the plantation at the time of my earlier stay in the village. Then he had just celebrated his consummation ceremony and set up house with his new wife. In the intervening years he has fathered six children, none of whom is yet old enough to play an active part in tending his two acres of wet land. Boma, who has no patrilateral kin in Wangala, explained to me that while he had been a plantation labourer he always managed to fit in his paid work with the needs of his own lands. Employment in the refinery makes such an arrangement impossible. If he were to work in the town no one would look after his land. Thus he did not take up the opportunity of regular factory work, although the steady wage would have made a welcome addition to his household's meagre farm income. Similar considerations determined the other Wangala plantation labourers' decision to concentrate on farming rather than risk jeopardising their stake in the rural economy. Wet land cultivation offers a considerable comparative advantage over wage income; average farm wages and profits per acre of cane cultivated in Wangala in 1969 amount to as much as Rs. 2,717 (see table 9) with an average subsistence labour input of no more than 85 days per year; at the same time the factory paid its unskilled labourers annually no more than approximately Rs. 1,200.

Wangala's poorer Peasant farmers with below average sized holdings were keen to enter regular paid employment only as long as their wages supplemented their farm income. Once they faced the choice of becoming *either* wage earners *or* full-time farmers they decided in favour of the latter, and what seemed to them a much more attractive, alternative.

Cane and paddy are the two most labour intensive crops villagers cultivate. Consequently, I estimate that annual demand for male agricultural labour has more than doubled: in 1955

52,086 male labour days could cope with all the cultivation, whereas by 1969 the necessary number had increased to 127,113. In the same period the male working population increased by 64 per cent to 490. The average number of yearly days each Wangala man needed to work in agriculture therefore increased from 174 to 258. Annual female labour requirements have increased by about 50 per cent from 19,296 to 29,565 while the number of females of working age has risen approximately 65 per cent to 436. The annual female *per capita* work load has therefore fallen from 73 to 67 days (see table 19). Here it must be noted though, that whereas household labour contributes about 50 per cent of total male labour inputs, as much as 90 per cent of all female labour is hired.

TABLE 19

ESTIMATED WANGALA ANNUAL FARM LABOUR
REQUIREMENTS (LABOUR DAYS)

| | 1955 | | 1969 | |
|---|---|---|---|---|
| | *Male* | *Female* | *Male* | *Female* |
| Jowar | 3,392 | 1,392 | 740 | 220 |
| Ragi: | | | | |
|    Dry | 4,692 | 6,120 | 2,331 | 693 |
|    Irrigated | 924 | 990 | 16,095 | 3,915 |
| Paddy | 22,116 | 6,384 | 46,740 | 12,300 |
| Sugar cane | 22,962 | 3,870 | 56,286 | 10,974 |
| Miscellaneous | — | 540 | 4,921 | 1,463 |
| Total | 52,086 | 19,296 | 127,113 | 29,565 |
| Working Population | 299 | 264 | 490 | 436 |
| Working Days per | | | | |
|    Adult per Year | 174 | 73 | 258 | 67 |

The *per capita* annual male labour requirement indicates that given the present cultivation needs Wangala's total male working force could be almost fully employed throughout the year. However, the greater part of annual farm labour requirements is concentrated within a few months of the year. This is unfortunate or Wangala's resident pool of labour depending on income from wages. It means that at the peak periods in the agricultural cycle Peasant farmers have to rely on labour originating outside the village to meet their urgent cultivation needs. Indigenous labour depending on wage earnings would prefer to have regular employment throughout the year, but this is impossible in a rural economy with seasonal changes in weather. The only possibility for such workers to secure more permanent village employment is to work as 'contract labour' (Epstein, 1962:74) for Peasant farmers.

Wangala's wealthier Peasants are all very keen to engage contract servants. In 1955 thirteen Peasant households had such an arrangement; this number has now increased to thirty-one. These Peasants altogether employ forty-eight servants; seventeen have one each, twelve have two each, one has three and another four. The annual cash wage of contract servants has increased by 50 per cent to Rs. 120; their rewards in kind have remained the same; they still get their food and two sets of clothing per year. The wealthiest landowners in Wangala frequently complain about the instability and fickleness of contract servants. They ignore the fact that only a single man can make do as contract servant for no man can hope to keep a wife let alone a family on Rs. 120 per year. Significantly, the only married men among Wangala's contract servants are locals, who have small plots of land to help them feed their families. Only five of the forty-eight servants are Peasants, of whom three are indigenous to the village, twelve are A.K.s, of whom nine are local; the rest are all outsiders belonging to an assortment of different castes, among them twelve Voddas. In 1955 not a single Wangala Peasant was prepared to work as contract servant in another's house; nowadays three Peasants are working in such a capacity. In their case it helps them pay off debts they owe their present employers. The three Peasants concerned are all small landowners, who have not sufficient wet land to enable them to cultivate cash crops and they therefore get into debt.

Contract service is advantageous from the employer's point of view. The annual cash wage of Rs. 120 plus the cost of food and clothes for his servant altogether amount to a maximum of Rs. 300. This is the equivalent of paying casual labour for 130 days work whereas the contract servant has to work at least 300 days per year. In justification Peasant employers are quick to point out that their servants are never fully employed throughout the year. On many days they have nothing to do but help with household chores; yet their basic needs of food and clothing still have to be met.

Labourers, on the other hand, do not find contract work so attractive. Those who work on an annual basis in Peasant households do so because of sheer force of circumstance rather than because of their positive preference for such work. Some are debtors to their Peasant master's household and, like Dalena A.K. domestics in Mandya, have to accept the service conditions to help reduce their debts and ensure further loans. The majority of Wangala's contract servants are keen to leave their employment; the fact that no more than six of the thirty-six outsiders working as contract servants in Wangala have been in their present employment for more than one year bears witness to this. As soon as they can find some other income earning opportunity they leave their employers; often they even leave without any immediate alternative open to them simply because they are so 'fed up' with the conditions of their work. Hence Peasants' complaints about the high labour turnover among their contract servants. Moreover, it helps to explain the continued existence of hereditary labour relationships between Peasant households and their A.K. dependents.

Peasant landowners need at least a minimum supply of local labour to call upon whenever required. In the traditional dry land economy village A.K.s could supply all the necessary labour. During the early years of irrigation Peasants needed more labour and consequently employed their hereditary A.K. dependents for more days in the year. At first, therefore, irrigation re-emphasised the economic interdependence between Peasants and A.K.s in Wangala. However, it soon became obvious to the former that the customary system of fixed rewards provided an obstacle to the introduction of new and more efficient cultivation techniques, as I described for the Japanese method of paddy cultivation (1962:65). Consequently, when canal irrigation was extended, enabling more Wangala lands to be irrigated, Peasant farmers needed more labour to cultivate their cash crops; they met the problem by employing migrant labourers. These workers give better value for money than do the indigenous A.K.s. They know that their employment depends on their performance. Frequently they form work teams and undertake to perform certain cultivation tasks in return for a rate for the job rather than on a daily casual wage basis. Moreover, they move on as soon as there is no more employment for them and do not put the same demands on their employers when they are not actually working for them as do resident A.K.s. However, Peasants do need at least a minimum of labour readily available at a moment's notice and migrant labour cannot be expected to stay around without being assured at least a minimum of subsistence.

The need for resident casual labour is particularly strong in years when canals provide little or no water and Wangala's economy is forced to revert almost to its pre-irrigation level. During such years migrant labour is not attracted to the region and Peasant farmers have to rely on their indigenous labour to help them cultivate their lands. Thus a Peasant may regard the 50 seers of paddy and the hay he gives to his hereditary A.K. household as some sort of risk premium he has to pay to ensure having at least a minimum supply of labour whenever he requires it. Peasants complain about the inefficiency and laziness of their hereditary labourers, possibly in many instances justifiably so. A proportion of Wangala A.K.s have at least some land. Due to population growth the average holding for Wangala A.K. households has declined from 1.53 acres in 1955 to 1.09 acres in 1970, while the proportion of their irrigated land has remained constant at about 40 per cent. The cultivation needs of their own crops frequently compete with those of their Peasant masters. Not surprisingly then, a Wangala Peasant may sometimes find his A.K. labourer reluctant to perform casual labour on the farmer's land.

A Peasant has in fact several good reasons for continuing the customary labour relationship with his A.K.: first of all, as just mentioned, it ensures a basic labour supply; second, he feels a social and moral obligation towards his A.K.; and last, but possibly most important, he depends on his A.K. for the performance of essential life-cycle rituals. The hereditary labour bond between a Peasant master and his A.K. dependent is therefore not of a purely economic nature but has strong social and religious overtones. As long as a Peasant has a surplus of basic food over and above his own household needs he will never allow his A.K.

dependent household to starve. Such is the responsibility the Wangala Peasant master shoulders for his A.K. labourer.

A.K.s naturally appreciate that their Peasant masters provide them with at least a minimum of social security. They praise their Peasant farmers for being always prepared to help them whenever they face the problem of extra expenditure: for instance weddings or funerals. In return the A.K. claims that he is always ready to work for his Peasant master when his labour is demanded. Wangala A.K.s resent the fact that village farmers have turned to employing migrant labour to an increasing extent, but they see no possibility of making their employers give them again more work or of finding employment elsewhere. Many Wangala A.K.s, in particular the younger men, appear keen to get more regular urban employment. However, outside their home village they are at a disadvantage in competing with so many other caste men all seeking jobs.

I discussed the work problem with Wangala's A.K. headman and asked him how many of his flock were prepared to take up jobs outside the village in offices or factories. His immediate and spontaneous response was most revealing. He said: 'How many jobs can you get for us? However many you manage to fix up, that many are ready to start work at a moment's notice!' His counter-questions illustrate two major aspects of the employment problem village A.K.s face: first, the lack of personal links with people in prominent positions in the nearby town – the A.K. headman was obviously hoping with my help to try and manipulate urban employment as Peasants are able to do by calling on caste loyalties; second, the severe competition from caste men for regular urban employment which exists in the region. I pursued this point by asking how many Wangala A.K. men, if any, had ever tried to get urban jobs. The A.K. headman assured me that many of them were continuously on the lookout for regular work, but without success. To illustrate their difficulties he pointed to the fact that during the many years the refinery plantation had functioned on Wangala lands no local A.K. managed to get work there. He stressed that this was not for any lack of trying on their part; they had done their utmost to get at least one or two of their people employed on the plantation, but always found that caste men were preferred.

The A.K. quest for regular work has, if anything, become

tougher these days. Their failure to secure jobs in the nearby town discourages them from venturing further afield. It also makes them more appreciative of the minimum social security they enjoy by remaining in the village. Understandably they are not willing to give up an assured minimum of subsistence within Wangala for a highly uncertain survival in the wider economy. This in turn makes A.K.s ready to carry on performing their traditional ritual roles in the village and in their Peasant masters' households. Moreover, they are prepared to continue accepting the customary social discrimination practised against Untouchables in South Indian villages. 'There is unwillingness to see the simple proposition, or to undertake commitment to its implications, that there is no method, short of charity, of ensuring everyone a minimum living without recognising one's right to work and earn one's living' (Dandekar, 1970:73).

Some authorities on labour relations in India maintain that 'the most important distinction to be made is between those arrangements in which the labourer contracts freely and those in which his bargaining power is abridged. A free labourer is one who is able to accept or reject the conditions and wages offered by the employer' (Thorner, 1962:21). Emphasis on such a distinction, however, assumes that there is always alternative work for labourers dissatisfied with conditions of employment. It does not take into account the severe shortage of jobs for unskilled labourers. 'Faced with the alternative of starvation, they succumb to the instinct of survival and accept whatever is offered them, whether equitable or not' (Dandekar, 1970:73). Therefore, Wangala A.K.s do not regard *free* labourers with envy, rather they thank their lucky stars for the persistence of hereditary labour relationships which yield them at least some protection against starvation.

Wangala A.K.s treat the *free* migrant Voddas as socially inferior: Voddas are not allowed to draw water from the A.K. well. Vodda labourers have no option but to accept the lowest status in the villages where they temporarily reside. They are by far the poorest section in Mysore villages, in terms of income and expenditure, yet they seem to be glad to be able to earn at least enough to keep themselves and their families alive. For them mere survival is a major problem.

## LEVELS OF LIVING

'At the root of prevailing inequalities in income is the inequitable distribution of the means of production. A major means of production in the Indian economy is land. . . . But there is not enough of it to redistribute so that everyone may employ himself on his land and earn a minimum desirable living. . . . The process of development during the past decade has affected different sections of the rural population differently. It has benefited the upper middle and the richest sections more than the middle, the lower middle and the poorer sections' (Dandekar, 1970:70). Consequently there has been a growing inequality in rural India. Yet the Planning Commission does not appear to have concerned itself with inequality trends in the last decade and assumes that the pattern of inequality in consumption as observed in 1967–8 will remain unaltered until at least 1980–1 (P.C., 1969:33). Dandekar's Report on Poverty in India takes the Planning Commission, as well as the National Sample Survey, to task for the unrealistic appraisal of inequalities existing in India. The Report concentrates on examining the level of *per capita* personal consumption of the different strata of Indian society as it emerges from published statistics. 'The National Sample Survey estimate of *per capita* consumption in 1967–8 is more than 10 per cent below the official estimate. This is conclusive and the conclusion is inescapable that the N.S.S. estimate of *per capita* consumption in 1967–8 is an underestimate and that it underestimates the consumption of the upper middle and the richer sections much more than that of the middle, lower middle and the poorer sections. . . . What part of the underestimation might be on account of underestimation of the consumption of the upper middle and richer sections and what part due to an overall underestimation of consumption of all sections is a matter of judgement and a certain subjective element is unavoidable' (Dandekar, 1970:37).

Such subjective judgement certainly plays an important role in revising consumption estimates which have been found inadequate, but it hardly has any part in the material I collected in Wangala and Dalena. My village data not only show the trend of consumption for the different strata in Mysore rural societies but also indicate changes in income pattern. The full extent of inequalities cannot be grasped just by examining different levels of personal consumption – though this is an important aspect of it – nor can future trends be forecast, without an understanding of income distribution. The differences in *per capita* personal consumption between the richest on the one hand and the poorest on the other are unlikely to reflect fully the extremes of economic differentiation in existence if the richest have a low income elasticity of current consumption, which is what I found in rural South India. Differences in *per capita* incomes indicate much more clearly the level of inequalities. Moreover, a comparison of income distributions over time illustrates the process of growing concentration of India's means of production, in particular land, in the hands of a small rich *élite* in spite of the various measures taken to prevent this.

For reasons mentioned at the outset, I have chosen to examine with the aid of case studies the changes in economic differentiation that have taken place in Wangala and Dalena during the last 15 years. The case method has become a valuable tool in social anthropological studies (Gluckman, 1967:XIV) but is still rarely used in the study of economic development. Economists usually rely for their analysis on macro-surveys, as India's National Sample Survey does; these lend themselves to statistical processing but can be subject to considerable error, as Dandekar has shown. The study of particular cases represents a much more modest approach than working with averages for large groups of people or whole populations. At the same time, if the cases examined can be shown to be typical of a larger section of the population, they can throw light on aspects of development which are hidden by statistical treatment of the data. Moreover, case studies by recording individual choices and actions taken bring development problems to life. 'Individuals are now seen as actors in a series of different circumstances who make greater or less use of (i.e. manipulate) an element of choice' (Van Velsen, 1967:143). This makes for a much more lively appreciation of development problems than mere quantitative analysis where individuals become engulfed in averages. I realise of course that detailed collection of reliable socio-economic data relating to individual cases is a painstaking process, but I hope that what follows will show that the effort is well worth while and may encourage other researchers in this field to advance the techniques and approaches of the case study method.

The various cases I discuss represent the four main economic strata in Mysore villages. In addition to other information on these cases, I collected a monthly household budget for June 1970; except for the poorest Vodda migrants, who are a new element in Wangala society, I contrast the 1970 figures with data similarly collected for the same households during my earlier stay in the villages. In order to eliminate the impact of the different size and age composition of households I utilised the concept of the consumption unit. As previously described I accepted Lusk's coefficient (1962:43).[1]

I evaluated 1970 Wangala expenditure and income in real terms at 1955 prices and 1970 Wangala cash income I deflated by an index of 2.85 to make allowances for price rises that have taken place in the intervening years. 1955 prices had risen by about five per cent a year later when I collected Dalena budgets; therefore I employ an index of 280 to deflate the 1970 Dalena household income data. A rural consumer price index of 285 for 1970 with 1955 as base year may appear to reflect an unduly high rate of inflation as compared with official statistics. For instance, the Mysore Consumer Price Index for Agricultural Labourers with a 1950–51 base shows for 1969 232 for food and only 211 for general items (B.E.S., 1970:189). There are, however, no details stated as to the weighting given to the various items which make up household consumption. Moreover, it is difficult to harmonise the Mysore Consumer Price Index for Agricultural Labourers with that of Wholesale Cereal Prices. Mysore cereal prices with 1952–3 as base year have risen from an index of 280.6 in 1966–7 to one of 309.4 within only one year (B.E.S., 1970:185). The Consumer Food Price Index for Agricultural Labourers on the other hand only shows a rise in index number from 230 to 231 for the very same year (B.E.S., 1970:189).

[1] *Lusk's coefficient*

| Age | Consumption unit |
|---|---|
| Men above 14 years | 1.00 |
| Women above 14 years | 0.83 |
| Either 10 years but below 14 years | 0.83 |
| Either 6 years but below 10 years | 0.70 |
| Either 1 year but below 6 years | 0.50 |
| Either below 1 year | Nil |

(M.O.L., 1951:15)

Official statistics indicate that wholesale prices of all agricultural commodities taken together have risen faster in Mysore than in India as a whole : starting from the same base year the Mysore index number was 236 in 1968–9 whereas the comparable number for the All-India index was only 199 (Bhagwati, 1970:75). 'This index, it must be added, tends to understate price increases in so far as the prices of controlled commodities are usually taken at the controlled rather than their "true market" level. . . . The index of consumer prices has followed a similar pattern' (Bhagwati, 1970:76). In view of the difficulties involved in unravelling official statistics on consumer price movements and Bhagwati's note of warning about the unrealistic picture they may present I decided to rely on my own data and compile a consumer price index specifically for Dalena and Wangala.

In 1955–6 I had carefully enquired into details of prices charged at Mandya fair and bazaars for the various commodities villagers bought. I repeated this exercise in 1970. On both occasions the various prices were first collected by three indigenous research assistants enquiring independently from different suppliers the prices, and in some instances even buying the commodities. Subsequently, we compared the prices we had established with those our village friends had paid for the various articles they purchased. In this way we managed to reach a consensus on the various prices (see table 20) which I feel confident represent the real market values. I then weighted the different items according to the proportion each constituted of middle-farmers' total cash expenditure. This resulted in a price index of 285 for 1970 Wangala budgets and 280 for Dalena budgets.

I outline and analyse altogether seven cases to represent the four economic strata in Mysore villages :

*Magnates (Peasant)*: Tugowda, the Wangala magnate, can be regarded as typical of the other two richest Peasants in the village; the three of them still constitute the *avant-garde* in village entrepreneurship. Similarly, Dalena's Lingowda is a good example of the way the four richest men in a dry land village operate to try and keep up with their counterparts in irrigated villages.

*Middle-farmers (Peasant)*: Jagegowda is representative of the middle stratum in Wangala society. As with so many others of

TABLE 20

COMPARATIVE PRICES OF ESSENTIAL HOUSE-
HOLD COMMODITIES
(Mandya fair and bazaars)

| Commodity | Unit | May 1955 Rs. | June 1970 Rs. | 1970 Index 1955 = 100 |
|---|---|---|---|---|
| *Staple Foods:* | | | | |
| Ragi | seer | 0.22 | 0.65 | 290 |
| Rice | ,, | 0.41 | 1.10 | 285 |
| *Pulses:* | | | | |
| Greengram | ,, | 0.50 | 2.00 | 400 |
| Horsegram | ,, | 0.22 | 1.00 | 455 |
| *Spices:* | | | | |
| Coriander | ,, | 0.33 | 1.25 | 379 |
| Garlic | ,, | 0.50 | 1.00 | 200 |
| Pepper | ,, | 3.00 | 10.00 | 330 |
| Salt | ,, | 0.10 | 0.17 | 170 |
| *Misc. Foods:* | | | | |
| Coconut | each | 0.19 | 0.60 | 319 |
| Groundnut oil | seer | 0.28 | 1.00 | 357 |
| Sugar | ,, | 0.25 | 0.75 | 300 |
| *Clothes:* | | | | |
| Dhoti | each | 2.00 | 5.00 | 250 |
| Blouse | ,, | 1.75 | 4.50 | 260 |
| Sari | ,, | 10.00 | 30.00 | 300 |
| Shirt | ,, | 3.50 | 10.00 | 290 |
| Shorts | ,, | 1.50 | 4.00 | 290 |
| *Sundries:* | | | | |
| Areca nuts | seer | 2.00 | 3.60 | 180 |
| Betel leaves | 100 | 0.16 | 0.40 | 250 |
| Country cigarettes | packet | 0.12 | 0.25 | 208 |
| Matches | ,, | 0.05 | 0.08 | 160 |
| *Household goods:* | | | | |
| Kerosene | bottle | 0.27 | 0.60 | 230 |

his kind, the increase in the size of his family has depressed his standard of living. Likewise, the study of Dalena's Ramgowda indicates the sort of options a small dry land farmer has within an irrigated region and how he is likely to respond to the various opportunities offered.

*Poor* (*A.K.*): The case studies of Wangala's Malla and Dalena's Naga illustrate the extreme difficulties under which village A.K.s are labouring to try and make a living. Their experiences and the way their lives have been affected by changes during the past 15 years clearly expose the fact that far from having been able to improve their position they have not only lost out in relation to village caste households but even their standard of living in real terms has declined. In this respect the households of Malla and Naga are representative of poor A.K.s in irrigated and dry land villages respectively; moreover, they appear to be typical of rural poor all over India. 'It is clear that the rural poor consist predominantly of agricultural labour households and small landholders with cultivated holdings of less than 5.0 acres and particularly less than 2.5 acres' (Dandekar, 1970:33).

*Poorest (Migrant Vodda)*: Vaji, the Wangala labourer, like most other migrants in search of work, is landless. In South India landless agricultural labourers made up half of the rural households living at less than Rs. 100 per year in 1956–7, whereas the comparable proportion for all India was only 41.91 per cent (Dandekar, 1970:31). Landless labourers were therefore more common among South Indian poor villagers already in 1956–7. Population growth since then has undoubtedly increased even further the numbers of South Indian landless labourers. The recent establishment of a migrant labour settlement in Wangala not only reflects the increased demand for labour but also indicates the greater number of people now looking for work. Vaji's case is typical of the many landless labourers in South India these days.

## Magnates (Peasant)

Tugowda is now a dignified elder in his early seventies. He speaks softly but his words always command respect. In 1955 he lived with his wife and four children : two sons and two daughters. In the intervening years his family has extended to three generations : the first-born son married and his wife and three small children have joined the household; the second son is an undergraduate at the University of Mysore; both daughters are married, one has moved to her husband's home, the other has brought her small baby and rejoined her father's household. Tugowda's family unit increased from six to ten; in terms of consumption units it grew from 4.86 to 7.19.

In spite of his age, Tugowda is a dominating personality and controls all the family ventures. Though fragile-looking he is still very active. To talk with him I had to pursue him to his land where he was supervising a team of migrant Vodda labourers in the cultivation of his crops. He told me there and then that 'to get your work done according to your requirements you just have to be on the spot and supervise your labourers'.

Tugowda's grandfather immigrated to Wangala; his father, like himself an only son, had acquired wealth before irrigation by acting as sales agent in sericulture. Tugowda joined his father in this venture and with their savings they bought more land, to which Tugowda was sole heir. He has been a shrewd entrepreneur all his life. He was among the first village Peasants to cultivate cane after irrigation made this possible. By the time I first moved into Wangala, Tugowda had already established himself as one of the richest Peasants there; he was then the leader of an informal political group which I called the progressive faction but to which villagers referred as 'Tugowda's party' (see p. 180).

In 1955 Tugowda owned six acres wet and one acre dry land and lived with his family in one of the typical small farm houses in the interior of the village. In the meantime he has purchased another 13 wet acres, on ten of which he is cultivating cane. The sale of cane provides his household with a monthly net income at 1970 prices of about Rs. 350 per consumption unit; sales of his surplus paddy add another Rs. 75 to this figure, amounting to a monthly net income from cash crops at 1970 prices of Rs. 425 per consumption unit. By using a deflation index of 2.85 so as to reduce this income to the 1955 price level we arrive at Rs. 149 (see table 21). Altogether Tugowda's monthly deflated income per consumption unit has almost trebled since 1955. Like many other Wangala farmers he has increased his subsistence output by diversifying it. His household's food consumption consists nowadays almost wholly of home-produced items. His current expenditure pattern indicates a low income elasticity of demand: the value of his household's monthly food intake per consumption unit has remained unchanged; in 1955 his household used up monthly about 50 lb. rice and 10 lb. ragi per consumption unit, by 1970 they had cut out altogether eating ragi and cooked monthly about 65 lb. rice per consumption unit. This substitution

TABLE 21

WANGALA MAGNATE (PEASANT);
TUGOWDA'S MONTHLY BUDGET PER CONSUMPTION UNIT* AT 1955
PRICES

INCOME

|  | 1955 May | | 1970 June | |
|---|---|---|---|---|
|  | Rs. | % | Rs. | % |
| Subsistence | 18 | 25 | 22 | 10 |
| Barter | 1 | 1 | 2 | 1 |
| Profits | 11 | 15 | 23† | 11 |
| Rent and Interest | 10 | 14 | 5† | 2 |
| Crop Sales | 30 | 41 | 149† | 76 |
| Animal Products | 3 | 4 | 1† | — |
| Total | 73 | 100 | 202 | 100 |

EXPENDITURE

|  | 1955 May | | 1970 June | |
|---|---|---|---|---|
|  | Rs. | % | Rs. | % |
| Food | 22 | 30 | 22 | 10 |
| Clothes | 8 | 11 | 10 | 4 |
| Sundries | 3 | 4 | 2 | 1 |
| Ritual Expenses | 0 | 0 | 4 | 2 |
| Household Overhead | 4 | 5 | 5 | 2 |
| Gifts | 2 | 3 | 4 | 2 |
| Rent and Interest | 0 | 0 | 0 | 0 |
| Miscellaneous | 0 | 0 | 12 | 5 |
| Savings | 34 | 47 | 143 | 74 |
| Total | 73 | 100 | 202 | 100 |

* 1955:4.86 C.U.  1970:7.19 C.U.
† Deflation Index:2.85.

of the dearer rice for the cheaper ragi increased Tugowda's expenses on staple diet items by about 20 per cent at 1955 prices; the daily calories intake per consumption unit of basic foods increased from about 2,700 to 2,980.

The only noticeable increase in Tugowda's regular household expenditure is the money he spends on the education of his son, which appears under the miscellaneous items, otherwise his expenditure pattern has remained unchanged. Consequently, his household savings have increased considerably : in 1955 he saved 47 per cent of his monthly income; by 1970 this proportion had increased to 74 per cent. Tugowda has not allowed his savings to remain idle : he has invested his money in several different ways. His first priority was to acquire more land : his 19 acres wet land are now worth about Rs. 100,000; moreover, he now owns two sturdy pairs of bullocks as well as agricultural implements together worth about Rs. 4,000. Second, he established a cane-crusher in 1968 which cost about Rs. 35,000. Third, he is investing in religious capital : some years ago he donated a small Shiva shrine to his village which cost about Rs. 1,000. Moreover, he told me proudly that he has pledged Rs. 20,000 towards the building of a large temple at a nearby place of pilgrimage. In this way he translates his material success into ritual status and general social prestige. He also lends money to villagers; in June 1970 he had approximately Rs. 11,000 outstanding in loans. His extensive money-lending gives strong support to his continued predominant social position in the village. Lastly, he invested in non-productive property; he acquired a prestigious plot by the side of the main road passing through the village and built on it an impressive two-storey house which cost approximately Rs. 40,000. This new house, like many others of its kind, combines the amenities of traditional quarters with modern building innovations. The rear is traditional, the front is modern. There are a few pieces of furniture such as table and chairs, and Tugowda explained that he is still in the process of equipping his home. It has electric light and in front is a well belonging only to this magnate's family.

Villagers still talk of the big weddings Tugowda arranged for his daughters. He spent lavishly on big feasts for hundreds of guests and bought costly clothes and jewellery for the brides and their 'grooms. He told me that he gave the parents of each of his two sons-in-law Rs. 3,000 in cash. Altogether, Tugowda claims that the two weddings jointly cost him about Rs. 15,000. Tugowda is still preoccupied with intra-village affairs. In this he differs greatly from his Dalena counterpart, Lingowda.

A tall and well-built man with an imposing personality, Lingowda is now in his early sixties and is still most actively involved in making money. His household, like Tugowda's, has also increased in size and now represents a three generation depth joint family. In 1956 he already occupied a spacious farm house supplied with electricity. His family was then composed of himself, his wife and three young sons as well as one of his young unmarried brothers. Now his eldest son is married and has one child. Lingowda has fathered two more sons in the intervening years while Lingowda's brother got himself married and established his own household. Lingowda's family unit therefore increased in numbers from six to nine and in terms of consumption units from 4.86 to 7.99. Already by 1956 he had proved himself an outstanding entrepreneur active in different spheres of activities. He was then one of a small number of village magnates all of whom were known to have made their fortunes on the black market. During the last war he established a flour mill at a rail junction not far from his home village. There 'black' grains could be milled, away from the watchful eyes of town administrative officials. To cater for the needs of cart and lorry drivers, who often were waiting in a queue to have their loads processed, he opened a small retail store. At the time of my earlier stay Lingowda was thus already a well-established entrepreneur. Moreover, he owned five acres of dry land within Dalena and six wet acres in neighbouring villages. He was then one of the most advanced cultivators and, as I have already indicated, was awarded a prize for producing the highest paddy yield per acre in the region. In the meantime he has managed to purchase four more wet acres for which he paid altogether Rs. 30,000. In 1969–70 he devoted half his wet acreage to cane and the other half to paddy. He still tries to keep apace with technological developments in agriculture : in 1969–70 he produced 330 tons of cane on five acres, making an average yield of 66 tons per acre, which was well above the regional average (see p. 95).

The increased wet acreage and his progressive cultivation have enabled Lingowda to extend his cash cropping. Lingowda's

TABLE 22

DALENA MAGNATE (PEASANT);
LINGOWDA'S MONTHLY BUDGET PER CONSUMPTION UNIT* AT 1956
PRICES

| | INCOME | | | | EXPENDITURE | | | |
|---|---|---|---|---|---|---|---|---|
| | *1956 May* | | *1970 June* | | | *1956 May* | | *1970 June* | |
| | Rs. | % | Rs. | % | | Rs. | % | Rs. | % |
| Subsistence | 24 | 21 | 34 | 17 | Food | 32 | 29 | 34 | 17 |
| Barter | 6 | 5 | 6 | 3 | Clothes | 9 | 8 | 9 | 4 |
| Profits | 30 | 27 | 63† | 30 | Sundries | 8 | 7 | 9 | 4 |
| Interest | 17 | 15 | 7† | 4 | Ritual Expenditure | 1 | 1 | 1 | — |
| Crop Sales | 36 | 32 | 96† | 46 | Household Overheads | 5 | 4 | 8 | 4 |
| | | | | | Gifts | 2 | 2 | 7 | 3 |
| | | | | | Interest | 15 | 13 | 0 | 0 |
| | | | | | Miscellaneous | 8 | 7 | 10 | 5 |
| | | | | | Savings | 33 | 29 | 128 | 63 |
| Total | 113 | 100 | 206 | 100 | Total | 113 | 100 | 206 | 100 |

* 1955:4.86 C.U. 1970:7.99 C.U.
† Deflation Index:2.80.

monthly net income per consumption unit at 1955 prices has almost doubled by 1970 (see table 22). Yet, like Tugowda, his expenditure pattern also displays a low income elasticity of current demand. Like many other rich farmers in the area, Lingowda has tended to substitute the more costly rice for the cheaper ragi in his household consumption – in 1955 they prepared monthly 38 lb. rice and 48 lb. ragi per consumption unit, the respective figures for 1970 are 52 lb. rice and only 36 lb. ragi. This resulted in a 15 per cent increase in the value of basic foods consumed per month per consumption unit and left the daily calorie intake per consumption unit practically unchanged at about 4,000 in the form of rice and ragi. The overall food intake per consumption unit in Lingowda's household has increased only slightly and by diversifying his dry land cultivation almost all his household's food consumption is nowadays home produced. The greater monetary value of food consumption per consumption unit in Lingowda's household, as compared with Tugowda's, represents a diet modified by urban influences including more meat : Lingowda keeps goats, sheep and chicken, which he periodically slaughters for his home consumption. By contrast, Tugowda keeps a vegetarian home, at least he claims to do so, and therefore little, if any, meat is consumed.

The increase in Lingowda's income, accompanied by an almost stable consumption pattern, has resulted in considerable household savings. He has invested his savings in different spheres of activities. First, he purchased more wet land. He would have liked to buy further wet acreages but, as I have described, wet land is hard to come by for dry land villagers. He is so keen to acquire more wet land that he follows up every rumour and every piece of gossip relating to some potential seller of irrigated land. His ten wet acres now have a market value of approximately Rs. 65,000. Moreover, he has one pair of strong bullocks worth about Rs. 1,200 and a pump set with which he irrigates some of his village dry lands as well as various modern implements used in cultivating his crops. These are worth altogether about Rs. 4,000. Second, he has established another and much larger rice mill besides a cane-crusher at a strategic spot along the major highway near his home village. The increased manpower that his sons provide enable Lingowda to cope with his various business ventures as well as looking after his wet and dry lands. His eldest son Nanjegowda, who failed to get an engineering degree, is in charge of his more recently acquired flour mill and cane-crusher while he himself and two of his younger sons look after the older mill, shop and lands. Lingowda's productive investment outside agriculture amounts now to approximately Rs. 100,000, yet his net gains from running these different ventures constitute less than one third of his net income from cash cropping, whereas his total agricultural capital of about Rs. 75,000 provides almost all the rest.[1] This helps to explain why even alert and outward looking men of Lingowda's type are so eager to extend their wet land holding so as to be able to grow more cash crops; cane growing still yields a greater return on capital than does operating a flour mill or cane-crusher.

Unlike Tugowda, who has invested in shrines and temples to raise his ritual status within Wangala, Lingowda is concerned mainly with the wider economy and polity. Consequently he spent a lot of money on financing his son's electioneering campaign when the latter was a candidate in the *Taluk* Board elections. It is generally recognised that the young man's success in getting himself elected was due largely to his father's generous support. Lingowda knows very well that his continued economic advance depends on his contacts with administrative officials in influential positions as well as with farmers in neighbouring irrigated villages. He was therefore prepared to spend money helping his son to achieve a formal position in the political structure.

These two brief case studies of magnates reveal several features of the way the richest farmers organise their lives. First of all, wet land farming is by far their most remunerative activity. It is only the limited availability of such land which leads them to invest outside agriculture in processing plants, shops and other rural services. Second, Tugowda, who lives in an irrigated village and has all his wet lands within its borders, spent a lot of his savings on elaborate weddings for his daughters and on financing shrines and temples and thereby reinforced his intra-village social status. By contrast, Dalena's dry land made Lingowda look outside his own village for opportunities to participate in the regional expansion. Consequently, he is no longer so concerned with intra-village prestige and instead prefers to spend his money on

---

[1] Here it must be remembered though that I have not included an interest charge in my calculations of returns from land.

launching his son on a political career. He wants to establish a niche for his family in the wider economy and polity. Last, but possibly most important, is the fact that in the richest farm households *per capita* expenditure on daily consumer necessities appears to have reached saturation point; they tend to spend at least part of their savings on improved housing facilities, wells, lavish weddings, and so on, which can be labelled consumer luxuries, but their consumption pattern in real terms changes only little as their income increases.

## Middle-farmers (Peasant)

Wangala's Jagegowda is an unassuming and retiring man in his early fifties. He does not show any signs of ambition and never complains about his lot but seems to accept as his well-deserved fate what the gods awarded him. He and his family still live in the same traditional type home in the centre of the village which they already occupied during my earlier stay there; the appearance of their home has hardly changed over the years. In 1955 the household was composed of Jagegowda, his wife and four young sons; now his two eldest sons are married and each of them has two small children; they all live together jointly, from one hearth. The family is now composed of 12 individuals and 9.55 consumption units whereas in 1955 there were only six individuals and 4.23 consumption units.

Jagegowda then had 3.75 wet acres and half a dry acre; he cultivated two acres cane and 1.75 acres paddy as well as dry ragi. When his first son married, which was before Wangala Peasants changed from a system of bridewealth to one of dowry (see p. 197), he got himself so much into debt that he had to sell 0.75 wet acre to appease his creditors. In 1969–70 he cultivated one acre cane and two acres paddy as well as some ragi as a second crop on his wet land. His total landholding is now worth about Rs. 15,000. He has one pair of bullocks worth about Rs. 1,200 and agricultural implements amounting to Rs. 500. The total value of his agricultural capital is thus no more than Rs. 17,000, which is considerably less than Tugowda's agricultural assets of Rs. 105,000. Like many other farmers of his kind, Jagegowda is just about managing to make ends meet. To do this he has had to adjust his household consumption : he has substituted cheaper ragi for more expensive rice. In 1955 his wife cooked monthly about 43 lb. rice and 10 lb. ragi per consumption unit; in 1970 she prepared approximately 32 lb. rice and 20 lb. ragi. This reduced the monthly value of basic foods per consumption unit by about 10 per cent at 1955 prices and reduced the daily calorie intake per consumption unit from 2,430 to 2,240 in the form of rice and ragi. The value of these basic items used to make up about 65 per cent of total food consumption, now it composes as much as 75 per cent in Jagegowda's household. This means that greater emphasis is now placed on the staple items just to fill their stomachs while their ability to vary their diet has somewhat declined.

Jagegowda's total monthly expenditure per consumption unit decreased by about 10 per cent since 1955. When his family was smaller he managed to save 18 per cent of his monthly income; now he just about breaks even (see table 23). The increased size of his household which necessitates greater overall expenditure on food, clothing and other essentials is responsible for the difficulties Jagegowda is now encountering. Yet as long as he can produce sufficient food crops to meet his household needs and also grow some cash crops to be able to make the essential cash purchases, he is likely to keep his head above water. However, his joint estate will probably be partitioned in the near future; his two married sons are not happy about living in the joint household and want to break up the unit. Jagegowda tries to persuade them that each family unit will be worse off independently than they are now sharing one hearth and all their landed property. In spite of his arguments the sons are adamant and Jagegowda seems too weak a person to withstand them much longer.

Dalena's Ramgowda is quite a different man from Jagegowda: he is a lively, extroverted man in his early forties. Already in 1956 he was eager to become an urban worker: he then persistently kept asking my assistance in his quest. I could not help him, but he persevered in seeking factory employment and finally succeeded in 1965 in getting a job with the Mandya refinery. As in Jagegowda's case, Ramgowda's housing too has remained unchanged, only the size of his family has increased: in 1956 he lived with his mother, wife and little boy; since then his wife has borne him two daughters. His household has thus increased from four to six in numbers and from 3.16 to 4.69 in terms of con-

TABLE 23

WANGALA MIDDLE-FARMER (PEASANT);
JAGEGOWDA'S MONTHLY BUDGET PER CONSUMPTION UNIT* AT 1955 PRICES

*INCOME*

| | 1955 May | | 1970 June | |
|---|---|---|---|---|
| | Rs. | % | Rs. | % |
| Subsistence | 13 | 38 | 12 | 46 |
| Barter | 2 | 6 | 2 | 8 |
| Rent and Interest | 2 | 6 | 0.30† | 1 |
| Crop Sales | 17 | 50 | 11.70† | 45 |
| Total | 34 | 100 | 26 | 100 |

*EXPENDITURE*

| | 1955 May | | 1970 June | |
|---|---|---|---|---|
| | Rs. | % | Rs. | % |
| Food | 14 | 40 | 12 | 46 |
| Clothes | 8 | 24 | 4 | 14 |
| Sundries | 2 | 6 | 3 | 12 |
| Ritual Expenses | | | 1 | 4 |
| Household | 3 | 9 | 2 | 8 |
| Gifts and Feasts | | | | |
| Interest | 1 | 3 | 2 | 8 |
| Miscellaneous | | | 1 | 4 |
| Savings | 6 | 18 | 1 | 4 |
| Total | 34 | 100 | 26 | 100 |

* 1955:4.23 C.U.  1970:9.55 C.U.
† Deflation Index:2.85.

sumption units. His landholding has remained the same : he still has only one and a half wet acres and two dry acres. He keeps to the same pattern of cropping : he grows half an acre of cane and one acre of paddy on the wet land he owns in a neighbouring village; on his two dry acres he tries to grow ragi which due to the poor rainfall in recent years has been a most frustrating exercise. This accounts for the drop in his subsistence output per consumption unit and his attempt to make up for it by bartering in June 1970 one sheep for 210 lb. ragi so as to meet his household's food needs. Ramgowda's wife prepares still about the same quantity of staple diet items per consumption unit, namely about 21 lb. rice and 30 lb. ragi per month, which together yield about 2,300 calories per day per consumption unit. In 1956 the value of rice and ragi accounted for about half of the household's food consumption; nowadays it composes 60 per cent. As in Jagegowda's case here too there has been a shift back on to relying on basic starchy foods and a decline in the variety of other items consumed.

Ramgowda has cut down his overall expenditure per consumption unit by 10 per cent; only in this way does he manage to break even these days. His household budget for June 1970 clearly indicates that without his factory wages he would have great difficulty in making ends meet (see table 24). In May 1955 he worked six days as agricultural labourer and his wife and mother worked each eight days as such. In June 1970 his wife worked three days for one of the wealthier farmers in the village and he himself earned Rs. 100 at the refinery. He explained that now that his son is a young farmer in his own right he expects him to take the full responsibility for cultivating the family lands. The son, however, is not very happy about this arrangement and would prefer to work in the town. This creates tension and difficulties between father and son and frequently necessitates Ramgowda absenting himself from his factory employment to ensure that his land is cultivated properly. During the previous twelve months he had to absent himself from his job for forty days for this very reason.

Jagegowda and Ramgowda provide good examples of the middle range of the middle-farmers in their respective villages. Jagegowda's economic status has declined because of the considerable increase in the size of his family, yet he still belongs to

## TABLE 24

### DALENA MIDDLE-FARMER (PEASANT); RAMGOWDA'S MONTHLY BUDGET PER CONSUMPTION UNIT* AT 1956 PRICES

#### INCOME

| | 1956 May | | 1970 June | |
|---|---|---|---|---|
| | Rs. | % | Rs. | % |
| Subsistence | 13 | 42 | 8 | 29 |
| Barter | | | 5 | 19 |
| Crop Sales | 8 | 26 | 6† | 22 |
| Wages: | | | | |
| Agriculture | 6 | 18 | 1† | 4 |
| Other | 0 | 0 | 7† | 26 |
| Miscellaneous | 4 | 14 | | |
| Total | 31 | 100 | 27 | 100 |

#### EXPENDITURE

| | 1956 May | | 1970 June | |
|---|---|---|---|---|
| | Rs. | % | Rs. | % |
| Food | 15 | 48 | 13 | 48 |
| Clothes | 5 | 17 | 5 | 18 |
| Sundries | 4 | 13 | 4 | 15 |
| Household | 3 | 10 | 1 | 4 |
| Gifts and Feasts | 1 | 3 | 0 | 0 |
| Interest | 2 | 6 | 4 | 15 |
| Savings | 1 | 3 | 0 | 0 |
| Total | 31 | 100 | 27 | 100 |

* 1955:3.16 C.U.  1970:4.69 C.U.
† Deflation Index:2.80.

the 70 per cent of Peasant households who have *sufficient* land to satisfy their requirements (Schönherr, 1972:36). In Wangala there are a number of Peasants falling into the category of middle-farmers who are considerably better off than Jagegowda. In most of these cases this is because their families have not increased by nearly as much as Jagegowda's. Therefore demographic accident plays an important role in the economic placing of Wangala Peasants, in particular middle-farmers. If, as is highly likely, Jagegowda's estate will be partitioned shortly, the emerging households will increase the number of Peasants without sufficient land to meet their basic requirements. In Dalena as many as 43 per cent belong to this category (Schönherr, 1972:35). Ramgowda is one of these. Without his factory wages he would have great difficulty in meeting his household needs. He, like so many other of his fellow villagers, is dependent on income derived from outside Dalena to keep his family going : irrigated lands and employment provide the major sources of such exogenous income for Dalena middle-farmers. Some Peasants in this category are better off than Ramgowda either because they have managed to acquire more wet land outside or because they also act as cattle traders or contractors; others again are considerably poorer either because they have even less land than Ramgowda and did not succeed in securing regular urban employment, and/or the size of their families has increased by much more than has Ramgowda's.

Jagedowda's case illustrates the way middle-range Peasants in an irrigated village are affected by increasing size of family and Ramgowda's case shows the vital importance of exogenous sources of income to dry land villagers.

## Poor (A.K.)

Wangala's Malla is an alert and lively young man in his early thirties. In 1955 he was still unmarried and lived together with his widowed mother and two younger siblings. In the meantime both Malla and his brother got married and they partitioned their one dry acre so that Malla has now only half a dry acre. Malla now lives with his mother, wife and two young children. In terms of numbers his family has increased from four to five but in terms of consumption units it has remained at 3.66.

Malla's father had acquired a quarter acre of wet land before he died. This his mother continued to cultivate and she insisted that it remains undivided in Malla's care. In addition, Malla managed to get another quarter acre of wet land in 1963 when he agreed to act as intermediary on behalf of Timmegowda, his Peasant master, in a land transaction. Timmegowda encouraged Malla to exercise his right to purchase newly irrigated land from the Government at well below market prices. The Peasant advanced Rs. 1,000 with which Malla bought one and a quarter acres wet land. Subsequently, Malla sold one acre of this land to Timmegowda and was allowed to keep the rest for his own needs. Both partners to the transaction were pleased for both gained by it : Timmegowda got one acre for Rs. 1,000 in 1963, when the market price of one wet acre in Wangala was about Rs. 3,500; Malla was happy because without any effort or money spent on his part he managed to acquire an additional quarter wet acre. Malla told me that his own example was but one of a number of similar cases where Wangala Peasants manipulated land transactions with the aid of their dependent A.K.s and either allowed the latter to keep a small part of the acreage they thus acquired, or they agreed to write off part or even all the debt their A.K.s owed them. Very few Wangala A.K.s are able to meet their basic household expenditure and they are therefore becoming cumulatively more indebted to their Peasant masters. In their eyes these land deals enable them to raise their heads once more, though they do not know for how long.

I mentioned to Malla that, had he been able to keep all of the one and a quarter wet acres for himself and cultivated cane on one acre, he might have been able to get sufficient money after one or two years to pay off the purchasing price of the land. Malla appeared fully aware of this possibility, but to him it was a purely theoretical one only. He explained that he could never have borrowed sufficient money to pay for the land in the first instance. He was aware of the favourable loan arrangements for members of Scheduled Castes but pointed out that to qualify for one an A.K. needs the signature of an official who he knows will not sign without a bribe of Rs. 150. Malla went on jokingly : 'If I had Rs. 150 ready to give in bribes I would not need a loan at all!' Moreover, Malla stressed that without strong bullocks and at least a minimum of working capital it would have been impossible for him to even attempt cultivating cane. Malla has no cattle at all and agricultural implements worth only about Rs. 60. He often gets a loan of his Peasant masters' bullocks or has to hire a pair to plough his wet land. Malla's lack of funds to purchase wet land and to finance cash cropping coupled with his indebtedness to his Peasant master prevented him from benefiting from the special privileges, in regard to the purchase of newly irrigated Government land, which the authorities try to vest in village A.K.s. Malla has thus gained only very little from the opportunities offered to Scheduled Castes to help them increase their landholdings, in spite of legislative measures introduced to help him and his fellow caste men do just that. The *Report of the Committee on Untouchability* recommends that: 'Scheduled Caste cultivators should be allotted additional land to ensure economic viability. The minimum land allotment should not be less than five acres. Scheduled Castes holding lands less than five acres should be allotted additional land, to make up a minimum of five acres' (D.S.W., 1969:124). The *Mysore Land Grant Rules* have proved ineffective in Wangala : almost all the newly irrigated land has passed into the hands of Peasant farmers and only two per cent of the additional cultivable acreage which has become available in Wangala since 1955 has passed into the hands of the local A.K. community. Sixty-nine per cent of Wangala A.K. households have insufficient land to produce their household needs (Schönherr, 1972:36). Malla is one of these poor villagers.

The additional quarter acre of wet land Malla has acquired enabled him to produce more of his household consumption : in 1955 his subsistence output at current prices amounted to Rs. 7 per consumption unit; by 1970 it had increased in real terms by about 15 per cent. Agricultural wages contributed 39 per cent of Malla's household expenditure in May 1955. During that month Malla and his brother together worked 23 days and earned a daily cash wage of Rs. 1.25; his mother and sister each worked 15 days for which they received daily in cash Rs. 0.50. Wage labour formed an important part in Malla's family's activities and constituted the biggest single item in his income. By contrast in June 1970 wages made up no more than 18 per cent of Malla's total household expenses at 1955 prices (see table 25). In that month his wife worked six days as casual labourer and earned

TABLE 25

WANGALA POOR (A.K.);
MALLA'S MONTHLY BUDGET PER CONSUMPTION* UNIT AT 1955 PRICES

INCOME

| | 1955 May | | 1970 June | |
|---|---|---|---|---|
| | *Rs.* | % | *Rs.* | % |
| Subsistence | 7 | 23 | 8.0 | 42 |
| Barter | 4 | 13 | 4.0 | 21 |
| Wages: | | | | |
| Agriculture | 12 | 39 | 3.3† | 18 |
| Miscellaneous: | | | | |
| Cash | 2 | 6 | 1.3† | 7 |
| Gifts | 2 | 6 | 1.0 | 5 |
| Net Borrowing | 4 | 13 | 1.4 | 7 |
| Total | 31 | 100 | 19 | 100 |

EXPENDITURE

| | 1955 May | | 1970 June | |
|---|---|---|---|---|
| | *Rs.* | % | *Rs.* | % |
| Food | 13 | 42 | 10.0 | 53 |
| Clothes | 7 | 22 | 2.5 | 12 |
| Sundries | 3 | 10 | 1.0 | 5 |
| Ritual Expenditure | 1 | 3 | 0.5 | 3 |
| Household Overheads | 3 | 10 | 1.0 | 5 |
| Gifts | 3 | 10 | 0 | 0 |
| Interest | 1 | 3 | 2.0 | 11 |
| Miscellaneous | 0 | 0 | 2.0 | 11 |
| Total | 31 | 100 | 19 | 100 |

* 1955 and 1970:3.66 C.U.
† Deflation Index:2.85.

Rs. 1.00 in cash per day and Malla himself worked 15 days at a rate of Rs. 2.00 per day. The number of days Malla's household members managed to get casual employment per month has thus been drastically reduced. Moreover, the purchasing power of daily wages has also declined considerably: Rs. 1.25 could buy $6\frac{1}{4}$ lb. rice or 12 lb. ragi in 1955; in 1970 the male daily wage of Rs. 2 could purchase no more than about $3\frac{3}{4}$ lb. rice or $6\frac{1}{2}$ lb. ragi. Thus in real terms the male daily casual wage was in 1970 no more than 60 per cent of its 1955 value; the purchasing power of female daily wages has declined by somewhat less, namely 25 per cent. These real wage indices largely coincide with those given by Bardhan for Mandya District as a whole: during the five years from 1962 to 1967 the daily real wage of agricultural labourers has declined by 14 per cent. Moreover, Bardhan states that during the same period employment of labour per acre has increased by only two per cent (1970:1241) in Mandya District. In view of the considerable increase of population this indicates a fall in wage employment per labouring household resident in the area.

Malla's household was severely affected by the decline in the numbers of days his family worked per month coupled with the fall in the purchasing power of daily wages. His household's income from wages had fallen by approximately 70 per cent at 1955 prices.

This drastic decline in Malla's real wage income is reflected in his considerably lower standard of living. He still lives in the same small thatched hut which now looks even more dilapidated than it did previously; he and his family walk around in clothes which are almost in shreds. Malla told me that he has arranged with his hereditary Peasant masters to give him ragi for his annual reward in kind instead of paddy, and whenever he has a chance he barters paddy for ragi. In May 1955 Malla's mother cooked about 20 lb. rice and 29 lb. ragi per consumption unit which yielded 2,140 calories per day; in June 1970 Malla's wife cooked $6\frac{1}{2}$ lb. rice and 40 lb. ragi per consumption unit yielding 1,960 calories per day. The staple diet of rice and ragi constituted 55 per cent of Malla's household food consumption by value during the earlier period; in 1970 the proportion had increased to almost 70 per cent. In relative terms food now occupies 53 per cent of Malla's household consumption by value at 1955 prices as compared with only 42 per cent during the earlier period; in absolute terms he has reduced the value of his food consumption by about 25 per cent from Rs. 13 to Rs. 10 per consumption unit, while reducing the calorific content of basic food per consumption unit by no more than 8 per cent. The total reduction in the calorific content of Malla's household's food consumption is probably considerably greater than that, as he had to substitute ragi for other items of food such as sugar and spices. I am afraid I am unable to give a more precise account here of his dietary changes.

Malla has had to reduce his expenditure per consumption unit on clothes, sundries, such as country cigarettes, betel leaves and areca nuts, and so on, and household overheads, such as pots and pans, by about two-thirds, just to try to make ends meet. The greater emphasis placed on food in his household expenditure illustrates the well known fact that people living at the lowest levels of income have to give first priority to food to ensure their survival. In spite of Malla's attempt to cut down his overall household expenses he still cannot pay everything out of his income and is cumulatively getting more and more indebted to his hereditary Peasant masters.

Malla feels very bitter about the fact that Wangala Peasants, even his own hereditary masters, now employ his own household labour for fewer days a month than they used to do and prefer to engage migrants. He complains that in spite of his efforts to find work he has not succeeded in securing anything like regular employment. Yet he appreciates his Peasant masters' generosity in advancing him money to keep his family going. Timmegowda, one of Malla's Peasant masters, explained to me that as long as he himself has at least a small surplus over and above his own family needs, he will always try and help Malla : he still remembers Malla's father who had worked for his own father and that there existed a give and take relationship between these two men. Timmegowda stressed that he feels morally obliged to continue this relationship. Moreover, through Malla's intervention he had managed to buy one acre of wet land at a bargain price. There may be similar attractive opportunities in future, so that Timmegowda is careful not to alienate Malla and risk missing such chances. The hereditary *halemakkalu* (old children) relationship between Peasant masters and their A.K. dependents persists in

Wangala simply because both parties regard it as advantageous for themselves.

Dalena's Naga expressed envy of the minimum social security his counterparts in Wangala and other nearby irrigated villages still enjoy. Naga is a quiet man in his mid-fifties, who looks and behaves as if all the energy has been drained out of him. He still lives in the same hut he occupied fifteen years ago, though since then it has deteriorated a lot. Then he lived together with his wife, three daughters and baby son; in the meantime his daughters married and moved to their respective husbands' homes, while his wife has borne him two more sons and one daughter. The size of his family has remained unchanged with six members, but in terms of consumption units it has increased from 4.19 to 4.69. In 1956 Naga had two acres dry land, and a pair of cows; since then he has had to sell one of his two dry acres as well as his cattle to pacify one of his creditors. He now has agricultural implements worth no more than about Rs. 50.

Unlike Malla, who can always approach his village Peasant masters for loans, Naga has to turn to professional money-lenders in Mandya or nearby villages. As he cannot meet even his running household expenses he has difficulty in paying interest let alone repay his debts. When I questioned him on how he manages to get money-lenders to continue advancing loans to him when he seems unable to repay them, he explained that last year he had sent his eldest son to work in the house of the Mandya money-lender: his wages of Rs. 12 per month went to pay off his debt and interest. Naga thought this a satisfactory arrangement. It enables him to borrow the necessary money just to keep his family. It provides periodic regular employment for at least one member of his family; while his son worked in Mandya he was fed and clothed there and therefore reduced the load on his shoulders. Lastly, but also very important, Naga could be sure of a free meal whenever he visited Mandya while his son was working there. For the urban money-lender Naga's son provided labour cheaper and more reliable than he could otherwise secure.

This creditor–debtor relationship is similar to the traditional *jeetha* system according to which 'agricultural labourers are advanced petty sums of money in time of their need. They are bound in such a way that they are not able to repay the debt out of their meagre wages, because under the terms of the bond they get food, clothes and small salary only. The result is that they are not only unable to repay the loan but also have to add to it. Even their children are obliged to take upon themselves the repayment and become involved in it' (D.S.W., 1969:159).

In 1956 Naga managed to produce 35 per cent of his household requirements on his own land : his subsistence output per consumption unit was then worth about Rs. 5 (see table 26). The sale of half his dry acreage coupled with the poor rainfall in recent years has reduced his subsistence output by 60 per cent to Rs. 2 per consumption unit in June 1970. This drastic fall in his output forced Naga to cut down his food intake : the value of monthly consumption expenditure per month per consumption unit was reduced by almost 40 per cent from Rs. 13 to Rs. 9 at 1955 prices. His wife used to prepare monthly about $6\frac{1}{4}$ lb. rice and 33 lb. ragi per consumption unit; now she cooks 2 lb. rice and 37 lb. ragi which still yield about 1,680 calories per day per consumption unit. Rice and ragi used to make up about 60 per cent of the value of Naga's household food consumption; nowadays this proportion has increased to 75 per cent. There is therefore very little money spent on other than staple foods; a calorie intake of less than 2,000 per day is hardly sufficient to feed a working man, yet this is all Naga can afford to have every day. His household consumption is for all practical purposes reduced to a minimum subsistence level.

During May 1956 he and his wife each worked two days as agricultural labourers on richer farmers' lands. In June 1970 he and his eldest son worked each five days as labourers in Mandya bazaars shifting bales of cloth and sacks of rice. They managed to get this casual employment through the intervention of one of Naga's money-lenders who was once more beginning to get worried that Naga was getting too much indebted. Naga and his son received each Rs. 2 per day, which was below the urban casual daily rate, but they were grateful of the chance of working and earning at least some wages. Naga kept emphasising that they had been extraordinarily fortunate this month to earn ten days' wages; normally they cannot get more than five or six days' work between them per month. Naga and his sons spend their days usually walking round nearby irrigated villages, or Mandya town, trying to pick up some news where they may find work. Most

## Table 26

### DALENA POOR (A.K.); NAGA'S MONTHLY BUDGET PER CONSUMPTION UNIT* AT 1956 PRICES

**INCOME**

|  | 1956 May | | 1970 June | |
|---|---|---|---|---|
|  | Rs. | % | Rs. | % |
| Subsistence | 5 | 35 | 2.00 | 22 |
| Barter | 4 | 30 | 3.00 | 32 |
| Gifts | 2 | 14 | 1.00 | 10 |
| Sale: Animal Products | 1 | 7 | 0 | 0 |
| Wages: Agriculture | 1 | 7 | 0.33† | 3 |
| Other |  |  | 1.33† | 14 |
| Net Borrowing | 1 | 7 | 1.84 | 19 |
| Total | 14 | 100 | 9.50 | 100 |

**EXPENDITURE**

|  | 1956 May | | 1970 June | |
|---|---|---|---|---|
|  | Rs. | % | Rs. | % |
| Food | 8 | 58 | 5.50 | 59 |
| Clothes | 1 | 7 | 0.50 | 5 |
| Sundries | 1 | 7 | 1.00 | 10 |
| Household | 2 | 14 | 1.00 | 10 |
| Gifts and Feasts | 1 | 7 | 0 | 0 |
| Rent and Interest | 1 | 7 | 1.50 | 16 |
| Total | 14 | 100 | 9.50 | 100 |

* 1955:4.19 C.U. 1970:4.69 C.U.
† Deflation Index:2.80.

evenings they return home tired and depressed by their failures. Naga's case is representative of Dalena A.K. households, 90 per cent of whom do not have *sufficient* land to produce what their own household requires (Schönherr, 1972:35).

Dalena A.K.s are considerably worse off than their Wangala counterparts. This emerges clearly from a comparison of their respective budgets. Naga's overall monthly household expenditure per consumption unit amounts to only about half that in Malla's household. Yet compared with landless migrant labour Naga still regards himself as fortunate; at least he has a permanent home in a village where the local language is his own and where he owns one acre of dry land which enables him to grow some of his necessary food.

## Poorest (*Vodda migrants*)

Vaji's case is typical not only of Wangala's 23 Vodda migrant households but of the thousands and thousands of Vodda who are landless in their native Madras villages and are thus forced to migrate in search of work. Their native tongue is *Tamil* which, although one of the group of *Dravidian* languages, is quite different from the *Kannada* spoken in Mysore State. Their language already, therefore, marks these Vodda migrants as outsiders in Mysore villages. Vaji complained bitterly that in Wangala not even the A.K.s allow Voddas to draw water from their well, while in his home village he lived in the main caste section and not with the village Untouchables.

Wangala's migrant settlement looks even poorer than the A.K. section; migrants' huts are smaller and their inhabitants are even more scantily dressed than A.K.s. Many small Vodda children run around naked, their bodies covered in sores, with protruding bellies, an obvious sign of undernourishment. Vaji himself has one four-year-old son who in his appearance is typical of many other children of these poorest households. The family consists of six members : Vaji and his two younger brothers, one of whom is already married and has his wife with him, as well as his own wife and little boy. These six individuals constitute 4.99 consumption units. They left their home village in Madras in 1965 and arrived in Wangala almost one year ago. They use their small hut as a base from which to explore employment opportunities in Wangala itself as well as in neighbouring irrigated villages.

The two women in Vaji's household form part of a team of 10 Vodda women who perform agricultural tasks as a group. In June 1970 this team was engaged for 10 days, yielding a cash wage of Rs. 20 for Vaji's household. The head of the family and his two younger brothers worked altogether seven and a half days during the month, for which they received Rs. 15. This meagre wage income deflated to 1955 prices yields no more than Rs. 2.40 per consumption unit per month, which covers only half the necessary expenditure on food (see table 27). Vaji and his wife

TABLE 27

WANGALA POOREST (VODDA MIGRANT): VAJI'S MONTHLY BUDGET PER CONSUMPTION UNIT* AT 1955 PRICES

| INCOME | | | EXPENDITURE | | |
|---|---|---|---|---|---|
| | 1970 | | | 1970 | |
| | June | | | June | |
| | Rs. | % | | Rs. | % |
| Wages | 2.40† | 38 | Food | 5.00 | 79 |
| Barter | 1.50 | 24 | Clothes | 0.40 | 6 |
| Gift | 2.40 | 38 | Sundries | 0.54 | 9 |
| | | | Household | 0.36 | 6 |
| Total | 6.30 | 100 | Total | 6.30 | 100 |

\* 1970:4.99 C.U.
† Deflation Index:2.85.

claimed that they receive the remainder of their necessary food in the form of gifts from wealthier Peasants for whom they work. A number of Wangala farmers complained that the migrants were stealing crops. It is difficult to verify either claim; what is certain, however, is the fact that migrant labourers do not have sufficient wage income to meet even their most essential requirements. Vaji's wife cooks monthly about 10 lb. rice and 160 lb.

ragi for her household, which together yield a daily calorie intake of no more than 1,500 per consumption unit. Vaji's expenditure on rice and ragi compose about 80 per cent of his total food consumption. Therefore, the calorific content of his household's daily food consumption is likely to be no more than 1,800 per consumption unit, which is well below his minimum requirements of 2,500 calories. The lack of sufficient nourishment is obvious when one only looks at these Vodda labourers, in particular their children. No one is prepared to risk lending them money as they have no permanent abode; they can pack up their few belongings and leave at very short notice.

The Vodda migrant labourers are thus by far the poorest section in Mandya District villages and are regarded by indigenes in the area as the scum of society and treated as such. Voddas have no choice but to accept the lowliest social position; their very survival is at stake.

The case studies presented here clearly indicate the process of increasing economic differentiation which has taken place in Mysore villages during the last ten or fifteen years. The wealthiest Peasant farmers have become considerably richer. The jaggery boom provided the possibility of a windfall profit to all farmers who owned more than two or three wet acres: the greater the cane acreage the greater the benefit a farmer derived from the soaring jaggery prices. This encouraged the wealthier and more enterprising Peasants to invest in more and more wet land as well as in cane-crushers to process their crop into jaggery. Every additional wet acre added to the income stream a farmer derived from his agricultural activities; every cane-crusher provided a new source of profits to its owner. All this is reflected in a cumulative process of concentration of wealth in the hands of a small *élite* of Peasant farmers. In a period of rapidly rising prices investment in land and processing capital enabled the wealthiest farmers, who still produce their subsistence needs, to ride on the tide of inflation.

Peasant middle-farmers managed on the whole to hold their own during this period of inflationary pressures as long as they either had at least three wet acres to enable them to grow most of their own food as well as some cash crops to be able to make their essential purchases of clothing and so on, or if, as is shown in the case of Dalena's Ramgowda, they managed to get regular employment to supplement their farming income. The fate of these Peasant middle-farmers is largely determined by the rate of increase in the size of their families : the more rapid the increase, the quicker the decline in their economic status.

The case studies of the poor A.K. households in Wangala and Dalena show that the greater a household's dependence on rural cash wages for meeting necessary expenditure, the greater has been the deterioration in the standard of living.

In developing economies wages often lag behind price rises and rural wages are notoriously slow in adjusting to rises in the cost of living. In periods when rural wages lag considerably behind price rises, agricultural labourers are bound to suffer, while landowners and entrepreneurs operate with an obvious advantage. The difficulties Mysore agricultural labour experienced are by no means peculiar to Mandya District. 'A distinguished study group set up by the Government of India in July 1962 has deliberated on the question of what should be regarded the nationally desirable minimum level of consumer expenditure. The study group recommended that a *per capita* monthly consumer expenditure of Rs. 20 (at 1960–61 prices) should be deemed the national minimum' (Dandekar, 1970:10). 'According to the Second Agricultural Labour Inquiry Report about 80 per cent of people belonging to agricultural labour households were below this minimum' (Bardhan, 1970:1245). Moreover, 'according to National Sample Survey data the percentage of people below the minimum level in rural India went up by about 40 per cent between 1960–61 and 1967–68. In no State has there been a significant decline in this percentage' (Bardhan, 1970:1861). All over India, therefore, the poor have become poorer while the rich have become richer. 'Unless greater attention is paid to the landless agricultural labour force, enhanced economic activity in the agricultural sector cannot be effective in bringing about a unified institutional system in the rural areas. . . . It is the proprietors who have generally been favoured by government development programmes while the economic status of the lower and Scheduled Castes have not improved' (Lannoy, 1971:261). On the basis of my own and other studies, Lannoy's last sentence seems too mild; the problem of the position of the landless is taken up in detail in my final chapter.

# 6 Political Change

## VILLAGE GOVERNMENT

State legislation has revolutionised, at least in the legal sense, the composition, constitution, rights and duties of village councils. The *Mysore Village Panchayats and District Boards Act, 1952* introduced adult franchise and substituted elected for hereditary authority; it made provisions for reserved seats for Scheduled Castes at village as well as at District Board level. Membership of District Boards was determined by indirect election from among the elected village councillors. I have already outlined the practical effect this new democratic legislation had on Wangala's and Dalena's political system as I found it in 1955. 'In order to bring about democratic decentralisation and to instil in the people a sense of participation in developmental activities . . . a new system of *Panchayat Raj* has been ushered in, with the enactment of the *Mysore Village Panchayats and Local Boards Act, 1959*' (M.S.G., 1967:378). The old District Boards were abolished and a new three-tier local administration established, consisting of Village *Panchayats, Taluk* Boards and a District Development Council for each of Mysore's 19 districts. This reorganisation of the local government structure effectively decentralised the administration : instead of having one District Board for Mandya District population, which according to the 1961 census was 899,210, there are now seven *Taluk* Boards; Mandya *taluk* for instance had a population of 183,403 in 1961 (M.S.G., 1967:65). Moreover, each *taluk* is divided into a number of constituencies and members are elected on the basis of adult franchise. Presumably to make for more effective village government the minimum size of population for a village *panchayat* has been raised to 1,500 and the maximum to 10,000. This means in many cases several villages are joined together under one village *panchayat*.

Dalena is linked with three neighbouring villages in one such group *panchayat*. The *1959 Act* specifies that at each level of local government administration there are to be reserved seats, first of all for Scheduled Castes and Tribes in proportion to their population and second, for a minimum of two women. At the last group *panchayat* election which took place in Dalena in 1967 the village was allocated the election of one of the two seats reserved for women. There were then approximately 490 voters in the village; each had to cast three votes, one of which was to be for a woman candidate. Eight candidates were nominated for the election; all were Peasants and three were women. Each candidate was allocated a symbol such as an umbrella or an elephant and each tried by some means or other to gain majority support : some gave feasts, others relied on their political reputation, and again others used political manipulation. Only one of the candidates was a hereditary lineage elder; he was the man villagers referred to as chairman. As we have seen, in 1956 he acted as *de facto* headman and carried out most of the functions expected of a *patel.* He still looks upon himself as *the* leader in Dalena, and is widely regarded as such. The other candidates included Nanjegowda, the headman's son, his brother, Kempegowda, as well as Kempa, who is now a magnate of considerable standing and at the same time is respected for his qualities of leadership. He is the innovator of diesel pump irrigation in Dalena (see p. 87). The three female candidates included Bukamma, whose Peasant husband, though not rich, is widely respected for his composure as an arbitrator, and Honamma, wife of an ordinary middle-farmer, generally regarded as a busy-body who likes to poke her nose into everything.

Different motives inspired each of the candidates to seek election : the chairman expected his election to reaffirm his dominant political position in the village; the *patel*'s son saw membership of the Group *Panchayat* as the lowest rank on the ladder of political promotion he was eager to climb; Kempegowda, the *patel*'s younger brother, sought some political basis from which he could better manipulate his economic activities; Kempa was keen to represent the villagers' interests on the wider scene and to try and secure the Government's help in improving village facilities; Bukamma yielded to pressure from followers of her husband, who regarded her as her husband's mouthpiece, and agreed to be nominated. Her husband himself refused to be drawn into fighting the election. Honamma wanted an official forum to exert her nosiness. Group *Panchayat* membership is purely honorary; members get no reward for attending meetings or for anything they do in their capacity as councillors. Thus there was no financial incentive for any of the candidates.

Electioneering in the village was conducted on a purely personal basis; no wider political issues or political parties played any part in Dalena's election campaign. Votes were fairly evenly distributed between the chairman, Kempa, Kempegowda and Nanjegowda. Each of them scored over 300 votes. The two successful male candidates were Kempa and Nanjegowda; Bukamma was elected to one of the seats reserved for ladies. The three successful candidates still represent Dalena in the Group *Panchayat*. The chairman lost by no more than twenty votes. His failure does not seem to have affected his self-confidence and assurance in his intra-village political dominance. He still thinks of himself as *the* village leader and spokesman, and is so regarded by many of his co-residents.

Kempa shows obvious signs of disillusionment with the performance of the Group *Panchayat*. He no longer attends meetings regularly and complains that it has no powers, only duties. During my recent return to Dalena, Kempa was asked to attend one of its meetings. He sent his apologies and decided to stay home. He said bitterly : 'What is the point of my attending this meeting. It is just a forum where people air their grievances but nothing is ever done about them !' The councillors from each of the villages represented try to impress on the others that the needs of their own village are the most urgent and should be given priority. Kempa stressed that the Group *Panchayat* has in fact only rarely the necessary funds to sanction any one of the numerous projects for which the various councillors are clamouring – schools, wells and so on. On the rare occasion when the meeting reaches consensus on the priority of one project, this has to be submitted to the *Taluk* Board, the next level in the hierarchical structure of local government administration in Mysore. If the *Taluk* Board agrees to support the specific recommendation funds are contributed by the *Taluk* Board and Group *Panchayat* on a 50:50 basis. Only in the case of roads are schemes the sole responsibility of the *Taluk* Board. Kempa pointed out that as far as he could see the Group *Panchayat* has no, or only very limited, rights but extensive duties : councillors have to see that tax is collected. Tax is levied on the population according to the capacity to pay : individuals pay about Rs. 0.50 per year, whereas, for instance, a flour mill is taxed at Rs. 120 per year. Forty per cent of the Group *Panchayat*'s revenue is handed over to the *Taluk* Board. Kempa's account of the way local government operates may be far from accurate; it certainly does not square with some of the provisions of the *1959 Act*. He may have the wrong picture altogether of the system of local administration. Yet it is important that this is the way he sees and presents it to his fellow villagers.

Nanjegowda is much more optimistic than Kempa about the functions of local government. He points to past achievements: for instance, the fine new school in Dalena. Moreover, he himself is also a member of the *Taluk* Board which has much wider jurisdiction than Group *Panchayats*. He is therefore part of a higher level in the power structure and does not share Kempa's disillusionment. Bukamma does not appear to have expected much from being a councillor. She hardly ever attends any of the meetings and if she does she sits there quietly without contributing to the discussion or saying anything.

Dalena villagers in general seem to be disappointed with the ineffectiveness of the Group *Panchayat*. They would like it to do much more and more quickly. This is a widespread complaint levelled by citizens anywhere against their own government. Dalena villagers on the whole do regard themselves as part of a wider society. Many of them feel that the local government authorities owe them better living conditions and are disappointed with the slow progress made in this direction. Nevertheless, most of them realise that their own village improvement depends on their being part of the wider polity.

By contrast, Wangala residents still regard their own village as an independent political entity. They display little interest in participating in the wider sphere of local government. Wangala is grouped together with four neighbouring villages into one *Panchayat*. At the first Group *Panchayat* elections held in 1964 Wangala elected three councillors. The village had then been chosen to be the seat of the Group *Panchayat*. Subsequently, it was decided to shift its administration to one of the other four villages which is more conveniently situated. This upset Wangala villagers so much that they decided to abstain from participating in the official local government. During the last elections held in 1968 no Wangala man contested nor do residents now pay local government taxes. Wangala elders argue that their village is sufficiently big to have its own local government and they see no reason why councillors from much smaller neighbouring villages should have any say in matters which are the concern of Wangala residents only. Their numbers in fact already slightly exceed 1,500, the minimum population stipulated in the *Act* for a separate *panchayat*. Village elders have filed a writ-petition with the Mysore High Courts asking for Wangala to be declared a separate and independent electorate. At present they are still awaiting the decision in their case.

Wangala's refusal to participate in the Group *Panchayat* and the men's insistence to have their own *panchayat* for their own village illustrates their political isolationism. The fact that they have opted out of the official local government administration, for the time being at least, clearly indicates that Wangala residents feel that their own elders manage their village affairs quite well without outside interference.

The hereditary lineage elders of the 'major' lineages still constitute the *de facto* village government. The emphasis on hereditary succession to political office is as strong now as it ever was. This is clearly seen in the case of Mallegowda. His grandfather was the hereditary elder of one of the major lineages in Wangala during my earlier stay there. His lineage then formed the backbone of what I called the conservative faction of which he was the leader. The old man had only one son, whom he groomed to succeed him in this position. At the time young Mallegowda, who was the eldest grandson, was no more than seven years old. Meanwhile the old man and his son died. Thus young Mallegowda, who is now only twenty-two years old, is the rightful successor to lineage eldership. Accordingly, the lineage elders of the other major lineages in Wangala as well as members of his own lineage insist that he participates in village *panchayat* meetings. Most of the other men who attend these meetings are not only elders in terms of political office but also in years. Mallegowda therefore feels out of place there. He confessed to me that he hates having to sit together with all these older men, many of whom he respects for their superior wisdom. He feels completely at sea in their talks and is too embarrassed ever to speak up in their presence. Yet he is yielding to the pressure exerted on him and agrees to be present at village meetings whenever he is asked to do so.

The matters discussed at such meetings are all concerned with intra-village affairs such as the upkeep of temples, disputes over land, caste offences and so on. The practice of *ad hoc panchayat* meetings to arbitrate in specific quarrels speedily on the spot is still continued : on such occasions a minimum of three or four elders of major lineages congregate to hear the dispute and, provided it is of not too grave a nature, they give their ruling. When I enquired in Dalena if such *ad hoc panchayats* still existed I at first got the stereotyped reply that these days the village is part of the Group *Panchayat* which handles all village business. However, when I questioned my informants on particular intra-village disputes it soon became obvious that in Dalena, as in Wangala, quarrels and difficulties that arise between villagers are settled by at least a few of the hereditary lineage elders.

I myself listened to such a case. Three lineage elders and the chairman gathered to hear a dispute between two cousins. Devegowda demanded that his patrilateral cousin Hanumegowda repay the debt of Rs. 100 which the latter's father had incurred from his own father some years back. Both fathers were now dead. Devegowda said his father had told him many times how he had lent Rs. 100 to his brother to help him buy a pair of cows and that he was still waiting for the repayment of the loan. Devegowda pointed out that Hanumegowda had inherited the cows and was still using them. He now appealed to the elders to help him recover this debt. Hanumegowda then argued that the Rs. 100 represented an old debt, which he himself had never incurred. Moreover, he pleaded that he just did not have the necessary cash to repay it. The elders then asked him if his father had told him of the debt. When he admitted this the elders deliberated the issue among themselves for some time and then ruled that Hanumegowda had to repay the Rs. 100 to his cousin and was given three months in which to do so. Hanumegowda was obviously displeased but gave no indication that he would not abide by the ruling.

Dalena villagers distinguish between matters of purely internal village concern and those with wider political implications. They continue to use the customary procedure to deal with the former, while they participate in the modern local government for the latter. By contrast, Wangala villagers are still too much concerned with their own village affairs to see any need for participating in the wider system. Their economic introversion is reflected in their political isolationism.

Here it must be noted, however, that Wangala villagers are selective in their response to institutional innovations. When they saw substantial benefits to be derived from a new institution, as was the case with the Rural Co-operative Society (see p. 108), they reacted positively and participated with outsiders. Where, on the other hand, the new institution offered no immediately obvious advantages, as in the case of the Group *Panchayat*, they abstained and continued their traditional village government.

## VILLAGE FACTIONS

'There are more faction fights in our villages these days than we ever had before irrigation came' was a statement I frequently heard during my earlier stay in South India; villagers used the English word 'party' to denote factions. This led me to examine the overt as well as the hidden content of a number of such faction fights. I then argued that the economic expansion resulting from the introduction of irrigation had caused an imbalance in Wangala between the economic, political and ritual status of individual households : political and ritual status was determined by hereditary succession; by contrast economic status depended on a number of variables such as the size of the ancestral estate, the number of heirs and most importantly on the individual's own drive and initiative. This greater flexibility in the economic sphere as opposed to strictly hereditary succession to political and ritual offices created in Wangala a cleavage between what I called progressives and conservatives.

In Dalena I found a similar division between modern-oriented Peasants on the one hand and traditionalists on the other. Here it was not a problem of the emerging rich wanting to establish positions for themselves in the village political and ritual system so much as the fact that the hereditary headman happened to be the most outstanding entrepreneur. He had gathered round him a small but economically most powerful faction. These men were beginning to operate on the basis of different principles than those motivating traditional village leaders. They looked to the wider economy for new opportunities and were keen to establish and strengthen their links with the wider polity; they turned to the urban courts for settlement of village disputes and called in the State police to protect a procession held within the village.

What has happened to factionalism in Wangala and Dalena since 1955? At the time of my earlier research in Wangala I was obviously witnessing the struggle for social recognition by Peasants who had recently been successful in the economic sphere. Interestingly, Spiro reports comparable developments for a Burmese village. 'The core of the Thamo-Hnamu faction consists of villagers who have recently entered the upper class, but who, because of their wealth, have become serious contenders for the prestige normally accruing to the traditional upper-class élite' (1969:408). In 1955 I witnessed in Wangala a quarrel between the two opposing factions over who should perform a certain ritual at the Kalamma village feast (1962:132). The issue was resolved by a duplication of the ceremony: leaders of the progressive faction organised their own Kalamma feast at which their men officiated the rituals while simultaneously the conservatives, joined by the neutrals, conducted separately the ceremony in the customary manner with hereditarily entitled men performing the rituals. Similarly in the Burmese village 'the first, and the most important, withdrawal of co-operation occurred in religious and ceremonial activities of which the most important was the split in the Buddhist sodality' (Spiro, 1969:410).

The factions which I labelled progressive and conservative were in fact referred to by villagers in each case under the name of their individual leaders. Wangala people talked in their vernacular of 'Mallegowda's' (conservative) and 'Tugowda's' (progressive) party. Similarly, Dalena residents talked of the 'patel party' and that of the 'chairman'. Naming of factions after their leaders seems to be a widespread phenomenon: Gallin, for instance, called one major faction in the Taiwan village of Pu Yen Hsiang the Public Office faction, 'although its membership identifies it by the name of its leader' (1969:389). Researchers seem to find it more convenient to give village factions more meaningful labels instead of following the practice of the villagers. Unfortunately, this often leads, as it did in my own case, to attaching insufficient weight to the indigenous way of emphasising the importance of informal leaders in naming their factions. Nicholas, who recognised this problem, stressed that 'members can be connected to a faction only through the activity of a leader, since the unit has no corporate existence or clear single principle of recruitment' (1965:28). The full significance of the leader's role in intra-village factions emerged clearly during my return visit to South India.

Wangala Peasants kept assuring me in 1970 that they had finished with faction fights: 'These days we all live together in harmony', they repeated. This seemed at first sight to be too good to be true, particularly in view of the fact that 'many authors feel confident in asserting that factionalism in Indian villages is increasing and that this trend will continue' (Miller, 1965:24). Only after a long talk with Tugowda and his two magnate friends, the leaders of the progressives in 1955, did I begin to understand what had been happening in respect to factionalism in Wangala. I questioned Tugowda about the Kalamma feast, for it was he who had been responsible for the duplication of this ceremony. He explained that the two factions continued to celebrate separately this and other feasts for about five years after I left South India in 1956. Each year the number of goats sacrificed at ceremonies by his faction increased while that presented for ritual slaughter by their opponents declined. This meant that more and more people became keen to attend Tugowda's feasts and fewer turned up for those organised by the conservatives. Finally, the traditional *panchayat* met and discussed the problem. After long deliberation it was decided that there should in future be only one ceremony to mark the village festivals. The old man grinned sheepishly when he ended his account by telling me that one of *his* men replaced the hereditary incumbent of the ritual sacrificer' at the Kalamma feast and similar ceremonies. Other informants verified the truth of his tale.

This account neatly sums up the political developments that have taken place in Wangala: the men who in earlier years were struggling for social recognition of their newly gained economic status have meanwhile achieved their ambitions. At the same time no young contestants have yet emerged in the village to challenge their economic dominance. Kinegowda, one of the *patel*'s sons, is about the only outstanding entrepreneur of the younger generation; he is busily trying to increase his family's wealth. However, because he is the son of the headman he already has all the social recognition he may want and therefore does not have to struggle to achieve it.

Tugowda, Beregowda and Charegowda, the three progressive

magnates of 1955, have not only retained, but even managed to strengthen their economic dominance in Wangala. They are still the richest men in the village. Significantly, in each case their children, who have in the meantime matured and married, provide additional managerial labour for the family estates. Each of the three magnate households now lives as a joint family. By contrast, the two magnates who in 1955 belonged to lineages neutral in the faction fight, have in the meantime partitioned their assets and consequently their households are nowadays no more counted among the richest Peasants. Kangowda, one of these men, used to be the chief money-lender in the village. Almost everyone was indebted to him and feared his aggressive insistence on payment of interest and repayment of debts. His estate had to be equally partitioned between himself and his four sons, and he disappeared from the village economic scene. None of his sons has inherited his drive and abilities. They do not display any ambitions to get rich like their father did. The fate of Wangala's magnates during the last 15 years emphasises that in a rural economy with limited supply of lands, where each son has the right to an equal share in the ancestral estate, the relative fortune of any one household changes as soon as the joint property has to be divided among a number of sons. Moreover, it makes it clear that factional opposition is closely tied up with the economic fortunes of individual Peasants. This accounts for the cyclical nature of Wangala's factionalism. If we assume that equilibrium existed in the socio-economic sphere at the time irrigation reached the village, which is what informants imply when they stress that pre-irrigation there used to be much more harmony in the village, then we can correlate the increase and decline in factional opposition with the economic and social progress of the three progressive magnates. These are three ambitious and able men who were in their prime years just when irrigation provided them with new opportunities. They all belonged to newcomer lineages without any established positions in village politics or ritual. In Indian villages 'whatever route may be chosen effective rise begins with the prospering of individual families. Hopes for higher rank are futile unless steeled with secular strength. Individual families can achieve real advance only as part of a larger group and so prospering families deploy their secular resources to achieve ritual gains for their group'

(Mandelbaum, 1970:631). This is precisely the way the three Wangala progressive magnates acted. It took them about thirty years before they managed to achieve social recognition and become part of the village establishment.

The major questions which have yet to be answered in this context are the following : 1. Why have there been no new contestants for political and ritual positions in Wangala? 2. How did the three progressive leaders manage to keep a stranglehold over economic advance in the village? 3. Why have no other younger and possibly abler men at least begun to challenge the dominance of these magnates? One possible answer is that the younger generation no longer attaches such great weight to intra-village ritual and political status; instead young men might now seek prestige and social recognition outside. This, however, does not seem to be the case in Wangala judging by the fact that, except for Kinegowda, the headman's son, no man resident in the village has as yet sought a position in the wider political sphere.

The only reasonable explanation I can offer is the fact that entrepreneurship is an extremely scarce resource in rural economies, particularly in South India. To be an innovator by definition implies non-conformity. In Wangala great stress is laid on conformity to traditional behaviour patterns. This accounts both for the sparsity of entrepreneurs as well as for the ganging together in Wangala of three innovators who were still at that time regarded as social outsiders. It appears to be much more difficult for a sole individual to branch out into new economic activities ostracised by fellow villagers than it is for two or three friends to do just this. When success rewards their enterprise and they are able to translate it into general socio-political recognition within the village they are in a good position to monopolise socio-economic leadership until their property is partitioned among a number of heirs. The estates of the three Wangala progressive magnates are as yet undivided. These three men now have such decisive dominance not only in the economic but also in the political and ritual sphere within their village that they control the decision-making process in Wangala's public field. Hence the greater harmony in the village these days as compared to fifteen years ago. Nowadays there are no effective challengers to the establishment. I suspect, though, that the whole process of intensive factionalism is likely to recur as soon as the present progressive magnates die and their estates are divided among their heirs. There will then once more be an open field for young and successful entrepreneurs to contest for positions in Wangala's hereditary political and ritual system and the whole process may repeat itself. 'The personal motivation toward challenge of immediate superiors is constant, and so is social competition' (Mandelbaum, 1970:627); what is restricted is the social field and the opportunities. 'Public power in the village is very limited: there is a relatively stable number of men over whom one can expect to exercise command and very restricted resources which one could conceivably control' (Nicholas, 1968:255). I am suggesting that the scarcity of successful entrepreneurs in Wangala accompanied by the limited political and ritual positions available makes for factional cycles, each of about forty to fifty years' duration.

In contrast to this cyclical development of factions in Wangala, Dalena's intra-village opposition has continued to intensify. In this dry land village where economic progress could be achieved only by reaching outside the village to participate in the regional expansion there are now hardly any occasions which affect all residents alike and serve to unite them. Consequently sectional interests are now more important than considerations of overall village welfare. Dalena's progressives under the leadership of the *patel* operate on the basis of different premises from those of their conservative counterparts. The headman has continued to be the outstanding entrepreneur. His business activities increasingly take him outside his home village. His chief concern is to succeed in the wider economy; he does not attach much importance to social recognition within Dalena. He and his small group of followers have very little, if any, social contact with their fellow villagers. Dalena's progressives, in particular the *patel*, have more or less opted out of the intra-village struggle for prestige. Conservatives under the leadership of the chairman are still wholly village oriented. He is a full-time farmer and his main concern appears to be the continuous reaffirmation of his political prestige within the village. He is the source of most data on Dalena's past and therefore makes the most knowledgeable arbitrator in disputes. The chairman and a few other important men in his faction have taken over the effective leadership in informal village politics. The *patel* hardly ever participates in any of the small *ad hoc panchayats* composed of hereditary elders; these meetings are invariably conducted by the chairman.

Dalena's diversified economy has given rise to a third force, to which I referred earlier when I discussed Chennu's case (see p. 128). There are nowadays in Dalena a number of young urban workers like Chennu, who aspire to political influence in the village under a progressive flag, but they have no common ground with Dalena's entrepreneurs. This third force, as yet small, is highly critical of the chairman's political manipulations, of which Chennu gave the following example. Sidlingegowda was a young man married to the daughter of the chairman's wife's brother. The marriage had not been consummated when the young bride-groom contracted tuberculosis and had to go into hospital. In order to have some ready cash he borrowed Rs. 2,000 from his wife's father against a mortgage on two acres of wet land he owned in a neighbouring village. During his four-year stay in hospital his father-in-law, with the help of the chairman, trans-ferred his wet lands into the name of the young man's wife. When Sidlingegowda returned to his home fully cured and was keen for his consummation ceremony to be arranged – his wife had in the meantime reached maturity – his father-in-law pointed out to him that he did not want his daughter to be married to a sick man. Meanwhile, the chairman was busy trying to initiate marriage negotiations with the family of another young man from a nearby irrigated village. Sidlingegowda was so enraged when he discovered that he had not only lost his wife but also his precious two acres of wet land that he went in great anger to his wife's home and there and then cut her throat. He was taken to court and given a 12-year prison sentence which is about to expire. Chennu became very heated when he told me of this case and emphasised that he was keen to reopen the issue of the land transfer.

In another episode that Chennu recounted, one of the chair-man's daughters drowned in the canal which by-passes the village. The young girl had been married to a Peasant from Dalena and she already had some children. The couple are reported to have quarrelled a lot, the wife having been very unhappy. She kept appealing to her father to help her separate from her husband but her pleas fell on deaf ears. One day during the early part of 1970 villagers heard quarrelling from the canal

banks; a little later in the day some Peasants came running into
the village shouting that the chairman's daughter was drowning
in the canal. Attempts to rescue her failed and the body was
recovered only the following day. The chairman and his followers
were obviously afraid of police investigations and quickly
arranged for the funeral. The police turned up the day after the
burial and the chairman assured them that his daughter's death
was straightforward suicide. The villagers wondered who had
informed the police. Chennu admitted to me that it was he who
had told the Mandya police of what he described as murder in
Dalena: he maintained that the girl's husband had pushed her
into the water and should therefore have to stand trial.[1] He was
obviously keen to have the case aired in public and the chairman's
part in it exposed.

Chennu has as yet not been successful in making his opposition
to the chairman effective in the village. Yet, time and circumstances are likely to work in his favour. He is a young man compared to the chairman, who is in his sixties. Moreover, he is a
factory worker and as such represents the modern Dalena Peasant. The increasing integration of Dalena in the wider economy
will draw more and more Peasants into urban employment. If
they follow Chennu's path and, like him, remain village oriented,
this third force of theirs is likely to gain momentum. They will
not have to worry about opposition from the *patel* and his small
group of outward-looking village entrepreneurs. They may have
to face competition from Dalena's traditionalists who look for a
political leader familiar with and concerned with the village's
past. However, before too long Dalena is likely to be swallowed
up by the expansion of Mandya town, which will clear the field
for Chennu, or men like him, to enter the political arena.

I have outlined here and tried to analyse the different ways in
which factionalism changed during the last 15 years in Wangala
on the one hand and in Dalena on the other. Wangala's discrete
rural economy has experienced a cyclical development in factional opposition. By contrast, Dalena's continuing process of
economic diversification has brought a hardening of the division
between progressives and conservatives; at the same time it has

---

[1] From Chennu's account it was not clear whether he claimed the dead
girl's husband had pushed her bodily into the water or if he thought that the
husband was responsible for her wanting to kill herself.

led to the emergence of a third force which, though still in its embryonic stage, is likely to grow quickly into an influential group within the village.

# 7 Social Change

## BACKWARD CLASSES AND SCHEDULED CASTES

The *Constitution of India* accords each citizen equality before the law and makes discrimination by virtue of caste, religion, race, sex or place of birth a punishable offence (1955:5). At the same time it provides for favoured treatment for Scheduled Castes and Tribes (1955:105). The situation bred deep resentment among non-Brahmin castes, who form the bulk of India's population. They were at a disadvantage, compared with Brahmins, in access to tertiary education and high-level appointments, while they did not qualify for preferential treatment reserved to Scheduled communities. Their political pressures exerted at Central and State Government levels resulted in the appointment by the Government of India of the *Backward Classes Commission* to determine the criteria by which sections other than the Scheduled Castes and Tribes could be treated as socially and educationally backward.

The Commission's *1955 Report* recommended that caste be used as the criterion of an individual's backwardness. 'It quickly became clear that the great bulk of India's multitude of castes considered themselves "backward" enough to be counted among the deserving poor and to share in any benefits that were being handed around. . . . In many States a great clamour arose, with all kinds of groups insisting that they too should be classified as "backward" and these included, it must be said, some pretty forward castes who felt that their jealously guarded ritual and social superiority should not be allowed to interfere with their right to get on the government gravy train' (Isaacs, 1964:104). The *1955 Report* 'listed 2,399 castes as backward, and recommended that these be made eligible for benefits similar to those enjoyed by the Scheduled Castes and Tribes' (Srinivas, 1969:113).

Lingayats and Peasants, the two dominant castes in Mysore State, managed to get themselves included on the list of Backward Classes. According to a 1959 Mysore Government Order, in addition to the reservation for the Scheduled Castes and Tribes, 57 per cent of government posts and of seats in technical institutions were reserved for 165 castes and communities listed as 'Other Backward Classes'. In a case brought before the Mysore High Court in 1960 the Chief Justice declared that this policy violated the Constitution (Smith, 1963:318). Consequently, the Mysore Government appointed in the same year a committee under the chairmanship of Dr R. Nagan Gowda to lay down criteria for the classification of backward classes. The Committee took 'caste' as the unit for consideration, and the backwardness or otherwise of a caste was to be determined by its representation in government service and the number of high school students per thousand of population. On this basis the Lingayats were declared a 'forward' caste while their chief rivals for power at the state level, the Peasants, were classified as 'backward'. Lingayats promptly mounted strong opposition and eventually the Mysore Government yielded to their pressure and restored to Lingayats the coveted 'backward' status (Srinivas, 1969:110).

Many Peasants in Wangala and Dalena complain that while previously Brahmins had monopolised seats in colleges and high-ranking public service appointments, nowadays Scheduled Castes enjoy this monopoly. Some Peasants resent A.K. boys getting scholarships to high school and university while they have to pay fees for their own sons. When I heard such complaints from some of my poorer Peasant friends in Dalena I enquired whether it had ever occurred to any of them to try and qualify as Scheduled Caste men. They were aghast at this suggestion and they all burst out simultaneously shouting 'We are Peasants and not A.K.s! – Even if the Government today offered free education and free wet land to any man who declares himself belonging to a Scheduled Caste, we would prefer to do without these advantages rather than lower our status to that of A.K.s.'

This outburst from a group of poor Peasant farmers highlights their attitude towards their A.K.s: they still regard them as the lowest stratum in society and are prepared to forego the most attractive economic gains if this meant having to take on A.K. status. 'There is a stigma attached to being Scheduled Caste, but it is fine to get the money without the stigma simply by being another "Backward Community" ' (Isaacs, 1964:106). My village Peasant friends strongly objected to the mere suggestion that they accept the cloak of a Scheduled caste just to take advantage of government favoured treatment; yet they have no doubts or scruples whatsoever about claiming special conditions for themselves as members of a 'backward' caste. For instance, Wangala graduates and undergraduates secured their university places by virtue of belonging to the 'backward' Peasant caste.

The non-dominant castes in Mysore complain that they do not have a chance to share in the benefits offered to 'backward communities'. For instance, one young Wangala Goldsmith bewailed the fact that he had not managed to go on to University as had a number of his Peasant fellow students. He is firmly convinced that had he been a Peasant he would have also been able to continue his studies instead of having to turn to his ancestral craft. In this connection Srinivas points out that the non-dominant castes naturally feel frustrated and bitter. Today, in Mysore, men from non-dominant castes style themselves as 'minor' castes, and complain about the 'ruthless manner' in which the Lingayats and Peasants are collaring jobs and the licences and permits necessary for every type of entrepreneurial activity. That this is a widespread feeling is borne out by the Nagan Gowda Committee's recommendation that the backward classes be divided into 'backward' and 'more backward' to ensure a fair deal for the latter. This feeling is not confined to Mysore but occurs also in Kerala and Madras (Srinivas, 1969:112).

A village Peasant who wants to qualify for any of the benefits offered to 'backward communities' must give proof of his caste membership. To establish this he not only has to be a prominent member of his caste in his village, or attach himself to such a man, but more important still he has to try and invoke caste loyalties among fellow caste men in high positions in State Universities and in the public service. For instance, Rampa, the young Wangala Peasant who has a master's degree in economics (see p. 224), became a retainer of one of his professors who was also a Peasant. He hoped that his professor would be able and prepared to help him obtain a Ph.D. scholarship. He was sadly disappointed. When I discussed Rampa's case with his professor the latter pointed out to me that he dare not try to show any favours to fellow caste men. He explained that Lingayats are the dominant caste in his university and therefore he, as a Peasant, has to watch his step very carefully. He had helped Rampa in the course of his studies as much as he could, but now he was unable to do any more for him. Rampa, not fully aware of all the political implications of caste, felt very hurt that his professor, whom he had hero-worshipped as a student, had let him down.

As can be seen, caste is still very much a living social institution not only in Mysore villages but also in the urban environment. The policy of giving relief on the basis of caste membership necessarily reinforces intra-caste links and removes any chance of diminishing the importance of caste as a principle of social organisation. In fact it provides legal justification for citizens to ignore one of the most important clauses in India's *Constitution*, ensuring each citizen equality before the law and prohibiting discrimination. The Central Government's conflicting policies, by giving new strength to an institution it supposedly had already abolished, is giving caste a new lease of life. Srinivas correctly emphasises that 'caste is an institution of prodigious strength; it will take a lot of beating before it will die' (1955a:133), to which I may add that even if it does die some day, there is no assurance that it will not be reincarnated in some other shape or form.

## THE ECONOMICS OF SANSKRITISATION

'Sanskritisation is the process by which a "low" Hindu caste or tribal or other group changes its custom, ritual, ideology, and way of life in the direction of a high, and frequently, "twice-born" caste' (Srinivas, 1969:6). Srinivas first introduced the concept of sanskritisation in his study *Religion and Society among the Coorgs of South India* (1952:30). It has become a most useful and widely employed tool in the analysis of social change in India. Most researchers interested in these questions have established a relationship between secular mobility and sanscritisation. Caste men, who had not raised their secular status, had no hope of achieving higher ritual status, however much they sanskritised their way of life. One of the major functions of sanskritisation was found to be the provision of a bridge between secular and ritual rank. 'When a caste or section of a caste achieved secular power it usually also tried to acquire the traditional symbols of high status, namely the customs, ritual, ideas, beliefs, and life style of the locally highest castes' (Srinivas, 1969:28).

Recent economic growth in rural India has increased economic mobility; some individuals and their caste groups gained more from this development than others. In this connection Bailey perceptively remarks that 'increased wealth leads to a desire for a greater say in the management of the community. At the same time the aspirants wish to assume the guise of respectability, and they do this by improving their placing within the ritual ranking of the Hindu caste system' (1957:197). Different criteria, however, determine secular ranking on the one hand and ritual status on the other: upward secular mobility operates basically in a competitive field where enterprising individuals and their families constitute the units involved; by contrast, ritual status is acquired by birth into a caste whose position in the hierarchical social structure is, at least in theory, regarded as fixed. Srinivas does stress though that 'the caste system is far from rigid. . . . Movement has always been possible, and especially so in the middle regions of the hierarchy' (1952:30). Yet the units involved in ritual mobility have to be whole castes or sub-castes which usually have to be large enough to operate as an endogamous unit. The different sizes of unit involved in the secular and ritual fields introduces considerable friction into the process of social change. The imbalance between secular and ritual status provides a clue to understanding the process of sanskritisation. This does not imply that poor members of a caste ranking high in the ritual hierarchy automatically lose their ritual superiority, which has an independent existence and power of its own (Srinivas, 1969:13). Villagers do not find it paradoxical that Brahmins may refuse certain cooked foods and sometimes other social gestures from other castes, even from the economically powerful ones (Beidelman, 1959:18). There is no inconsistency between poorer high castes maintaining their ritual superiority and *nouveaux riches* medium-range castes trying to raise their relative ritual status.

'A feature of rural life in many parts of India is the existence of dominant landowning castes' (Srinivas, 1969:10). In Wangala and Dalena Peasants have decisive dominance for they represent numerically, economically, politically and ritually the most important single social group in these villages. None of the Functionary castes is numerically important, nor has any of them managed to achieve high economic status. The only other numerically important group are the A.K.s. I discuss their caste position and their relationship with Peasants in a subsequent section (see p. 211). Neither in Wangala nor in Dalena is there any caste which as yet can successfully challenge Peasant dominance. Srinivas emphasises that 'the mediation of the various models of Sanskritisation through the local dominant caste stresses the importance of the latter in the process of cultural transmission' (1969:14). There are now a number of accounts available which describe and analyse the way locally successful castes use sanskritisation as a means to translate their raised secular status into ritual recognition, but little has been written so far on how sanskritic changes of life style are actually adopted by the wealthiest section of a locally dominant caste and how these begin to filter through the various economic strata within the dominant caste in the whole region. Here, therefore, I concern myself with examining the process whereby the richer Peasants adopt certain sanskritic customs and their poorer caste fellows have to follow suit.

Sanskritisation is a many-sided process, particularly when it affects intra-caste relations; different aspects manifest themselves in different situations. In Dalena and Wangala the adoption of Brahminical names and the change-over from bridewealth to dowry are the most obvious signs indicating how wealthier Peasants attempt to adopt features of the sanskritic life style, thereby distinguishing themselves from the rest of their caste fellows. During my earlier stay in the villages all male Peasants bore the names with the suffix '*gowda*', which denoted their caste, although in colloquial usage it was often dropped. There were then only a limited number of personal names used, of which Kempa, short for Kempegowda – literally meaning 'red Peasant' – was the one name which occurred most frequently. Nowadays there are a number of young Peasant boys in Wangala, and also some in Dalena, with names such as Ramakrishna.

The full significance of these new names became clear to me only when I talked with a ten-year-old Wangala Peasant boy. He had given me his name as Rama and not being aware yet of the new naming practice I called him Ramegowda. This bright youngster at once pointed out to me that his full name was not Ramegowda but Ramakrishna and that he bore the name of one of the most important Indian deities. He did not even try to hide how hurt he was that I had called him *gowda* instead of by his proper Brahminical name. A crowd of other young Peasant boys of Rama's age or slightly older, who were gathered around and had listened to our conversation, all joined in to make sure that I had grasped the importance of the point. Kempegowda, Rama's father, a Peasant immigrant to Wangala, who runs one of the two most successful cafés there, explained to me subsequently that Rama was his first son after his wife had borne him three daughters and he had already given up all hope of ever having a male offspring. Consequently, he decided to name the new baby after the god of creation, Krishna. This may explain why Kempegowda called his son by that name, but a contributory factor was without doubt the father's attempt to raise his family's social status so as to achieve finally full acceptance into Wangala Peasant society. Thus changes in personal names represent an attempt at sanskritisation. This is particularly striking in South India, where sharp linguistic differences exist between typically Brahmin names and names common among non-Brahmin peasantry (Beteille, 1967:96). Ramakrishna was the first Wangala Peasant whose name did not have the suffix *gowda*; by now there are at least ten more village Peasant boys with similar Brahminical names. Significantly, all of them are sons of wealthier middle-farmers.

Another sign of sanskritisation among village Peasants is the change from bridewealth to dowry. On my first field trip the full responsibility for arranging a wedding and meeting most of the expenses rested with the bridegroom's family. When I then collected details of the different types of wedding expenditure I hardly had to question the bride's parents, for they spent very little on the occasion. The customary bridewealth (*tara*), handed over by the bridegroom's father to the father of the bride, then symbolised the passing of authority over the bride from her father to her new husband's kin-group. In 1955–6 I witnessed a number of elaborate wedding ceremonies at which the bridegroom's family spent lavishly so as to show off their newly gained wealth. The richer the household, the more elaborate the feast it offered to the village and the greater the expense on clothing and orna- ments for the bride. Middle-farmers competed among themselves for novel ways of displaying their wealth, and the magnates had to keep pace. One magnate purchased an expensive woollen Western-style jacket and a pair of shoes for his son. The son proudly and bravely sweated in his heavy jacket and limped his way between his house and the temple on aching feet unused to footwear. On another similar occasion, one of the richer middle-farmers hired an old car to come 30 miles to the village to drive the bridal pair in procession through the bumpy village streets.

Against this background I was greatly astonished to discover on my return to Mysore that among Wangala Peasants bride-wealth had altogether given way to dowry (*varmana*). Among Dalena Peasants the poorer were still struggling against a dowry system but the wealthier had already accepted it. Unfortunately I arrived back in Mysore at the end of the wedding season. I managed to witness therefore only one wedding in Dalena. This took place on the very day I first returned, when the daughter of one of the *patel*'s younger brothers married a young Peasant from one of the nearby irrigated villages. The bride's father told me proudly that he was giving Rs. 3,000 in dowry to the 'groom's father and that he was spending at least another Rs. 3,000 on jewellery, clothes and a lavish feast for hundreds of wedding guests. I was immediately struck by this change for during my earlier stay in Dalena I had observed the wedding of the son of one of the *patel*'s classificatory brothers. On that occasion the marriage took place in the groom's home and was financed entirely by his parents. By contrast, the recent wedding was conducted in the bride's home and her parents footed the bill. When I began to enquire into this change it did not take long to find out that Dalena's Peasant chairman had been the first in the village when, five years earlier, he gave Rs. 2,000 to his son-in-law's family when his daughter got married. The richer Peasants followed suit, but the poorer farmers have tried to resist the change. The latter argue that dowry not only makes it harder for fathers to find husbands for their daughters, but it makes it well nigh impossible for them to compete in the inflationary dowry system. They complained that a farmer without any wet land just cannot raise the minimum of Rs. 3,000 which seems to be required to marry off a girl under a dowry system. Significantly, during the past two years two Dalena girls and one young man married under the customary system of bridewealth. The three families involved belonged to the poorest section of Dalena Peasants and the respective marriage partners also all originated from dry land villages in the neighbourhood. Dry land farmers appear to be too poor to adopt a dowry system. In fact some of them mentioned that they were trying to have the problem discussed at one of the next *panchayat* meetings where they hoped a regulation might be introduced to stop the spiralling of dowry payments and to revert to the customary bridewealth. These men pointed out that they thought it wrong for the bride's family to have to pay her groom, when they are losing an important productive helper while the groom is gaining one in his new wife. Women are still the mainstay of dry land farming and therefore, they argue, a girl's family should be compensated on her marriage for parting with her, rather than to have to pay the groom an additional dowry. However, despite their efforts to withstand the tide of change, it is likely that they will have to give way before long. Sooner or later they are bound to discover that they cannot find husbands for their daughters unless they abide by the new rules of the Peasant marriage game.

This is precisely what has happened in Wangala. Boma, one of the poorer Peasants, who used to work on the Wangala factory plantation, told me that the recent marriage of his eldest daughter had landed him deeply in debt. He had tried very hard to find her a husband without having to give dowry, but without success. The girl was already 15 years old and had reached puberty. His wife was urging him to arrange a marriage. He finally settled the wedding by paying Rs. 1,000 dowry to the groom's father, giving a watch and clothes to the groom worth Rs. 500, buying clothes and jewellery for Rs. 850 for his daughter and spending Rs. 1,200 on the actual wedding ceremony and accompanying feast – about Rs. 3,550 altogether. He has only two acres of wet land and therefore hardly produces enough to meet his current household needs let alone to pay such heavy marriage expenses. He has three more younger daughters and dreads the time when their turn comes to get married.

Boma and many other Wangala Peasants attribute the change from bridewealth to dowry to an unbalanced demographic development. They see it in terms of too many girls chasing too few grooms. Population statistics do not bear this out. Since 1951 the proportion of females in Mandya District has remained stable at about half the total population. However, in view of the fact that there is not the same urgency for young men to marry as there is for girls, fathers of sons are in a much better position to hold out for the highest bidder than are the fathers of girls. Thus, seen from the viewpoint of the individual Peasant in search of a groom for his daughter, it looks as if the demand for grooms outstrips their supply.

In Wangala it was Beregowda, one of the most enterprising Peasants (see p. 64), who initiated the change to dowry payments. He related that soon after he had opened his cane-crusher he decided he wanted to marry his daughter to his own wife's brother, then a college student from a neighbouring village. When he approached his in-laws with his suggestion he was told that other parents of young girls also had their eyes on the young man. They had been offered Rs. 700 by one such eager father. Beregowda bid Rs. 1,000 and 'clinched the deal'.

Beregowda explained that three considerations had motivated him to take this step: first, he was keen to get an educated husband for his daughter; second, his daughter had not been trained to work in the fields (Epstein, 1962:71) and, far from being an economic asset, she would be a liability as a wife; finally, he said, Brahmins had always given their daughters dowries. At the same time Beregowda stressed that the institution of bridewealth is still formally observed: as part of the Peasant wedding ritual, *tara* is handed over. Moreover, a girl's maternal uncle still has first claim to marry her and if she is marrying another man her maternal uncle is expected to attend the wedding and give her away so as to indicate publicly that he is relinquishing his claim and has no objection to the union taking place.

Peasants, who have invested in the education of their sons, now expect to be rewarded when the young men get married. Rampa, until now the only man from Wangala with a master's degree, is a case in point. His father had spent about Rs. 2,500 on financing his tertiary education. Shortly before Rampa was due to complete his degree his father began negotiating a marriage for him. Rampa is not only educated but also a very pleasant and handsome young man. His father, therefore, felt confident that he could demand a premium price on the marriage market. A wealthy Mandya Peasant, who owns some land in Wangala, happened to be looking for a husband for his daughter just about the same time. He knew about Rampa and had approached his father about the possibility of a union between their children. Assuming that his son would feel duty-bound to abide by the superior judgement of his elders, Rampa's father acted without consulting his son. Rampa, however, had other plans; he was keen to continue his post-graduate studies and get a Ph.D. degree, and when he was told of the marriage negotiations he bluntly refused to comply with his father's wishes. His father was terribly upset and told Rampa that he thought it high time that he was repaid all the money he had spent on his son's education. But Rampa was adamant. His father appealed to Peasant elders in Wangala and Rampa was called before a traditional *panchayat* meeting. The elders sought to make Rampa see reason and accept his father's advice and marriage arrangements. But still Rampa held out and refused to oblige his father. After hours of discussion at a meeting which lasted into the early hours of the morning, the elders advised Rampa's father to try and postpone the wedding until the young man was ready for it. A few weeks later Rampa learned that he had failed to get a Ph.D. scholarship and he accepted a lectureship at a Mandya college. This appointment added to his prestige, though in terms of actual salary it did not mean very much.

In the meantime his father continued to try to persuade him to accept the marriage, all the while maintaining negotiations with the girl's father. Finally, some months after I had left South India, Rampa succumbed and agreed to the marriage. He wrote and told me that his father-in-law had bought for the young couple jewellery worth about Rs. 5,000 and clothes for another Rs. 5,000. The marriage took place in the luxurious Mandya home of Rampa's in-laws. More than 5,000 guests attended the wedding and were treated to a feast which altogether cost about Rs. 10,000. Though Rampa said nothing of any dowry payment I strongly suspect that his father was not left empty-handed by Rampa's rich in-laws. Moreover, his father-in-law had registered two of his wet acres in Wangala in his daughter's name as well as a valuable housing site in Mandya on which the young couple will have their own home built. Rampa's father-in-law is even prepared to finance the young man's doctoral studies abroad should he succeed in making the necessary arrangements.

Rampa's future now seems well provided for and his father is proud of having organised it all. Many other Wangala Peasants are proud of Rampa's achievements too. However, so far as the village society is concerned, Rampa has moved completely out of it. He regards himself as an urban resident now and takes no more interest in village life. He wears the now customary urban dress of shirt, trousers and shoes and seems somewhat ashamed of the primitive conditions still prevailing in his home village. The gap between this educated young man and his village kin and friends has become unbridgeable.

The changeover to a system of dowry I attribute to the interaction between four important variables. First and fundamental is the increased wealth Mandya Peasants now enjoy. It is this which enables them to spend more lavishly on weddings in their struggle for social recognition. Second, it has become a matter of prestige for wealthier Peasants that their womenfolk do not work on the land; young girls no longer trained to do field work become capricious and demand more and costlier items of jewellery. Where formerly a Peasant wife was an economic asset, she has now become a liability. Accordingly, the groom's family now want to be paid for taking over the responsibility of keeping her where previously they had been prepared to compensate her father for the loss of her productive contribution. Third, there is now a small but growing number of young educated male Peasants whose parents feel justified in claiming compensation from their son's in-laws, as I have outlined in Rampa's case. Lastly, Brahmins, who provide the reference group for village Peasants, practise a dowry system; imitating Brahmin customs means sanskritising one's style of life in the hope of raising one's social status. As Beregowda put it: 'What is good enough for Brahmins is good enough for me!'

It is difficult to weigh the part each of these variables played in bringing about the change from bridewealth to dowry, but what seems certain is that the interaction between the changed economic conditions under which the wealthier Peasants now live and their desire to raise their social status by sanskritisation is responsible for bringing about this dramatic shift in social custom. The richer Wangala and Dalena Peasants regard the sanskritisation of their life style as an avenue for translating their economic success into social recognition. It is significant to note that the initiator of Brahminical names in Wangala is a wealthier middle-farmer, whereas the *avant-garde* in adopting the inflationary dowry system are the richest Peasants. It did not cost Kempegowda any money to give his son a Brahminical name; by contrast Beregowda needed hard cash to be the first Wangala Peasant to pay dowry, and so did Rampa's father-in-law.

On the basis of the preceding examination it is possible to suggest that whenever sanskritisation affects relations within the dominant caste it is likely that only the wealthiest will make costly innovations, while life style changes, which involve little or no extra expenditure, will be initiated by the up and coming among the middle classes; irrespective, however, of which section was responsible for introducing the change, it will ultimately permeate right throughout the total membership of the caste in the whole region.

## FAMILY STRUCTURE

### Joint family

Many studies of Indian society have pointed to the decline of the joint family as a result of economic growth. Bailey says with reference to Bissipara, the Orissa village he studied, that 'the joint family cannot survive divergent interests and disparate incomes' (1957:92); Kaldate states that 'in the process of social disorganisation the changes in family organisation tend to take the form of changes from the larger or joint family system to the small family system' (1962:104); Lannoy remarks that 'wherever there has recently been a radical betterment of the economic conditions of sectors of the Indian population, correspondingly great changes have been found in the pattern of family life. Structurally there is a change from the joint to the nuclear system' (1971:124).

In my own earlier studies I also remarked on the decline of the joint family system : I found then only ten per cent of Wangala's and eight per cent of Dalena's households containing more than the members of the elementary family and an occasional grandparent. On the basis of this data I advanced the general argument that in subsistence economies a joint estate is a necessary precondition to the existence of joint families. Moreover, the adoption of cash crops by joint family subsistence farmers creates strains between the component families and leads to the partitioning of the joint property and household (1962:177).

Unfortunately it was not possible for me to conduct a 100 per cent village census on my return to Wangala and Dalena; I therefore have no overall comparative data for 1970 which could show the trend of change in family pattern. My colleagues at the

University of Nürnberg employed a different definition of the joint family from the one I had accepted; their data is therefore not comparable with my own earlier findings. In my enquiry I treated as joint families only those where all of the following conditions in a unit larger than the elementary family were observed : 'common property and income, co-residence, commensality, co-worship and the performance of certain rights and obligations' (Desai, 1956:147); my German colleagues restricted their definition to common property, common income and co-residence.

My recent observations, however, bear out much of my earlier hypothesis. Landless families and those with insignificant size landholdings have for the most part remained elementary units. On the other hand, growing cash income has increased the tensions within joint families in the middle-range. A considerable proportion of families which during the last fifteen years have extended to three generations have either already been partitioned or are on the verge, or in the process, of breaking up. Jagegowda's family is a good example of the difficulties the head of such a joint family encounters when his sons are not satisfied with the joint activities or the distribution of income within the family unit (see p. 156).

Wangala's Karigowda represents another case of the same kind. He is a man now in his late sixties who had seven wet and two dry acres; each of his four sons had married during the 1960s and has a family of his own. Karigowda, a quiet widower for many years, was a hard-working farmer himself and expected his sons to pull their weight in the joint enterprise, as soon as they were old enough to do so. His two elder sons, however, were a great disappointment in this respect; they were lazy, the old man complained, and only wanted to spend money rather than help earning it. The two younger sons, who actively helped their father in the cultivation of the joint estate, kept asking for partition of the joint household : they felt it was not fair that they and their father did all the work while the two elder brothers spent most of the joint family income. The old man, therefore, agreed to the break-up of the joint household, which took place shortly before I returned to Wangala. The land was divided among the four sons, each receiving one and a half wet acres and half a dry one; the father retained only one wet acre for himself and has joined his youngest son's household. Most of the joint productive and non-productive property was also equally divided : jewellery heirlooms and household equipment were distributed among the four sons' families; the same was done with most tools and agricultural equipment. Only larger capital items, such as a cart, continue to be jointly used by the brothers. Karigowda had two pairs of bullocks : the stronger and more valuable pair was taken over by two of his sons to use jointly, while he took the weaker pair with him when he joined his youngest son's family. The fourth son was just then negotiating to purchase a pair of bullocks for himself, having received some monetary compensation for having forgone his share in the family cattle. Karigowda's traditional-type farm house which was built to accommodate one family has been rearranged : each of the four separate families has now its own hearth and occupies a corner of the house. Jagegowda and Karigowda are typical of Peasant middle-farmers' families. Though the partitioning of joint property by them is uneconomic – it creates a large number of individual productive units well below optimum size – it is, significantly, among middle-farmers that the break-up of joint families is most frequent.

By contrast, all of the Wangala and Dalena magnates, who were already among the wealthiest in 1955, live now in joint households. As already mentioned, Wangala's Tugowda is the head of a joint family; his eldest son participates actively in the management of the joint estate. He respects his father's entrepreneurial abilities and accepts the old man's superior wisdom and judgement in the household's decision-making process. Beregowda, another Wangala magnate, who has managed to retain his dominant economic position in the village, has no sons, but only two daughters by his second wife. Both the girls are now married : one has moved to her husband's home in a neighbouring village and the other resides with her husband in Wangala. Beregowda has continued to live jointly from one hearth with his ten years younger brother, who is married and has two adolescent children. The household is now composed of Beregowda and his two wives, as well as his younger brother and his family. Such fraternal joint families are even rarer than the three-generation-depth units. Beregowda explained that by the time his brother got married, he himself had already become resigned to having only daughters and no sons. This meant that he had to forgo the chance of own sons growing up and helping him run his various ventures. He stressed the importance, as he saw it, of having near kin as partners rather than having to depend on strangers. Thus when his brother married and suggested partitioning the paternal property, which was only a small part of the wealth Beregowda had by then acquired, Beregowda offered to continue the family as one unit. This enabled him to have a reliable partner in his ventures and benefited his younger brother, who has nothing like Beregowda's entrepreneurial abilities, by giving him a right to share in much larger wealth than he would otherwise have been able to accumulate.

Charegowda, the third Wangala magnate, who has maintained his economic dominance, has likewise had to extend his household beyond its elementary size. He has two sons now aged fifteen and eleven years who, he complained, are still too young to take an active part in his household's various economic activities. His first-born child was a daughter, who married her mother's brother about eight years ago. Charegowda then felt the need of a reliable partner in his growing ventures – he had acquired four more acres wet land – and therefore suggested to his brother-in-law, whose attachment to his family had been reinforced by marriage to Charegowda's daughter, to join his household at least temporarily until his own sons were old enough to play their part in economic activities. The young man readily accepted what seemed to him an attractive offer. He was one of four sons of a Peasant who altogether possessed no more than four wet acres in a neighbouring village. Charegowda promised him that he would set him up with at least two wet acres as a separate family as soon as his own sons were old enough to participate in the joint venture. In the meantime they all live jointly from one hearth.

These examples illustrate a number of important points. In the first place, it is clear that magnates fully realise the economies of scale to be derived by living in joint families. Secondly, they appear to trust only their near kin as reliable partners in their economic ventures. If the elementary units making up a magnate's joint family are not lineally related, as in the case of Beregowda and Charegowda, then it seems essential for the peripheral partners to be offered attractive economic opportunities if they are to accept joint living conditions. On the other

hand, in lineally related three-generation joint families, persistence depends largely on the personality of the head of the household and the sort of relationship he establishes with his sons and
their wives. Tugowda is a good example of a magnate who has
succeeded in this respect. His sons look up to him for he has a
most impressive personality and are prepared to listen to him and
take his advice. At the same time Tugowda is a clever manager
who knows how to delegate responsibility to his sons. A magnate
has in fact to walk a tight rope trying to avoid being too
domineering and efficient on the one hand, thereby alienating his
sons so that they may insist on partitioning the joint property;
on the other he has to be a decisively entrepreneurial type, otherwise he would never remain a magnate.

Wangala's Kangowda, who is now in his early sixties and who
was a magnate in 1955 – then one of the shrewdest and most
feared money-lenders in the village – exemplifies the type of man
who lost his dominant economic status because he alienated his
sons' allegiance. Kangowda owned in 1955 seven wet and four
dry acres; in the early 1960s he purchased four more wet acres
and one of his dry acres also became irrigated. In the meantime
four of his six sons married and had children of their own. In
particular, the three eldest sons were getting more and more
resentful of their father's domineering and self-centred ways. He
was not prepared to let them participate in making decisions
which they claimed affected their very own welfare. Consequently they insisted on having the joint estate partitioned.
Kangowda was so deeply hurt when his sons made him partition
the estate that he almost completely withdrew from active participation in economic activities. In 1969 he shared out his land
among his sons, each getting two wet and half a dry acre. He
kept none for himself and together with his wife joined his
youngest married son's family. From having been a fiery and
forceful entrepreneur he has now become a meek and mild old
man of whom no one takes much notice any more. Although in
1955 he was probably even wealthier than Tugowda, he has now
completely disappeared from Wangala's economic stage while
Tugowda has gone from strength to strength. Kangowda was
apparently too grasping a man and had to suffer for it; Tugowda
on the other hand seemed always a much kinder and less self-
interested man who through his personal qualities has succeeded

in maintaining the affection and admiration not only of his sons but also most villagers.

Dalena's Lingowda, similarly, managed to keep his sons' devotion and they still live jointly. He, like Tugowda, is a most impressive man. He is tall and well built and has an imposing appearance. None of his sons has ever mentioned the possibility of partitioning their joint estate. When I discussed with him his business ventures and enquired which of his sons he thought would continue in his footsteps after his own death, he told me that he kept advising his children to remain a joint entity even when he himself was no more, otherwise the wealth which their household had managed to accumulate would soon be dissipated and none of them would be left with very much. He stressed over and over again the importance of reinvesting funds in business enterprises rather than spending all the profits lavishly on unnecessary consumer goods. He foresaw that if his sons insisted on partitioning their joint property after his death none of them would be left with sufficient liquid funds to replace worn-out machinery or invest in additional productive assets. They would therefore be forced to sell off at least part of their investments which, he forecast, would be the beginning of a cumulative decline in their wealth. The joint family makes for a larger productive unit, which in turn facilitates intra-familial division of labour.

In rural societies, where each son has the right to an equal share in the paternal estate, enterprising men are likely to reach the peak in their careers when their sons are old enough to be active participants in the joint activities and yet still dependent enough not to insist on claiming their individual share in the joint property. As long as individual magnates can exert control over their sons and give them a sense of belonging to one of the leading households in their village, there is a good chance for the kin unit not only to retain its dominant economic position but even to improve it. The cyclical nature of family development inevitably leads to periodic partitioning of joint families. Nicholas perceptively argues that 'a family in which property is held jointly between a father and his married sons is not likely to partition because the power of economic decision-making remains with the father. . . . A family in which property is held jointly among brothers, however, has more than 50 per cent chance of dividing. Only if such a family has above average wealth is it likely to be able to moderate its internal conflicts, and only if it has above average wealth is economic cooperation among household members likely to be an important unifying factor' (1961: 1060). My own data help to substantiate this hypothesis : it is the richest Peasants who appear to feel the need most to form and maintain joint households, whereas middle-farmers are less likely to try to keep their families joint.

The greater importance of the extended family among the richest sections of a community appears to be a fairly general phenomenon. König recounts for a village on the east coast of Tenerife, one of the Canary Isands, 'that there, too, the "entrepreneurial" class, formed of former fishermen, kept their joint family system' (1970:603). Similarly, Agarwala, reporting on a Bombay settlement of Marwadis, a caste traditionally engaged in commerce and trade, states that 'the family pattern of this community is what is known as joint family'. He goes on to say that they always try and see 'that all the brothers or members of the family get their jobs and start their business or carry on their profession as far as possible in the same city. If residence is not available under the same roof they see that they get it nearby so that the advantages of a joint family may be enjoyed' (1962:144). This makes it clear though that we are not dealing here with the conventional type of joint family where 'the different kinsmen along with their spouses and children occupy the same dwelling, eat and worship together and enjoy property in common' (Driver, 1962:112) but rather with an adaptation of it. The Marwadis appear to have learned to differentiate on the one hand between the unit of production and income and on the other that of consumption. Such differentiation is essential to enable large wealthy families to benefit from the economies of scale while at the same time permitting diversified living arrangements for participating elementary families to suit their individual tastes. This difference between co-operation in production coupled with separate consumption arrangements has enabled some of the wealthiest business families in industrialised societies, such as the Rothschilds or Rockefellers, to maintain their economic predominance over a number of generations.

*Share family*

I have already mentioned that new types of families, but not necessarily elementary units, are emerging to meet the new needs of society. This process is likely to become increasingly complex in South India as the economic base of villagers changes. For many Peasant farmers it is realistic to assume that the nuclear family is not a self-contained unit, viable on its own. 'It needs to build bridges outwards so that it may fulfil various needs' (Bailey, 1960:352). The new type of family arrangement, which I found in Dalena, and which for lack of a better name I call 'share family', provides one example of an adaptation of the conventional joint family to new economic circumstances.

The share family differs from joint families in as far as the family no more lives jointly under one roof; it differs from the elementary family because it involves a number of near kin – agnatic or affinal – who each live separately with their families, but who have agreed to share the responsibility for their incomes as well as their expenditure. Chennu is one of a number of Dalena wage earners who has such a share agreement with his brother who lives as a full-time farmer in the village. Another is Honegowda, who shares with his wife's younger brother; the latter works for the Public Works Department as an irrigation overseer, but still has eight acres of dry land in Dalena. Honegowda cultivates this dry acreage and gives about half of the yield to his brother-in-law in return for which he gets sufficient cash out of the latter's wages to meet his own household requirements. Honegowda explained that his brother-in-law has little time to cultivate his dry lands, but he was not prepared to sell or to relinquish his claim to this land. None of Dalena's wage earners is prepared to part with his village land however unproductive it may be. Consequently, a number of these Dalena wage earners have made arrangements with their kin who are still full-time farmers.

The farming members of the family undertake to cultivate the land belonging to the urban worker and usually let him have at least part of the yield; in turn the wage-earning relative reciprocates by meeting the necessary cash requirements of his rural kin. These share arrangements are usually highly flexible, without any fixed terms laid down. So far hardly any quarrels have arisen within these share families. This new type of family organisation is regarded as mutually beneficial by all concerned. It enables the Peasant who works for wages outside the village to keep a foothold within it, which seems to be of great importance to these village wage earners. At the same time it allows the farming members of the family to concentrate on cultivating their lands without having to worry about earning cash. This makes them prepared to keep their cash demands within manageable limits. Moreover, many Dalena wage earners try to provide as many modern amenities for their rural kin as possible within their own limited budgets. Thereby they not only continue to have a stake in the rural economy but also remain part of the village social system; they eagerly participate in the internal struggle for prestige (see p. 185).

Singer reports a similar adaptation in families to new situations. 'The urban and industrial members of a family maintain numerous ties and obligations with the members of the family who have remained in the ancestral village or town or have moved elsewhere. And within the urban and industrial setting a modified joint family organisation is emerging . . . The urban "branch" may become a new "stem" sending out new shoots into other cities or towns. . . . Family histories of successful Madras industrial leaders suggest that the traditional joint family system and many of the practices associated with it offer some distinct advantages for organising an industrial enterprise' (1968:445).

Some authorities regard the newly emerging family types as only transitional forms. Kaldate, for instance, states that 'many recent studies have gone to assert that although structurally the traditional family appears to break down, functionally it is not so. These try to maintain that the joint family is not disintegrating in order to function as independent units (nuclear) but adapting to new patterns which have the same degrees of jointness' (1962:103). He goes on to say that 'these are joint in structure either lineally or collaterally. Residentially they are nuclear . . . These forms are of temporary nature and in course of time would become nuclear families altogether' (1962:106). Though this may be true in the long run, for immediate purposes it is not very helpful to regard these changed family types as of only transitional nature. It is important to analyse the operation and function of the share families, because they seem to play a big part in facilitating economic diversification in rural households. Beteille points out that 'it is not known to what extent the family continues to have a common budget even after it has become territorially dispersed, but this appears to be true for a large number of cases' (1964:241). Taking the Marwari as an example, he states that their 'strategy of commercial enterprise has been so organised that its most effective operation can be carried out by a group of individuals who have complementary functions to perform and are held together by the firm and cohesive ties of kinship' (1964:243).

The close productive integration accompanied by only a loosely knit living arrangement enables the elementary families participating in such a share union to have the best of both worlds: each gains from the resulting division of labour and specialisation, while each is free to live its life according to its own judgement. The organisation of a share family is comparable with that of a private company in which all the shares are held by members of one family only. Each participant in a share family, like each shareholder, has an interest in the overall prosperity of the unit in which they all join. Kolenda, who conducted a comparative examination of the Indian joint family by analysing twenty-six individual studies, seems to have been concerned mainly with the structural aspect, for although in Table 20 eight different categories of household are listed no mention is made of the share household type (1968:369). I suspect that with increasing economic diversification in Indian urban, as well as rural, settlements the share family will gain in importance and may become before too long the predominant type of family.

Bailey claimed that 'the relationships which nuclear families have within a joint family serve three ends. These are: first, economies of scale, second, economic security and third, political security' (1960:351). The share family which I found in Dalena offers all these advantages while eliminating the disadvantages which are part and parcel of the conventional joint family in a period of economic growth and change. Not every society is as inventive in adapting its family structure to meet new needs. Arab families do not appear to have managed to adjust their family system equally well. Cohen reports that 'with increasing occupational differentiation there is thus cultural and social differentiation of households. These developments have been associated with the rapid break-up of the traditional joint family . . . For what is involved here is not just a difference in the source of income, but a difference in the way of living attending the two kinds of economic activity' (1965:50).

The persistence in India of the joint family among the richest and the development of the share family in households where co-operating units pursue different types of economic activities, contradict relevant statements made by some leading sociologists: Durkheim, for instance, talked of the 'law of contraction', meaning thereby that all families are likely to change from larger family associations to the restricted nuclear family (1921:20). Similarly, Parsons states that 'there has been a historic trend to whittle down the size of kinship units in the general direction of isolating the nuclear family' (1961:257). Data on past and present family organisation in India certainly limits the general applicability of the hypothesis that economic diversification and industrialisation necessarily lead to the restriction of the family size to its nuclear core. In view of this I now add two more clauses to the hypothesis I put forward in my earlier study :

(1) 'In a subsistence economy the joint family is associated with joint estates; correspondingly, if a family in this type of economy does not own an estate, it cannot expand beyond the elementary size;

(2) 'if a cash crop is introduced into a society of subsistence farmers holding estates on the basis of joint families, the conversion of the subsistence into a cash economy will necessarily produce competition between the component families and lead to the breaking of wider kinship ties' (1962:178).

(a) Such break-up of the joint family is most likely to occur among the middle-farmers. By contrast the traditional type joint family will continue among the wealthiest village *élite* at least until these rich farmers begin to differentiate between productive activities on the one hand and living arrangements on the other.

(b) Adaptations to the customary joint family are likely to occur whenever the wider kin unit offers mutual advantages to the participating members which each would have to forgo by operating in isolation from his extended kin : the share family is but one example of such mutually beneficial adaptation.

## RELATIONS BETWEEN PEASANTS AND A.K.s

'Untouchability was declared "abolished" by Article 17 of the new Indian Constitution of 1949, a charter largely drafted by Ambedkar as Law Minister in Nehru's first post-independence cabinet. The practice of Untouchability was declared "forbidden" and "punishable in accordance with law". The Untouchability (Offences) Act of 1955 spelled out many of the particulars and fixed penalties for infractions. It established the legal right of former Untouchables to enter Hindu temples and to draw water from public wells and streams, to have access and use of every kind of public facility, including shops, cafés, restaurants, hotels, hospitals, housing, all forms of transportation, to wear whatever kind of clothes they wished or enter any occupation they desired. Penalties of imprisonment and fines were laid down not only for anyone who obstructed the exercise of these rights but used "words spoken or written" that might have obstructive effect' (Isaacs, 1964:48). Consequently, village A.K.s who rank as Scheduled Caste are legally entitled to equal public rights with their caste fellow villagers. The drama incident which occurred during my earlier stay in the village (see p. 38) clearly indicates that this legal entitlement was no more than a purely theoretical proposition as far as Wangala village A.K.s were concerned : as economically dependent labourers they could not succeed in their rebellion against their Peasant masters within the borders of their own village. They were legally empowered to take their village Peasants to court for social discrimination against them, but none of them dared to do so. Years have passed since the memorable A.K. drama performance in Wangala. On my return there I asked the A.K. headman if they had performed any more dramas in the meantime; he smiled sadly and told me that they had learned their lesson once and for all – Wangala A.K.s would never again venture upon a drama performance.

The reluctance on the part of Scheduled Castes in villages to exercise their legal rights against their landlords or employers appears to be a widespread phenomenon in India : Beteille reports that 'a Harijan tenant or agricultural labourer who dares to behave as the equal of his master on social or ceremonial occasions may find himself deprived of his source of livelihood' (1967:99). More generally, the *Report of the Commissioner for Scheduled Castes and Scheduled Tribes* remarks that 'due to their economic dependence on caste Hindus, the Scheduled Caste persons concerned generally do not risk approaching the police, who also, it is reported, do not at times properly register the cases reported to them' (M.P., 1962:8). The difficulties a village A.K. faces in claiming his legal rights against his Peasant master emerge clearly from a case I came across as a result of my co-operation with the Nürnberg university team.

My German colleague, who was interviewing political leaders in the region at the time of my return visit, was told by one of the prominent A.K. organisers in the area that he had known about the drama incident in Wangala but had not interfered at the time because no Wangala A.K. approached him for help. However, he added that things had changed since then and one Wangala Peasant had actually been imprisoned a few years ago for having hit a village A.K. This report rather surprised me in view of the obvious continuing subservience of Wangala A.K.s to their village Peasants. I first enquired among my Peasant friends who flatly denied that any such incident had ever occurred. Subsequently, I mentioned it to a few of my A.K. friends who clearly remembered that one of their men had been hit by one of the Peasants, but this had not resulted in a court case as the A.K. organiser had stated.

What had happened was that about three years ago one Wangala young A.K. ordered a cup of coffee at one of the village cafés. When it was handed to him outside he looked in and seeing the place empty he decided to venture inside and sit down. While he was sitting on a bench a Peasant, who happened to be the young man's hereditary master, entered. The Peasant immediately ordered the A.K. to leave and threatened that he would hit him if he was not quick about it. The young A.K. lingered somewhat whereupon the Peasant got hold of a coconut lying on the ground and indeed hit him. The A.K. then threatened that he would complain to Mandya police that a Peasant had assaulted him. A few *panchayat* members, who had been attracted to the scene by the noise, immediately held an *ad hoc* meeting. The A.K. headman was called and it was pointed out to him that if his young subject insisted on taking his complaint to Mandya police this would seriously upset the good relations which existed in the village between Peasants and A.K.s. The Peasant who had committed the offence insisted that he had been justified in hitting an A.K. for breaking customary caste rules and most Peasants present agreed with him. What had probably been quite an innocent action on the part of the young A.K. came to be regarded as the heinous deed of a rebel and he was treated as such. His Peasant master made it clear to him that if he insisted on taking the case to Mandya police, he in turn would insist on immediate repayment of all the money he owed him. This finally clinched the matter. The young A.K. accepted the situation, and the whole matter was hushed up. Yet the event continued to feature prominently in local A.K. gossip. Its account became increasingly more devoid from reality and thus was related in its distorted form by the A.K. politician active in the area.

The Peasant master decided some months after the incident to sever his hereditary relationship with the young man's household. Another local A.K. immediately stepped into the breach and his relationship to his new Peasant master has taken on the character of a hereditary link. The young A.K. 'rebel' was deprived of one of his hereditary Peasant masters and consequently of one lot of annual rewards in kind. His 'defiance' of his Peasant master has thus cost him dearly. In this case, as in the drama incident of fifteen years ago, Peasants used economic sanctions to maintain their socio-political dominance in the village.

Wangala A.K.s seem to accept their social inferiority as the price they have to pay for the assured minimum subsistence which they enjoy and which is part of their traditional hereditary relationships with local Peasants. It is probably true that they inwardly resent their lowly social status; outwardly they certainly accept it except for the odd sign of rebellion such as that just cited. Not even the A.K. headman dares to address a Peasant without being spoken to first; Wangala A.K.s unquestioningly accept the custom that they are polluting and therefore have to drink out of containers specifically kept for their use when they buy coffee at a café. Isaacs' account of what a Scheduled Caste Chamar from Uttar Pradesh, who was a Member of Parliament, told him, clearly indicates how widespread and deep-rooted is the belief in Untouchable pollution : 'Once when I went back to the province and visited a village where there were caste Hindus I found they were ready to sit and eat with me. I was very pleased with this. But when I came outside, I noticed a man of my own caste whom I had seen there before when I arrived. He was sitting out waiting. I asked him why he was waiting there. He told me he had brought the *thali* – the brass bowl – and glass for me to use, and was waiting to get them back so he could go home' (1964:64). If village caste households in Uttar Pradesh were not prepared to make an exception to the rule of Untouchable pollution even for their own Member of Parliament, it is highly unlikely that the dominant Peasant caste in Mysore villages will in the near future be prepared to discard this pollution concept *vis-à-vis* their economically dependent A.K.s.

The ritual and social status of Wangala A.K.s has remained unchanged during the last few generations in spite of new legal provisions and economic opportunities meant to raise them from their social inferiority. Even now no Wangala A.K. would ever dare to attempt drawing water from a caste well. Nor will he allow a Vodda to take water from the one and only A.K. well. The right of a villager to draw water from a well clearly marks off his social status. In this context the *Report of the Commissioner for Scheduled Castes and Scheduled Tribes* comments that 'in certain areas the prejudice is so strong that separate wells have to be provided by the government for different classes of Scheduled Castes living in the same village. This fact weakens to some extent the campaign for the removal of Untouchability' (M.P., 1962:7).

Wangala A.K.s may resent their social inferiority *vis-à-vis* their village Peasants, but at the same time they themselves strictly discriminate against Vodda migrants. This emerged clearly when I discussed the problem of water supply with Mana, Wangala's A.K. headman. Mana pointed out that their one well was not sufficient for their growing community; moreover, he said it was too far for their women to carry water all the way uphill to their homes. The construction of this well was started just before I left Wangala in 1955. I remember that village A.K.s at the time wanted the well nearer their homes, while the expert the government sent to explore the water level decided that since their huts occupied about the highest elevation in Wangala's housing area it would require too deep a well to reach water if it were put in their section. Accordingly, a plot some hundred yards down hill was selected for the well and although the A.K.s were not very happy with this spot they agreed to have the well built there. Mana and his fellow A.K.s are still convinced that it was I who had been instrumental in arousing the authorities' interest in their plight and got the government to agree to subsidise the building of their very first well. Consequently, on my return Mana tried his best to enrol my help in arranging a second well for them. I innocently asked Mana if, when they got a second well, they would allow Voddas to use it. Mana's spontaneous reaction was to deny categorically that Voddas should ever be allowed to draw water from an A.K. well. His reaction was almost identical with the one the Wangala Peasant chairman displayed when I suggested to him if the Peasants might not, now that so many of them have their own wells, permit the A.K.s to draw water from the village caste wells. Mana, the A.K., and the Peasant chairman were each horrified at the idea of allowing people, whom they regard as below themselves in the caste hierarchy and consequently as polluting, to use their respective wells.

In Wangala and nearby irrigated villages discrimination against Scheduled Castes appears to be still more strictly observed than in other parts of South India. For instance, when Malla, my A.K. friend, invited me to come to his home and I suggested we should walk first through the main part of the village he refused to accompany me through the caste streets because, he explained, he was wearing sandals (old and tattered ones) and Peasants do not allow their A.K.s to cover their feet. This contrasts with Beteille's statement that even in South India the issue of Scheduled Castes wearing upper garments, silk cloth, sandals and umbrellas is no more a living one. 'In these matters the *Harijans* seem clearly to have won their battle. Diacritical distinctions in the matter of dress are now rarely enforced by the caste Hindus upon the Scheduled Castes. When the latter continue to retain their former style of life it is more because they lack the economic resources to acquire the symbols of upper caste society and less because they are coerced by the latter to retain their traditional marks of society' (1967:100). Though it is true also for Wangala A.K.s that poverty is largely responsible for their shabbily dressed appearance, Malla's case clearly shows that it is not just lack of money which accounts for the difference in style of dress between Peasants and A.K.s.

In Wangala the social distance between Peasants and A.K.s is as wide as ever. By contrast, in Dalena it has narrowed considerably. The Dalena A.K. postman walks through the caste streets wearing sandals and none of the Peasants takes any notice of it. Moreover, when I went to see the Peasant whose house I had rented during my earlier stay in Dalena I found this A.K. postman inside squatting on the floor checking his accounts. The young A.K. told me that he uses this Peasant house regularly as his office and no Peasant has raised any objections to it. The same Peasant landlord, who used to object to my receiving A.K.s in his house while I rented it from him fifteen years ago, now seemed quite pleased with the arrangement whereby the A.K. postman made use of his house. When I reminded him of his earlier objections to A.K.s entering his house and enquired what had happened to alter his attitude, he explained that times were changing : now the government strongly opposes discrimination against Scheduled Castes. Accordingly, he saw no reason why he should not allow an A.K. to enter his house. He was quick to point out, though, that no A.K. is allowed anywhere near his kitchen. This indicates that the Peasant landowner in this case, like many others of his village caste fellows, has found a compromise which squares with the customary pollution concept and at the same time makes allowances for the new policies concerning Scheduled castes.

The admittance of A.K.s to Dalena caste cafés represents a similar compromise : A.K.s can sit next to caste men in the café, but the coffee they drink is still served them in containers specifically reserved for their use. The A.K. postman sat down unperturbed next to a Peasant in a Dalena café when I was asked to join them. In this respect the attitude of Dalena Peasants has changed radically during the past few years. In 1956 the newly appointed Revenue Inspector for Dalena happened to be an A.K. and so was the school teacher. When the new Revenue Inspector first visited Dalena the chairman invited him for a coffee at the local café knowing perfectly well that the new official would have to decline because he would have to stay outdoors and drink out of a glass specifically reserved for A.K.s while his Peasant host would sit indoors. This incident became a favourite joke told by Peasants at village gatherings to the general amusement of all who listened. Dalena Peasants now no longer object to sitting down in a café side by side with A.K.s, but, as in the case of the

Chamar Member of Parliament, they still observe the rules of pollution by insisting that Scheduled Castes use separate containers for drinking.

The more liberal attitude Dalena Peasants now display towards Scheduled Castes may give the impression that their village A.K.s are now better off than what they used to be. This impression, however, is soon dispelled if one talks with a number of Dalena A.K.s. They are quick to point out that this more liberal Peasant attitude affected only the very few A.K. men who had managed to secure regular employment outside the village. The rest, who depended for their meagre livelihood on dry land farming and casual labouring, were all too poor to worry much about social discrimination against them. What concerns them far more is their extreme poverty and their complete lack of social security. Some of them envied their fellows in Wangala who in their eyes still lead a sheltered life. They pointed out that Wangala Peasants continue to call their A.K.s *halemakalu*, old children, and treat them as such according to custom : they provide them at least with a minimum of basic security in return for which they expect to be shown the traditional respect due to them. In the eyes of Dalena A.K.s this arrangement was fair enough. Mason sums up precisely the A.K. problem in Wangala and Dalena when he says 'the *Harijans* in the village were not free; they were virtually serfs. But the relationship, which was hereditary, did operate on both parties, if the patron exploited, he also protected . . . As hereditary patronage gives way to cash nexus, to competition and contract, insecurity grows more rapidly than social esteem – and real advance is for a very few . . . their poverty is even more crushing. Legal emancipation does not bring a job' (1967:18).

The majority of Dalena A.K.s clearly feel that theirs is largely an economic problem; they explicitly told me that 'you cannot eat social acceptance; we want to get either some wet land or regular employment to help us earn sufficient to keep our families; we are not really concerned about being allowed to enter caste temples, houses or cafés. We want to feel certain that even if the rains fail we will have enough to keep alive.' Judging by this outburst, Beteille correctly puts it that 'in the last analysis it may be argued that the fundamental problem facing *Harijans* . . . is an economic one. It is a problem of landlessness, poverty and unemployment' (1967:117).

Economic improvement, though basic to the difficulties village A.K.s face at present, does not provide, however, the total solution to all their problems. This emerges clearly from the experiences of the few fortunate A.K.s who have managed to raise their economic status to the average level of at least that of the middle-range castes : as soon as Scheduled caste men have solved their immediate economic problems they begin to worry about social acceptance. Man cannot live by social recognition alone, nor is material welfare all he wants. Yeera, the one Dalena A.K. who is now a clerk in Mandya and has moved there, tries his best to dissociate himself from his fellow A.K.s (see p. 130). Similarly, the young Dalena postman feels himself a cut above his fellow caste-men in the village and is very pleased with the opportunity to join Peasants in their homes and cafés. The full significance of the economically successful Scheduled Caste-man's struggle for social acceptance was brought home to me when I met Kuram, an educated Pulaya Scheduled Caste-man from Kerala State where he occupies a high-ranking administrative position. He complained bitterly that even in the socialist-oriented Kerala society Scheduled castes are not accepted on equal terms. Kuram got his education and official position on the basis of being a member of the Scheduled caste. He would like to get away from his past, but cannot do so. He had to prove his Scheduled Caste status 'by supplying a properly attested certificate to show that L is what the government is presumably trying to help him escape from being. He has to certify that he is an ex-Untouchable before the government can help him become something else' (Isaacs, 1964:114). Kuram still lives in a village not far from the administrative centre where he works. However, with two sons growing up, he is keen to move to the town to enable them to benefit from urban schooling. He is ambitious for them to go to university. He told me that he had been trying for a few years to purchase a plot of land in the town so that he might benefit from the government building subsidy to help him put a house up there. As blocks of new sites come on the market he tries to make a bid for one, but he never succeeds. Most landlords in the area know his caste and are not prepared even to consider his application for a site. On the rare occasion when a landlord did not know Kuram's caste and agreed to negotiate the sale of a house site with him the deal fell through when he faced the question 'what is your caste?'

The landlord was most apologetic when he called off the negotiations; he had obviously liked Kuram, who is a well dressed man with an educated manner of speech, but had to explain to him that it would never do for a landlord to sell a new housing site to a Scheduled caste man because this would automatically depress the price of his land : no caste man would be prepared to buy a site in a block where a Scheduled caste man is also going to live. Consequently, the whole block would have to be allocated to Scheduled caste households and there are not so many of them with sufficient money, like Kuram, who can meet the price caste men can pay. Kuram sympathised with the economic considerations which motivated urban landlords to prefer caste customers for housing sites, but this did not make it easier to accept the indignity. He is beginning to be seriously worried that his sons may ultimately miss out on going to university simply because their village schooling is not of sufficiently high standard to qualify them for university entrance. Moreover, he is eager to move to town to try to become a fully accepted member of urban society. His Scheduled caste status has so far prevented him from achieving his ambitions.

Kuram's experiences throw into relief the severe social discrimination even the few economically successful Scheduled caste men have to face; neither their economic nor their administrative status ensures them automatic social acceptance. No Dalena A.K. has so far managed to occupy anything like Kuram's official position; for most of them mere survival is still an urgent problem. They cannot as yet even conceive of the enigma of social recognition. However, if and when at least a few Dalena A.K.s manage to achieve higher positions in the administrative structure, it is likely that they will be subjected to difficulties similar to those Kuram has to suffer. For the poorest A.K. economic advancement seems an insurmountable obstacle; for their better-off caste fellows social acceptance represents an even more intractable one.

Government policies may be effective in raising the economic status of the poorest Scheduled Castes and ensuring them legal recognition of their equal rights, but no legislation by itself can ever ensure changes in deep-rooted social customs. The attempt by Indian central authorities to introduce egalitarianism in what is fundamentally a hierarchically oriented society is thus doomed to be unsuccessful for a long time to come.

## EDUCATION

General education is often regarded as a powerful solvent of social differentiation, in particular that based on hereditary criteria. In theory equal educational opportunities should ultimately play an important part in eliminating caste differentiation. However, Isaacs' study of educated city people who are of Untouchable origin shows clearly that, although they are generally able to gloss over their caste origin in their professional or business practice, their family life and intimate relations are with similarly educated people of like caste birth (1964:157). As Mandelbaum puts it, 'they have a way of passing in public while not passing in private . . . Educated people cannot separate themselves from their *jati* community because without a community all a man's relationships are awkward' (1970:472). This illustrates how social pressures operate through the medium of family and marital relationships and thereby perpetuate social differentiation in urban societies in spite of higher education. 'Marriage out of caste is still quite rare and radical in all parts of Indian society, and all the more so, of course, where ex-Untouchables are concerned' (Isaacs, 1964:98). Marriage conventions which have dominated the life of village communities for many generations appear to be still sufficiently powerful to survive even in the new and more impersonal urban environment. All this indicates the impact of village conventions on the newly established urban educated society. However, in this book I am chiefly concerned with the analysis of exogenous changes affecting South Indian villages. Therefore, I attempt here to examine the impact of the modern secular education system on village societies.

In 1955 most Wangala Peasants still wanted and needed their sons' help in cultivating their wet crops. Accordingly, even those boys who by then had attended schools beyond primary education were expected to take up farming as soon as they turned fourteen. Dalena farmers could even in earlier days more easily spare their sons, because their labour was not essential for the intra-village dry land farming or for wet cultivation outside. Therefore there were already in 1956 a number of men in Dalena who were literate even in English, and one young Peasant was then a student of physics at Mysore University. Though the educational differentiation was then much greater in Dalena than in Wangala, the overall literacy rate was very much alike in the two villages – in Wangala and Dalena about 12 per cent of the population over five years old were literate. In the intervening years there has been a considerable increase in school attendance in both villages. This is reflected in an overall increase in literacy: in Dalena now 22 per cent and in Wangala 19 per cent of all residents over six years old have attended, or are still going to school (Schönherr, 1972:27).

The increased wealth of many farmers has reduced their dependence on subsistence labour and has encouraged them to invest in their sons' education. In 1955 only about 40 per cent of Wangala boys between the age of five and fourteen years were attending school; now as much as 52 per cent of Wangala boys between six and twenty years enjoyed schooling (Schönherr, 1972:28). Seventeen of a total number of 174 school-age boys attend high school, and of these only two are A.K.s. Not a single Wangala girl goes beyond primary education. Schooling for girls is still regarded by Peasant farmers as an unnecessary luxury. The literacy rate is, accordingly, much lower among village women than among their menfolk : in Dalena and Wangala the proportion of females above the age of six with any schooling is no more than seven per cent; by contrast 41 per cent males in the same age group in Dalena and 35 per cent in Wangala have some schooling (Schönherr, 1972:28).

Mysore State literacy in general 'rose from 19.3 per cent in 1951 to 25.3 per cent in 1961. . . . With 17.3 per cent literacy . . . Mandya is a backward district in the field of education' (B.E.S., 1970:167). Thus while the Authorities made all efforts to realise the economic potential of Mandya District, education seems to have been sadly neglected. The *Mysore Compulsory Primary Education Act*, 1961, makes primary education compulsory for all children and lays down that it must be provided free. One of the most important provisions of the Act is the establishment of primary schools within a walking distance of one mile from the home of every child in the State (M.S.G., 1967:396).

Dalena's primary school is housed in an impressive new building which was put up in 1960 at a cost of Rs. 41,000; the money was raised by joint contributions from individual villagers, from *panchayat* funds and the National Extension Service. Dalena

residents are proud of their school and regard it as a symbol of
the good old days before the introduction of Group *panchayats,*
when it was still left to the individual village to decide on
priorities in capital expenditure. Nowadays, they complain, it is
difficult for councillors from any one village to convince their
fellow councillors from other villages that their own project
should take precedence over all others listed.

Wangala's primary school is housed in the old disused Public
Works Department bungalow which I occupied during my earlier
stay in the village. The school has three full-time teachers who
receive their pay from the State. All of them are outsiders; one
is a Peasant, the others Lingayats. When I visited the primary
school on an ordinary school day I counted thirty-six children,
of whom only two were A.K.s. These numbers, the head teacher
assured me, represented only about one-third of total enrolment,
but he went on to say 'attendance is not very regular and generally far from 100 per cent'.

In 1955 there was not a single individual in Wangala who was
literate in English. A number of schoolboys then used to bring
their English homework to me and I tried my hardest to help
them in their struggle to learn the language. A few of these boys
have in the meantime continued their studies; there are now five
Wangala university graduates, all of whom are Peasants; four
more are undergraduates, of whom three are Peasants and one
is an A.K.

The State educational framework has thus provided increasing
opportunities to which a growing number of villagers respond
positively. I give below three cases of educated young men from
Wangala which show clearly the impact of higher education on
village societies in general and A.K.s in particular before going
on to discuss the sort of education that would be most efficient in
improving village life.

Tama, the one and only A.K. student from the village, is taking
a commerce degree at the University of Mysore. I had long talks
with his parents and met him once in Mysore. He is a bright and
alert looking young man of about twenty years of age, the
youngest of three brothers. He started his schooling in the village
primary school which he attended together with two other A.K.
boys and many Peasant youngsters. Tama was quick to point out
that although all children sat together in the same classroom,

Peasant children never played together with A.K.s in their leisure time. This strict separation between caste and A.K. children is still noticeable. Whenever I walked through Wangala's caste streets I was surrounded by a crowd of caste children but as soon as I crossed over into the A.K. section they stayed behind and in turn I was taken over by a group of A.K. children, who accompanied me through their settlement and similarly let me go when I returned back into the caste area.

Already in primary school Tama displayed his scholarly abilities and being a Scheduled Caste boy he qualified for a high school scholarship. His father, who has only half a wet and one dry acre, had a hard time to scrape enough money together to provide Tama with the minimum necessary school clothing and the boy walked daily to and from the nearest high school about one and a half miles away. The difficulties some A.K. parents encounter in equipping their sons to attend high school, although they have been awarded scholarships, prevents many an A.K. boy from taking advantage of his scholarship. Two such cases were brought to my notice in Wangala. In this connection the *Scheduled Castes and Scheduled Tribes Appointments Committee Report* states that 'dresses and school equipment should be provided during the educational period. For this purpose comprehensive educational planning for these communities may be necessary' (G.A.D., 1962:23).

Tama's parents worked hard to see their son through high school. Now he has a university scholarship with a special living and clothing allowance, which makes him independent of support. His parents, in particular his mother, seem ambivalent about their educated son : on the one hand they are obviously proud of his achievements and happy at the thought of his ultimately getting a regular Public Service appointment, on the other they regret that education is alienating their son from his village home. His mother kept complaining : 'We hardly see our son now while he is studying in Mysore; once he will have finished his studies we'll probably never see him again'. When I talked to Tama I found confirmation of his mother's fear. He is obviously getting more and more estranged from his parental home; his very appearance, wearing shirt and long trousers, distinguishes him from village A.K.s. He complained that on the rare occasions that he visits his home he feels he has nothing in common any more with his family or other fellow A.K.s there. Tama hopes to find a position in the Revenue Department once he graduates. He knows that his chances of realising his ambition are pretty good : he is aware of the proportion of public appointments reserved for Scheduled castes and of the small number qualifying. Tama stays in an A.K. students' hostel in Mysore. He confirmed what Isaacs writes that 'at the present time in the city of Mysore a student has trouble in finding a place to live : when you go to a house to rent a room, the first question is, what caste are you? And when you say you are Scheduled Caste, they say, no rooms. Nobody rents to a Scheduled Caste' (1964:63).

Tama's parents told me that they were trying to negotiate a marriage for their son but that they were afraid he would not accept their arrangements. True enough, Tama confided in me that he was not prepared to marry the girl his parents would choose for him, whom he suspects is an ordinary uneducated villager. He wanted ultimately to marry an educated girl. He realises that she will have to belong to his own caste, but he is determined to try and get a knowledgeable wife. He hopes to achieve his ambition through the contacts he is establishing among fellow A.K. students, some of whom have schooled sisters.

On the whole, therefore, Tama's future looks pretty secure: he knows his aims and how to achieve them. However, as far as his fellow village A.K.s are concerned, his education will be altogether inconsequential : all it will do is to relieve the pressure of population on their meagre land resources by one individual. Judging from his present attitude it is highly unlikely that Tama will keep any contact with his rural home; he is already determined to opt out of the village system and make a life for himself as an urban member of a Scheduled caste. Therefore Tama's education, though it has a decisive influence on his own personal future and through this possibly on urban development, will have very little – if any – impact on the life of the village A.K. community.

The case of Rampa indicates that even sons of richer Peasant middle-farmers may only marginally affect their rural societies if they have academic ambitions. Rampa was awarded a first-class master's degree in economics at the University of Bangalore. He specialised in International Trade and was keen to continue his studies and read for a Ph.D. degree but failed to get the necessary scholarship enabling him to do so. Consequently, he accepted the offer of a lectureship at one of Mandya's colleges. He has married the daughter of a rich landlord residing in the town (see p. 198), and made it clear to me, in his almost perfect English, that he had no intention whatsoever of returning to Wangala and settling down to help farming his father's estate. He has already indicated to his younger brother that he will leave his own share in the ancestral estate in the latter's care. In terms of income, Rampa's academic salary does not offer an attractive alternative to farm earnings, but he seems already firmly committed to urban academic life and wants to sever the ties with his village kin and friends. He did yield to his father's wishes and marry the girl chosen for him; however, he did so not out of any respect for traditional custom, but because he thought the marriage offered him a chance to become a fully-fledged townsman completely detached from his rural background. Unlike Chennu, the Dalena unskilled factory worker, who now resides in Mandya but is still wholly village-oriented (see p. 129), Rampa hardly displays any interest in intra-village matters. Significantly, on the occasion when he was asked to come before Wangala's traditional *panchayat*, where he had to face all the important village elders, he was not prepared to yield to their arguments and stuck to his own decision. It is highly unlikely that an uneducated young Peasant would have dared to behave the way Rampa did. He is always conscious of his superior education as compared to the rest of Wangala Peasants. His very appearance marks him off from them: he walks around dressed in spotless white shirt and trousers as well as socks and shoes; sometimes he even sports a tie.

Rampa's field of specialisation, International Trade, has no immediate relevance to rural problems. Though his father and most of his fellow Wangala Peasants are extremely proud of his academic success, they never approach him for advice or help, save on the rare occasion when he might help them draw up a petition to one or other of the administrative authorities. His education, like Tama's, has turned him away from the village and towards the town; in as far as education is expected to help improve rural living conditions, these young village graduates are a sad disappointment.

The third example illustrates the desirability of encouraging young villagers to study subjects of more immediate relevance to rural activities instead of taking general arts or commerce degrees.

Kinegowda, the younger son of Wangala's *patel*, is now about twenty-nine years old. He is one of the boys who attended middle-school during my earlier stay in the village. I then regarded his attempts at learning English as hopeless. In the meantime, however, he went on to study economics at the university of Mysore, where he graduated in 1964; but he is still unable to talk or understand English. After graduating, Kinegowda taught at a high school for three years. He was not happy as a teacher; he did not like his work and was even less satisfied with the meagre pay he received. In 1967 he resigned and decided to return home and devote his interests to farming his family lands full time. His higher education has obviously widened Kinegowda's horizons; he has gone out of his way to learn improved methods of cultivation; he has hired a bulldozer to level his lands and a tractor for ploughing; he has been applying fertiliser freely to his land. The high price of fertiliser gave him the idea of setting up in business retailing fertiliser in competition with rural co-operative societies. At the beginning of 1970, Kinegowda opened a fertiliser shop at the outskirts of Mandya on the road to Wangala. When I spoke to him later in the year he was pleased with his success and said that the majority of his sales were to fellow farmers from his own village. He was not only happy about his business success but obviously also proud of his role in educating other Wangala cultivators in the use of fertiliser.

Kinegowda, his young wife and their one baby live together under one roof with the rest of the *patel*'s family. Theirs is an elaborate new house supplied with electricity. Kinegowda has arranged a sort of office for himself in one of the small rooms leading from the porch of the house. The *patel* is proud of his educated son and leaves the management of his own property to him. The component members of the headman's family jointly own about 26 acres of wet land; in the village land records they have four separate entries: the *patel* has 10 acres, his wife 4 acres, their eldest son $3\frac{1}{2}$ acres and Kinegowda $8\frac{1}{2}$ acres. In fact Kinegowda told me that he had only recently acquired his land when the Wangala refinery plantation was auctioned. He and his brother cultivate their own land independently and both of them help their parents in tending theirs. The young graduate has bought himself a scooter for Rs. 5,000 on which he proudly drives through the countryside. At the last *Taluk* Board elections he decided to stand and he competed with, and was defeated by, the son of Dalena's headman. Kinegowda had had far less contact than the Dalena man with other villages in the neighbourhood and therefore failed to rally sufficient support. He attributed his opponent's success to Dalena *patel*'s greater affluence and readiness to finance his son's costly electioneering campaign; Kinegowda claimed that he could not afford to spend so much money on wooing his electorate, nor did his father offer any financial support.

Kinegowda, like so many other landowners in irrigated villages, has clearly indicated that he is keenly interested in farming in particular and in rural life in general. His university education has undoubtedly made him alert to improved farming methods and the wider economy and polity of which he sees his own village as part. The time and effort he spent on finding out about more efficient ways of cultivating their customary crops makes it obvious that in his case it would have been much more beneficial had he trained in agriculture or agricultural economics rather than in reading for a general economics degree.

Indian authorities realise the need for more education in agricultural sciences: *The Report of the Education Commission* states explicitly that 'the tasks before agricultural development are . . . clear . . . We must change food habits, lessen our dependency on the vagaries of the monsoon and the winter rains, diversify and improve the quality of our products on our farms, forests and fisheries and push through a rural improvement programme to transform the life in the villages from one of feudal backwardness into that of modernised communities . . . Those goals can only be achieved through the application of science and technology to the problems of agricultural production and rural betterment . . . We must . . . provide for high quality education and research for agriculture' (M.E., 1966:348). Yet only in 1965 did Mysore State establish a University of Agricultural Sciences; before this there had been only two agricultural colleges and one veterinary college in the State. These colleges became affiliated to the newly established Agricultural University and in 1966 had altogether no more than 1,000 undergraduates, which represented less than two per cent of all undergraduates in Mysore during that year while 77 per cent of the State's population still lives in villages (B.E.S., 1970:166). This small percentage reveals the lack of emphasis and interest in higher agricultural education in Mysore State. It is reflected in the fact that none of Wangala's graduates or undergraduates has read or is studying agricultural sciences. If Kinegowda, or any of the other Wangala young Peasants, had studied agriculture instead of more general subjects, these trained and qualified men would have by now probably applied their expertise to farming their own lands; their fellow villagers are more likely to imitate better farming techniques practised by one of their own men than accept the advice of an outside extension official. Although university education alerted Kinegowda to improved farming, he had not received any scientific training in it. Kinegowda's case suggests that young village students, who do not display great potential for theoretical work, might do much better by learning agricultural sciences rather than conventional university subjects.

Kinegowda explained, when I asked him why he had chosen to study economics instead of agriculture, that his teachers had advised him to do so. The Mysore Agricultural University had been established only after he completed his degree. Moreover, he added : 'to get a degree in economics, commerce or general arts is a matter of prestige, whereas a degree in agriculture is an occupational qualification without any prestige attached!' Kinegowda's remarks bear out Isaacs' statement that 'any manual labour in India is still held to be part of a lower estate and it is the primary function of education, many still think, to emancipate them from it. In Bombay the law stipulates that no one who has passed the matriculation examination may be kept in a manual job' (1964:95). There seems to be no provision in the curriculum even of village primary schools to teach pupils the rudiments of efficient farming.

Indian educational authorities appear to assume that no villager would want to study agriculture just to become a better farmer and that agricultural graduates must necessarily be absorbed into the employment structure as extension officers or in similar jobs. The *Report of the Education Commission* estimates a required output of 13,000 agricultural graduates by 1975–6 who are expected to represent no more than three per cent of all graduates in that year (M.E., 1966:366). This seems an altogether wrongly slanted education policy for a country like India where about 70 per cent of the working population are occupied in farming activities and primary produce contributes 51 per cent (M.I.B., 1969:158) to domestic net product.

# PART THREE
# TOMORROW

# 8 What the Future Holds

SUCCESSFUL planning forecasts have to rely on the projection of past trends into the future. This requires full appraisal of the interplay of the various social and economic variables affecting change. But even in the most favourable circumstances many factors converge to make prognostication a hazardous and uncertain exercise. Adequate statistical information is clearly necessary, but in under-developed countries is often simply not available to planners. Thus, speaking of employment in India the *Fourth Five Year Plan* points out that 'No comprehensive surveys were available of the situation in urban and rural areas at different points of time which would make it possible to check the validity of the estimates made. The estimates carried over from Plan to Plan appeared less and less firmly based' (P.C., 1969:341). In this kind of situation planning comes to rest on sheer guesswork.

Detailed studies of local communities might seem to offer a sounder basis for prediction, but are subject to rather different kinds of limitation. There is for example the question of 'representativeness' and the problem of generalising from a situation in which there can be no guarantee that all the relevant variables are present. There is the further, and related, fact that the more restricted the form of observation, the greater the likelihood of the local situation under study being affected by intrusive factors; a good example is the case of jaggery discussed earlier in this book. As against this the validity of an analysis, however interesting, cannot be established unless it is subjected to testing. In what follows, therefore, I have attempted, subject to some of the limitations I have mentioned, to extrapolate from present trends observed in Wangala and Dalena an outline of further developments in the two villages in the immediate future.

Wangala and Dalena can be regarded as representing two types of village in an irrigated region. Therefore a reasonably accurate forecast of their future development may throw light on the changes that can be expected in similar villages in the rest of South India. Rural development must necessarily be viewed within the framework of the interaction between the modern development-oriented and egalitarian all-India policies on the one hand and traditional socio-economic organisation on the other. Dumont in his recent study of the caste system stresses the hierarchical nature of Indian ideology and though he himself points out that his book is not 'immediately relevant to the very urgent problems of contemporary India' (1970:XV) his analysis underlines the immensity of the task which is being undertaken there: to introduce egalitarian concepts in a society with an altogether hierarchically-oriented ideology is a very difficult and consequently slow process. It is likely that in the throes of change the poorest will suffer greater hardships than ever before. No one can say how long it will take before Indians begin to regard themselves first and foremost as individuals instead of what is still their present practice, as members of hierarchically arranged groups; how long it will take before in India *Homo Aequalis* will replace *Homo Hierarchicus* is anybody's guess. What is certain is that political forces, in particular under the guidance of Mrs Gandhi, are trying their utmost to speed this radical change on its way. The measures introduced to effect this may not be the most efficient but the genuine interest among many political leaders cannot be doubted. There just does not seem to be any one panacea for India's vast socio-economic problems; the most to be hoped for is to be able to suggest means to ameliorate major areas of difficulties. This is the topic of the final chapter. In the remainder of this section I try to outline the likely pattern of continuing development of Wangala and Dalena in the immediate years ahead.

## DALENA: TOMORROW

Dalena's population has increased at an average annual rate of at least $2\frac{1}{2}$ per cent over the last fifteen years. Family planning, though widely advocated in Mandya district, has not been accepted by many villagers. Sen Gupta shows that in a sample of 58 Dalena men and 58 women no more than 20 per cent felt decidedly positive about family planning.[1] It is hardly likely that family planning will become a widely accepted practice in Dalena within the near future. Therefore we must expect natural popula-

[1] Personal communication dated 29.11.1971 from the Institut für Soziologie und Sozialanthropologie, University of Erlangen-Nürnberg. Publication of this material is in preparation.

tion increase to continue at least at its present rate. Unless migration takes on unprecedented proportions, Dalena's population is likely to double within the next thirty years. There is little chance that within this period, if ever, canal irrigation will bring water to Dalena land, though of course there is always the possibility of more efficient pump irrigation being introduced to irrigate the village dry land and thereby increase agricultural productivity. If this were accompanied by the introduction of high yielding varieties of millet and paddy seeds comparable in result with the high yielding wheat varieties, Dalena might be able to produce overall sufficient crops to feed its population for the next ten or fifteen years. However, in view of past trends these favourable expectations seem over-optimistic.

More realistic is the assumption that population will continue to grow much faster than the increase in village food production. Wealthier farmers may succeed in buying more wet land in neighbouring villages, but the area involved will be decreasing over the years as the demand for wet land is growing, and altogether it will add only little to the total village product. In view of their partible inheritance the increasing population will be reflected in more and more subdivisions of estates which will make the size of individual farm units smaller and less economic.

The decreasing supply of farm output per family in Dalena will put increasing pressure on a growing number of households to seek income from other sources. This is likely to lead to greater economic diversification among villagers. More and more of the smaller Peasant farmers will seek income other than from cultivating crops. Assuming that the regional economy continues to expand, Mandya will probably have a population of over 150,000 by the year 2000. This urban growth is bound to concentrate along the already existing major highway, which will mean that before too long Dalena is going to be swallowed up by urban suburbs in very much the same way as villages which used to be in the vicinity of Bangalore have by now become part of the city. The greater productivity of irrigated land and its consequently higher value will prevent urban settlement from expanding over much of the nearby wet land. Therefore Dalena and similar dry land villages near Mandya will offer ideal conditions for urban growth. Some of the village land will probably remain devoted to agriculture while the greater proportion of it will be bought by urban developers on a larger scale or sold or rented in small plots to individual settlers.

Dalena's change from being a separate village to becoming an urban suburb will, however, be a slow process. In the meantime every year more villagers will seek and possibly get regular urban employment. Younger men will probably predominate among those who get regular work outside agriculture. If, as is likely, the greater proportion of them, like Chennu, remain village-oriented, this will lead to the spread of share families as well as to a new type of progressive faction in Dalena. The present progressives are all entrepreneurs; by contrast, the new type of progressives will be workers. Thus there are indications of the development of intra-Peasant caste cleavages emerging along class lines. Beteille studied the relationship between caste, class and power in a South Indian village in Tanjore district. In this multi-caste village he found that 'the cleavages most clearly represented are those of caste rather than of the economic or political systems. People belonging to the same group of castes (e.g. Brahmins) live together, but not necessarily people belonging to the same class (e.g. landowners). This is understandable because, at least in the village, a caste or group of castes constitutes a community, whereas this is rarely, if ever, true of a class' (1965:43).

It will be interesting to see what form and what expression class cleavages within the Peasant caste in Dalena will take, for in contrast to Beteille's Tanjore village, here the class section will also be reinforced by caste and group ties. Judging by past experience it is likely that the leaders of Dalena's Peasant workers faction will be readier to make concessions to the demands of the more conservative Peasant farmers than will the entrepreneurial faction. It is possible that the entrepreneurs may want to opt out altogether from intra-village political competition and instead concentrate all their interest and energies on establishing a firm foothold in the wider polity. However, in a democratic political system, wooing of the electorate is an important part of political activity. Should Peasant entrepreneurs therefore ignore intra-village politics altogether they will make the cardinal mistake of any politician who loses the support of his home base.

There will be for a long time to come in Dalena a group of Peasants who will be predominantly conservative and who will continue to regard as the good old days the time when their village was a separate socio-political entity. At the same time the new progressive Peasant worker faction will want to maintain and reinforce much of village custom to keep the old ritual prestige structure alive and to secure a high place within it. As the older Peasants, who have most knowledge of their traditions, die, it is reasonable to expect that it will be the new workers' faction which will take over the role of conservatives in trying to resurrect their old village society. This will probably sharpen the intra-village conflict between progressive Peasant entrepreneurs and Peasant workers.

Simultaneously, other forces will be at work helping to bridge this intra-caste class conflict. The growing need for more Peasant farmers to seek income from outside agriculture will reinforce intra-Peasant caste loyalty. The network of a Peasant's relations with fellow caste men will be widened and each link strengthened and manipulated as the need arises. As long as it is legitimate for Peasants to claim certain benefits on the basis of being members of a 'backward community', caste differentiation will gain in strength. However, even if all benefits to 'backward communities' were to be removed and the concept of 'backwardness' altogether abolished, there is very little chance of caste disappearing within the foreseeable future as a basic principle of socio-economic organisation in the Mandya region.

The persistence of a caste-conscious society will have the worst effect on A.K.s in Dalena. In the traditional village system A.K.s certainly always formed the poorest section, but, as Dumont rightly emphasises, inequality must not be confused with exploitation. The system used to assure subsistence to each proportionately to his status (1970:32). Past economic changes have already removed this minimum social security for A.K.s in Dalena and nothing positive has been put in its place. Unless increasing population in the region should be offset by an equal or greater rate of overall economic expansion, competition for employment will be intensified. A.K.s will be at a disadvantage in this competition, even though legislation lays down that they are to receive preferential treatment at least in public employment. Only if official policy changes to using economic criteria instead of caste as the decisive qualification for favoured treatment may the poorest villagers be able to secure regular employment. In the meantime their best chance of earning wages will be as casual agricultural labourers. As we have seen, the supply of labour in agriculture has increased much more than the demand for it. This has led to a reduction in real wages which was facilitated by inflation : rising prices enabled farmers to reduce real wages without reducing the money wage, thereby they avoided certain socio-economic resistance that they might otherwise have had to face. Since we must expect population increase and inflation to continue in South India in the near future, real agricultural wages will continue to fall until they reach bare subsistence level, unless drastic steps are taken to prevent a further deterioration in the standard of living of the poorest landless labourers.

To summarise the way I see the near future of Dalena : an increasing economic diversification reflected in an intra-Peasant class cleavage and a further deterioration in the economic conditions of the local A.K.s. These economic changes are likely to be reflected increasingly in more radical socio-political changes. Discrimination by village Peasants against A.K.s may become considerably less as their economic interdependence disappears. Yet the social distance between them is likely to remain as big as ever.

## WANGALA: TOMORROW

Wangala's population, like Dalena's, must be expected to continue growing. Wangala men are even less interested in family planning than are their Dalena counterparts : Sen Gupta shows that in a sample of 72 men no more than three felt decidedly positive about family planning.[1] Wangala's population will probably double in about twenty-five years. If in the meantime a high yielding variety of paddy can be successfully introduced this will obviously increase the carrying capacity of irrigated land. Otherwise at least 800 wet acres will be required by the year 2000 to produce enough food to feed Wangala's population with its staple diet of rice and ragi alone. In view of their subsistence orientation farmers will replace cash crops by subsistence crops as population pressure necessitates a greater food acreage. At

[1] Personal communication dated 29.11.1971 from the Institut für Soziologie und Sozialanthropologie, University of Erlangen-Nürnberg. Publication of this material is in preparation.

least, past indications point to such a trend. Though Wangala has been incorporated in the cash economy, farmers are still only secondarily cash croppers; their first concern is to grow sufficient subsistence food. Only if they have more wet land than is required to feed their household do they plant cash crops.

A decline in the acreage under cane will reduce the villagers' cash income. The few wealthiest Peasants will be least affected: though they too will devote an increasing acreage to subsistence agriculture they will still have surplus wet acres to plant cane. Caste middle-farmers will be the most affected group; the extent to which individual households will be impoverished will depend on the size of their wet landholding and the rate of increase in the size of their families. The continuing splitting up of joint families and the increasing number of nuclear households which will emerge will lead to smaller and smaller estates. The smaller the individual farm unit the greater will be the pressure on the farmer to seek income from sources other than cultivating his own land. Some of these impoverished Peasants, particularly those who will have received secondary education, will seek regular employment. However, bearing in mind their strong attachment to the land, they will continue to keep a stake in the rural economy in the way we have seen Dalena urban workers do. Therefore, it is likely that an increasing number of share families will be formed among this section of Wangala Peasants. The magnates, on the other hand, will continue to keep their families 'joint' for as long as possible so as to avoid the splitting up of their estates.

Wangala magnates will remain concerned predominantly with organising the cultivation of their wet land, and with operating crop processing plants in their own village. Consequently, they will continue to concentrate their political interests on intra-village problems. The wider polity will remain of marginal concern to them only. If the State offers help or services which Wangala Peasants find useful they will be prepared to co-operate; otherwise they will continue to mind their own business. This isolationist attitude is likely to come under attack from those Peasants who will have secured regular urban employment in the meantime. However, since the majority of these too will probably be concerned with preserving village traditions, as their Dalena counterparts still are, they will not press their demands too hard.

As long as the richest Peasants derive their wealth from village land, intra-village factions will follow a cyclical course of about two generations' depth.

It is of course always possible that external democratic influences may help to separate the village power structure from its economic base. Beteille reports that this has already happened to a certain extent in Sripuram, the Tanjore village he studied; yet even of his more politically-integrated villagers he says that 'one should not, however, emphasize too much the divergence between political and economic power. In order to acquire and retain political power it is necessary for a person to have some economic standing'. He goes on to pose the question 'to what extent are the ones who have acquired political power also on the way to acquiring control over land?' to which he cannot offer an answer (1965:204). In Sripuram the new democratic legislation strengthened the position of the non-Brahmin majority *vis-à-vis* the small number of wealthy Brahmin absentee landlords. There 'political conflicts seem to have followed more closely the cleavages of caste than those of class' (Beteille, 1965:207). In Wangala there are no Brahmins, and Peasants have what Srinivas calls decisive dominance (1969:10), which is unlikely to be challenged by the only other sizeable, but still much smaller, A.K. community. Therefore, in Wangala, even the adoption of a truly democratic political system is unlikely to upset the traditional power structure controlled by Peasant magnates.

University graduates from Wangala are unlikely to exert much influence over village affairs. Most of them will probably seek regular Public Service or teaching appointments outside. The indications are that, unlike their less educated fellow villagers in urban employment, the graduates will sever their ties with the village completely and, becoming contemptuous of village ways of life, will try to become fully-fledged townsmen. The few graduates who may be attracted back to the village will probably be sons of established magnates or they will use their broader education to try and join the wealthiest. They will therefore reinforce the traditional socio-economic system of the village.

Wangala's increasing population, accompanied by a swing to food production and a declining cane acreage, will automatically reduce the average number of labour days per resident. Mechanisation of agriculture may further reduce village labour requirements. This will make Wangala a less attractive place for migrant labourers and may once more result in a greater reliance by Peasants on their local A.K. dependents. Consequently traditional hereditary relationships which exist between Peasant and A.K. households might again be strengthened. Wangala A.K.s will therefore continue to enjoy a minimum social security. Their income will probably fall back to mere subsistence level. An increasing number of village A.K.s will seek regular urban employment nearby, but unless conditions radically change in the regional employment pattern only very few, if any, are likely to succeed in getting such jobs.

Haswell states categorically that 'labour supply is inelastic at the subsistence wage' (1967:90) and explains the phenomenon in terms 'of the lack of basic physical stamina caused by malnutrition and disease which induces apathy and the unfamiliarity with the industrial discipline of having to work regularly and continuously' (1967:43). Though there is a great element of truth in her explanation, she does not seem to have taken into account the risk even the poorest villager runs by uprooting himself and leaving the shelter of his home. Wangala A.K.s are understandably reluctant to risk jeopardising their assured minimum survival by migrating in search of work in a completely unfamiliar environment. They therefore tend to restrict the radius within which they look for regular employment to commuting distance. They have not yet had a chance to develop faith in the stability of urban employment: they know that if they move into the town and then lose their job they will have a very hard time scraping enough food together to keep themselves and their families alive. While in the village they feel reasonably secure that in the last resort they can always depend on their local Peasants' charity.

This basic feeling of security influences Wangala A.K.s to accept their low ritual and social status in the village against which they may otherwise be tempted to revolt. There is hardly any danger of Wangala A.K.s taking any violent action against their Peasant masters in the near future. In this connection Rudolph and Hoeber rightly say that 'most village Untouchables remain subject to vertical mobilisation by dominant castes upon whom they are economically dependent' and elaborating on this they point out that 'vertical mobilisation by dominant castes, horizontal mobilisation by caste communities and differential mobilisation by parties, even those with revolutionary ideologies, will not easily produce revolutionary consequences' (1967:154). There may be a few occasional rebellious attempts by local A.K.s against Peasant dominance, but judging by past events these are likely to be easily squashed by their economic masters. The biggest problem facing Wangala A.K.s is the fact that not only are they inferior in terms of economic, ritual and socio-political status, but even in terms of numbers they cannot constitute a viable challenge to Peasant superiority. Therefore, even if Wangala Peasants adopted democratic village government based on universal adult franchise, local A.K.s have no hope of securing a majority of councillors so as to have their interests adequately represented.

Thus on the whole I do not envisage any radical socio-political changes taking place in Wangala's foreseeable future. Unless alternative sources of income reduce the pressure of population on landed resources and/or a new high yielding variety of paddy can successfully multiply the productivity per unit of land, there is going to be a steepening decline in the rate of economic growth per head. Economic differentiation will be heightened: the few wealthiest Peasant farmers will become richer, while caste middle-farmers will become poorer and A.K. labourers may be reduced to a minimum subsistence level. Except for a limited number of Peasant farmers who may secure regular urban employment and commute from their village home, intra-village agriculture will remain the dominant economic interest and activity of Wangala residents. This economic introversion will be reflected in continued political isolationism.

# 9 Some Palliatives in Socio-economic Development

INDIA's *First Five Year Plan* already stated explicitly that 'planning even in the initial stages should not be confined to stimulating economic activity within the existing social and economic framework. That framework itself has to be remoulded so as to ensure progressively for all members of the community full employment, education, security against sickness and other disabilities and adequate income' (P.C., 1952:11). If the experience of Wangala and Dalena is in any way representative of larger areas of rural India, then it is clear that planning has failed in one of its major objectives. I have shown that social inequality in these two villages has continued almost unchanged while economic differentiation has considerably increased during the last fifteen years: the poor have become poorer not only relatively but also absolutely.

The *Fourth Five Year Plan* reiterates these aims in slightly different terms: 'the broad objectives of planning could thus be defined as rapid economic development accompanied by continuous progress towards equality and social justice and the establishment of a social and economic democracy' (P.E., 1969:5).

Reading the four development plans one cannot help wondering whether their authors really believed these laudable objectives could ever be attained or whether they were merely paying lip-service to an ideal which either they never truly accepted or never expected to achieve. Certainly, India's planners face a vast and unenviable task. It it not easy to convert a poor and hierarchically-oriented people, who place great emphasis on ascribed status and live in a stagnant economy, into a modern, progressively egalitarian and democratic nation with a cumulatively growing economy. Even so, I believe that many of the planners' difficulties stem from their remoteness from grass-root levels.

In the introduction to this book I pointed out some of the

deficiencies in present macro-planning and stressed the need to learn from micro-research which treats communities as systems and is therefore able to indicate the interaction between the various socio-economic variables in the process of growth. The bulk of this book presents such a small-scale study. It describes and analyses the socio-economic development and changes which occurred in one dry and one irrigated Mysore village during the past fifteen years. In this final chapter, I focus on some of the implications of my findings where these touch on matters of policy.

## REGIONAL DEVELOPMENT

Irrigation is of vital importance in many parts of India where rainfall is too little and/or too irregular to allow farmers to realise anywhere near the full potential of their land. India's *Fourth Five Year Plan* states explicitly that 'one of the major impediments to full exploitation of the possibilities of intensive agriculture is the lack of assured and dependable water supply throughout the year. . . . The development of irrigation has thus a very important role in the development of Indian Agriculture' (P.C., 1969:182). It is generally recognised that Mysore State has still wide scope to expand irrigation facilities. 'The utter inadequacy in respect of irrigation can be judged from the fact that the State's net sown area covered by irrigation in 1966–7 was only 10 per cent as compared to 19.5 per cent in the country as a whole' (B.E.S., 1970:205). Thus there is the great likelihood that more irrigation schemes will be started in Mysore and other parts of South India.

Those responsible for new irrigation projects might be well advised to study Mandya's regional economy before finalising their plans. There the economic integration of irrigated and dry land villages into a regional economy was the result of spontaneous indigenous response. I am not aware that any planner there ever considered that dry land villages might become servicing centres for their neighbours farming irrigated lands. Yet this is precisely what happened in Dalena. Village leaders, and potential entrepreneurs in particular, watched enviously as their fellows in neighbouring communities waxed richer and gained in prestige by cultivating wet land. They resented being left behind. Social competition pervades village life. Men get considerable personal satisfaction from the results of status striving (Mandelbaum, 1970:627). In order to keep pace with their neighbours Dalena men looked for economic opportunities outside their village and diversified their activities.

Irrigation raises the productivity of land and increases the need for supplementary services. It would be wasteful if wet land farmers had to divert their attention from cultivation to provide the additional services themselves. Every irrigation scheme, will, at least at the margins, touch on land that cannot be irrigated. The comparative disadvantage of dry land farming in an irrigated region makes alternative income earning opportunities more attractive to these villagers. It is thus important that planners utilise and foster the competitive drive of villagers for the benefit of the region as a whole : special loans and training facilities may be provided for small-scale entrepreneurs from such dry land villages. This could help to facilitate and speed up the integration of irrigated and dry land villages into a regional economy.

Where planners are concerned with social as well as economic changes, as they often are in India and elsewhere, they need to bear in mind that to increase productivity of land does not necessarily result in a redistribution of wealth and/or a more egalitarian society. Wangala's development over the years shows this clearly. This should, of course, not discourage the extension of irrigation schemes; quite the contrary, from a development point of view it is essential that the wet land acreage should be expanded as far and as fast as topographical factors permit. However, there is a far greater chance of reducing social discrimination in rural South India if economic diversification precedes egalitarian social legislation. Rural economic diversification almost inevitably results in an extension of villagers' economic relations beyond their home base and leads to a change in intra-village customary roles and relations. It is this factor, more than any other, which makes radical social change possible.

As we have seen, even the most revolutionary social legislation is likely to be ineffective in village communities where the economic base and therefore roles and relations continue unchanged. Equally, we need to remember that social changes do not necessarily bring in their wake economic improvement in the lot of the poorest section of the community. I have shown that Dalena A.K.s are considerably worse off than are their Wangala counterparts, despite the more radical social changes that have taken place in the former. Other complementary developments are essential to ensure that changes in traditional South Indian village organisation, which provided all residents with a minimum basic security, do not result in a greater impoverishment of the lowest socio-economic strata.

Regional development can provide a useful base from which to initiate socio-economic changes which may help to put into practice the government's new development-oriented and fundamentally egalitarian ideology; it may help to convert South India's *Homo Hierarchicus* into *Homo Aequalis* at least by reducing social discrimination.

## NON-AGRICULTURAL EMPLOYMENT FOR LANDLESS LABOURERS ONLY

India's rapidly growing population puts a heavy load on her economic planning. About 70 per cent of the population still lives in villages. The high level of rural under-employment and the limited availability of cultivable land will make it necessary for most of the increasing additional labour force to be absorbed into employment outside agriculture. Contrasting the abundance of labour with the scarcity of capital might lead one to expect the establishment of more labour-intensive rather than capital-intensive processes of manufacture. Yet studies of industrial change in India indicate 'a trend toward both higher capital-output ratios and capital-labour ratios over time' (Rosen, 1958:146). In other words, in spite of the abundance of labour in India manufacturers prefer to substitute machinery for labour. An explanation for this tendency must be sought in the high cost of labour.

Although wage rates in India are low compared with Western countries, so is the level of available skills and consequently workers' productivity. Moreover, there is a high absentee and labour turnover rate among urban employees. If a man is absent from his job for many days per year, he is likely to lose or leave it, in which case he will not acquire any proper training or skill in it. If a remedy to this problem is to be sought, we require first to establish the factors responsible for the high rate of industrial absenteeism and labour turnover. Unfortunately I was not able to conduct a study among Mandya's urban labour force. Yet my close acquaintance with Dalena villagers, many of whom work in the town, enables me to throw at least some light on the behaviour of Mandya employees who commute from their villages in the vicinity.

The argument on which this section is based first took shape in my mind during a conversation I had with the General Manager of the Mandya refinery in 1955.[1] He explained to me that the high absentee and labour-turnover rate, particularly at times in the year when men are required to perform operations on the land, induced the management to substitute machinery for labour as far as possible. It therefore seems that it is the lack of an urban-committed labour force which accounts for the instability in work performance. A large proportion of urban workers are, like Chennu, still village-oriented, and many do in fact keep their stake in the rural economy. This is particularly important in decentralised industrial development, as in the case of Mandya, which became a processing and servicing centre for the growing rural hinterland. Kropp, who studied in six North Indian villages the problem of mobilising rural labour for industrial development, remarks that decentralised urban growth results in a great number of workers travelling daily between their home in the village and their place of work. In all communities complete migration of labour force is of very minor significance (1968:179).

The attachment of urban workers to their land affects also the migration pattern to India's larger cities. Zachariah in a study of migrants in greater Bombay found that even of the more stable urban workers over the age of 35 one-third of the male migrants left the city again after three or four years; even factory workers remained in the city for no more than ten years before returning home to take up ancestral land (1968:102). There seems to be a rapid turnover migration in which the volume of population migrating out of a city in a given period is comparable to the volume migrating into it. In this context Mitra states that 'the top industrial layer of urban India goes by this process, thereby exposing the precariousness, vulnerability, and instability of industrial skill, experience, knowledge and human worth in the principal metropolitan areas of the country' (1967:610). To understand the pull that land exerts over urban workers one has

---

[1] I published an earlier version of this discussion (1959:967).

to be familiar with village systems from which urban workers are drawn. Dalena provides a good example here.

In 1955 altogether twenty-six Dalena men were in regular urban employment; twenty of them worked in the Mandya refinery. They were all Caste-men. Nineteen of the twenty factory workers owned some land in the village, ranging from half an acre to six dry acres. The only landless factory worker was an Oilpresser who resided in the village. By 1970 there were forty-one Dalena men in regular urban employment, of whom thirty-three were Peasants, all of whom owned some land.

In order to illustrate what drives a small landholder to seek employment in the town and yet retain his interests in farming I relate the case of Halli. Halli, a young Peasant, is typical of the group of Dalena factory workers and probably of many more workers all over India. He is now in his early forties and has been a factory worker on and off for half his life. In these years he had two periods of about fourteen months each when he stayed in the village altogether.

Halli first made his way to Mandya in search of work when he was fifteen years old. His father had died when Halli was a young boy and he stayed with his mother and elder brother Chenna in Dalena, while his father's brother cultivated their estate. When the latter died without issue Halli and Chenna between them inherited one wet acre in a nearby village and three dry acres in Dalena. By that time Chenna was old enough to take over the cultivation of the estate. He encouraged Halli to seek work in the town, pointing out that when they both got married their small estate would not yield sufficient to support two families. Halli was too young then to be left in charge of the estate had Chenna tried to go out to work. For a long time Halli walked daily to Mandya in search of work. Finally he was fortunate enough to meet a Peasant from another village, who as a servant in the staff quarters at the refinery found Halli a job as a houseboy to a Brahmin engineer working at the factory. Halli had to move into his new master's home, but he regularly took most of his wages back to his mother and brother. After four years as a domestic servant Halli managed to get his master to secure him a job in the factory. This change of employment enabled Halli to return to live in Dalena.

After his period of regular employment in the town Halli

envied his brother being his own boss and he longed for the freedom of life in the village. On the other hand he had tasted the fruits of urban employment and was not prepared to relinquish his regular income altogether. When Halli returned to Dalena he stayed with his mother and Chenna and his new wife. While he worked in Mandya his mother had been ill in Dalena so they had agreed to get a wife for Chenna; for a woman was essential for the cultivation of their land as well as to look after the household. By this time, Halli's desire to keep his stake in the rural economy had become pronounced; he was keen to share in the cultivation of the jointly owned estate, but Chenna wanted no interference. In order to participate in the cultivation of the estate Halli had to take days off work – for instance when lands had to be ploughed after a heavy monsoon shower in June. Halli complained that he contributed most of his wages to the joint household and got little for it. Chenna, for his part, complained that Halli was a useless farmer : he felt bitter because he had to do all the work himself and share the proceeds with Halli. After many quarrels the brothers agreed in 1954 to partition. Each took an equal share of the joint landholding, but Chenna kept the bullocks, ploughs and other tools, on the grounds that he had cultivated their lands alone in all those years Halli had been working in Mandya. His mother joined Halli who built a partition in their common house to separate his household from that of his brother. His new responsibilities as independent farmer occupied Halli to such an extent that he absented himself from factory work for weeks at a time. As long as he had no bullocks or tools he had to borrow or hire from friends or relatives.

To establish himself in the village Halli arranged in 1956 to marry the second daughter of Hangowda, one of the rich farmers and political leaders in Dalena. His father-in-law had eight daughters and no son. This raised Halli's hopes that he could become a full-time farmer by cultivating part of Hangowda's estate, and ultimately to inherit a portion of it. Hangowda, on his side, allowed his daughter to marry a man from a lineage socially inferior to his own and from a poor household within the lineage at that, solely because Halli was a factory worker. Despite the fact that Hangowda was generally known in the village as a traditionalist, he sought for his daughter not an ordinary villager but a man who would look after her in the modern urban style. But this is not the only paradox in this case. Halli managed to marry higher in the social scale because he was a factory worker, and he used his work in the factory to achieve higher prestige within the traditional social system of the village.

In the intervening years since 1956 Halli's mother died and his wife bore him five children. His expectations of becoming a whole-time farmer have been sadly disappointed. Hangowda has married two of his younger daughters to sons of wealthier Dalena farmers and he has drawn these sons-in-law into helping him cultivate his own estate. Halli was upset about this and when he put his complaint to Hangowda the latter told him that as a factory worker he could not be expected to be a good farmer. This influenced Halli twice to give up his job in Mandya and to try and settle down to full-time farming on his own land as well as on land Hangowda allowed him to cultivate. However, Hangowda and his farmer sons-in-law were so critical of Halli's farming that he decided to return to urban employment, farming his own land part-time only. He told me that he was fortunate to get taken back twice on to the factory's payroll, but because of the breaks in his employment he was still, in 1970, after more than twenty years of urban work, employed at the lowest rank and wages of unskilled labour; he had missed out on promotion. Halli failed to become a successful worker; on the other hand, he is not a good farmer either.

Halli's case sets out the dilemma faced by a poor farmer who lives in a village and works in a town. In the first instance, the small size of the estate induced him to seek an income outside his village. But his attachment to the soil and his preference for the free and easy way of rural life compared with the discipline of urban employment made him want to utilise his factory earnings to become a farmer of standing in the village. Thus Halli belongs fully neither to the village nor to the town. His job at the factory prevents him from being a good farmer, while his interest in farming stops him from being a committed factory worker. Morris did not seem to consider the strong attachment to the soil that even poorer farmers have when he said that 'historical evidence indicates that the transformation of a rural traditionally organised population into a committed industrial labour force has not been socially difficult in India. The desperate poverty of the countryside made available a large labour supply that was eager to move into industry as opportunity appeared' (1960:199). Unfortunately, there is no reliable data available on the proportion of urban workers who still have a stake in the rural economy, but I hazard a guess that at least 60 per cent of urban employees still have some share of land in their home village.

Halli's preoccupation with his small estate of uneconomic size is responsible for his frequent absenteeism from his factory employment. If his brother were to die today, he would most likely give up his job and return to full-time farming. There are a number of men in Dalena who, on the death of either their father or brother, left their urban jobs and returned to look after their lands. Cultivation did not yield anywhere near as much as they drew in wages, yet they preferred to come back to farming. It is men like these, I believe, who are largely responsible for the high absentee and labour-turnover rate in urban employment. The difference in the work performance between landholding and landless urban workers is striking. While the former regard wage-earning as nothing more than a stopgap measure and are therefore not interested in training to acquire urban skills, the latter are much keener on their work and never miss a day unless they are really sick. Yeera, one of Dalena's landless A.K.s, who was a peon in the Mandya engineering department in 1956, attended classes to learn to read and write. Since then he has been promoted to a clerical position in the same department and has moved to town (see p. 130). In contrast to Halli and the other landholding Peasant workers, Yeera, the landless A.K., sees his line of advancement in terms of his urban employment. He is therefore a much more conscientious urban worker than are his landholding fellow villagers.

In spite of the fact that landless men make better labourers, caste loyalties within the regionally dominant Peasant community in Mandya district result in Peasants, most of whom have at least some land, exerting a prior claim to urban employment over and above landless men. The law of partible inheritance, which entitles each son to an equal share in his father's estate, operating at a time when population is growing rapidly and only little more land can be brought within the margin of cultivation, is bound to lead to a greater subdivision of estates so that many will be well below optimum size. This in turn will induce many owners of such uneconomically sized estates to seek urban employment while retaining their interest in farming. This dual loyalty will be reflected on the one hand in instability in work performance and on the other in inefficient cultivation. Increasing pressure of population on land will therefore deepen the problem that a landowning urban workforce constitutes.

An urban worker's attachment to his land is certainly not the only reason for the high absenteeism and labour-turnover employers complain about, but it is one of the major causes of it. Having established this, it should now be possible to suggest a means whereby the instability in the labour force arising from the workers' continued interest in their small landholding may be eliminated or at least reduced.

Briefly, what I am proposing here is that the Administration should substitute economic criteria for caste as the determining qualification for preferential treatment; namely, landlessness instead of caste. 'Since 1961 the Central Government has pressed for adoption of economic criteria. . . . The Government statements and actions indicate that it means to do so by shifting over time from a caste to an economic criterion so that by the end of the Sixth Five Year Plan in 1981 no caste (or tribe) will be Scheduled' (Rudolph, 1967:149). The regulation which I suggest here therefore fits in with the intentions expressed by Central Government Authorities. But they seem to think in terms of making household income the decisive economic criterion. In 1961 the Home Ministry wrote to the State Governments asking them to do away with the caste criterion and adopt instead income (Srinivas, 1969:113). Though a laudable idea, I am afraid it may turn out too slippery a tool to use; income is unlikely to provide as concrete and reliable a proof of poverty as landlessness in rural India.

The idea of making special provision for the employment of landless labourers is not new. It was already embodied in the *Second Five Year Plan* when, in regard to employment opportunities, it stated that 'agricultural workers, especially those who are without land, should be specially considered' (P.C., 1956:111). There was, however, no mention of how such a policy might be implemented nor have any efficient steps been taken since to achieve this end. The emphasis so far has been on trying to help Scheduled Castes and Tribes as well as Backward Classes. I have already suggested how this has helped to strengthen caste, an institution which government seeks to abolish. Landlessness, on the other hand, as an economic condition, is not tied to caste, and may indeed cut across caste lines, since a Peasant and an A.K. may be equally landless. The effect of such a move would be to obviate the difficulty that present policy perpetuates, as experience has shown, of getting caste-men into positions of authority and power to implement provisions favouring Scheduled Castes and Tribes. I suggest it should be a lot easier to make them prepared to help landless people, the majority of whom may in fact belong to Scheduled communities.

The landless should be given preference in filling vacancies for employment not only in towns but also in the construction of bridges, roads, canals and other public works. If progressive land taxes were also introduced, as I am suggesting (see p. 259), local revenue would increase and could be used to improve the infrastructure. In turn this would increase the public works labour requirements.

As part of the suggested measure all employers outside agriculture may be compelled by law to engage only workers who can produce a certificate issued by the land record authorities of their native district to prove that they belong to a landless household. Most rural settlements in South India are served by village accountants, who could be empowered to provide such certificate free of charge whenever warranted.

Even without a detailed examination of all the possible ramifications of such a measure it is easy to foresee a number of technical difficulties. There would be, in the first place, the problem of defining non-agricultural employment and evasion of such legislation is likely on this account. There might be a further problem of deciding whether such legislation should apply to all or only certain grades of employment. Perhaps in the initial stages it could be confined to unskilled labourers only. It is possible too that at the outset the implementation of such policy would encourage bribery among those seeking to establish their landlessness. Yet these and other possible drawbacks should be far outweighed by the favourable consequences which are likely to result ultimately from it in the sphere of socio-economic development.

First of all, it would result in an urban-committed labour force keen to train and acquire skills. This would be reflected in a greater employment stability and consequently greater efficiency and productivity of labour which would reduce unit cost of labour. Ultimately this should influence industrial entrepreneurs to prefer labour-intensive to capital-intensive production processes. An increasing number of urban-committed employees would want to acquire skills. Many would probably take a lively interest in town life; they would participate in the various urban associations and consequently become politically conscious and aware of their democratic rights as citizens. Therefore, the urban employment of only landless labourers is likely to have an overall beneficial impact not only on industrial development and urban growth but also on the spread of democratic institutions.

Second, we must examine the likely effects of such a policy on the rural hinterland. Let me take Wangala as an example: 31 per cent of all the village households are landless (Schönherr, 1972:36), of which about half are composed of local A.K.s who have hereditary labour relationships with Peasant farmers. An important aspect of such a relationship is that Peasants are obliged to provide their A.K. dependents with at least a minimum of security. As we have seen, Wangala A.K.s now have to live almost at bare subsistence level. Their continuous attempts to secure regular employment indicate that given the opportunity of work in Mandya many would accept it most willingly. After they had gained confidence in the permanency of their employment they would most probably move into town and, like Dalena's Yeera, become committed to work and life there. However, even while commuting from Wangala there would be nothing to keep them away from regular work attendance; unlike landowning villagers they would have no land to induce them to stay off work. Alternative employment opportunities for Wangala landless A.K.s are likely to result in the disappearance of hereditary labour relationships between them and Peasant farmers. Consequently, this would leave farmers in the village free to introduce labour-saving devices, such as for instance the weeding hook, which will reduce the cost of cultivation. This in turn would increase the demand for the services and some of the village craftsmen who would be able to produce weeding hooks and similar small-scale equipment. The reduction in numbers of Wangala resident landless A.K.s would therefore increase the efficiency of the remaining agricultural workers and therefore the marginal product of labour. Unless their numbers were made up once more by migrant workers they would be in a much better bargaining position to demand higher wages than they are now.

The urban employment of only landless labourers would therefore not only increase the efficiency of urban but also of rural workers, as well as encourage village craftsmen to produce more small-scale equipment. Kropp reports from North Indian villages near growing towns that some of the village craftsmen set up independent trading enterprises, partly with mechanical multiple production. Only a few of them leave to join expanding industries as paid workers, for their income is considerably higher than what they could earn in wages (1968:177).

It remains to consider what would happen to the smallholders who now work outside their home villages or those who desire to do so. The authors of India's latest plan put the smallest landowners under the same heading as the landless. 'The Fourth Plan recognises that the typically non-viable small farmers fall basically into the same category as landless labour and that for the large class of sub-marginal farmers, agricultural labour and landless labour the same remedy lies in the provision of supplementary occupations and employment opportunities' (Dandekar, 1970: 151). Planners do not seem to appreciate that there is a big difference between even the smallest landowner and a landless labourer, though it is of great significance in economic expansion. On the basis of my study in Dalena, where many men are small farmers and at the same time urban workers, I have shown that the provision of supplementary occupations for sub-marginal farmers, as the Plan suggests, is likely to result in inefficiency not only in work performance but also in farming. To improve the productivity of industry and agriculture I am proposing to make the smallholder face the choice of either selling his land or forgoing the chance of earning a regular wage.

It may be argued by some that as long as there is a scarcity of jobs outside agriculture it is not advisable to encourage the owner of even the smallest plot of land to relinquish the shelter of village life; he has no assurance that he will in fact find regular employment outside. This is certainly an important consideration to bear in mind. It illustrates the fact that *not the same*, but radically *different* remedies are necessary to help landless labourers on the one hand and smallholders on the other. The only practical way to aid the former is to enable them to secure employment. Agricultural research and extension may provide the solution to the latter's problems. Farmers 'should . . . be induced to adopt modern techniques, but these should be deliberately chosen to take account of the present vast underutilisation of labour and the rapid growth in the labour force' (Myrdal, 1968:1239). For instance, it may be possible to develop some high-priced labour-intensive cash crop which flourishes on small plots. This would increase the profitability of small farms and make alternative employment less attractive to their owners. This suggestion is not as far-fetched as it may appear at first sight. Israeli agricultural extension services have managed to help smallholders in this way: they have encouraged them to grow flowers to supply metropolitan markets during the European winter. These flowers are best grown on small plots, they require a lot of labour and sell at high prices. I am, of course, not suggesting that Indian villagers should start cultivating flowers; what I am saying is that imaginative agricultural research associated with assessment of, and alertness to, opportunities may suggest a way to make small holders into viable farmers.

Under present conditions men owning no more than one or two dry acres cannot possibly hope to provide for their families from the yield of their small acreage. Many of the owners of tiny estates may prefer to sell when confronted with the alternative of either continuing to farm and struggle along below subsistence level or on the other hand of selling the land and getting a job outside agriculture. In such cases it is likely that one farmer will buy the property of his less efficient or more adventurous brothers; he will devote his interests to farming all their ancestral land while his landless brothers will be free to take up urban employment. In time such practice may result in the law of partible inheritance being accompanied by the arrangement which is prevalent in Norway, whereby the eldest son has the right to buy his younger brothers' shares in the ancestral estate. Such change may help to prevent the further subdivision of farms into uneconomic size units.

Provided urban growth proceeds at a high enough rate while at the same time the profitability of small holdings is increased, we can expect that the policy of giving landless workers preference in urban employment will not only attract a work-committed labour force but also increase the efficiency of output in the rural hinterland, as well as encourage the establishment of small mechanical workshops in villages and towns.

Having examined the likely effects on the urban as well as the rural systems of the suggested employment policy, I now turn to analysing its possible impact on social change. I have stressed throughout this discussion that I suggest making economic criteria rather than caste the determining qualifications for preferential treatment. The majority of landless labourers is made up of Scheduled Castes whose social status the Government of India has been trying to raise by special legislation favouring Scheduled Castes. However, as I have shown for Wangala, political legislation is likely to remain ineffective in raising the social status of Scheduled castes in villages as long as they are still economically dependent on the higher castes. While urban jobs are scarce and discrimination operates against Scheduled Castes, urban employment will remain the prerogative of the regionally dominant caste. Employment outside agriculture of only landless labourers would favour the employment of Scheduled Castes and would therefore tend to undermine the economic support for caste differentiation in rural areas, where caste is still at its strongest. The first attack on caste differentiation should come in the economic rather than in the political or social sphere. Only after Scheduled Castes have been given an opportunity to free themselves from the economic dependence on the higher castes in villages may their social status be raised by political or general social legislation. What A.K. would dare to draw water from the village caste well or enter the village caste temple, rights which the *Constitution* assures to him, when his very livelihood depends on the village caste men who still feel strongly about the differentiation between castes and Untouchables? The importance of economic dependence in social organisation far outweighs that of political rights.

In suggesting a policy for the employment of only landless labourers I have been arguing on the basis of my experience in Mysore villages where the problem of the small *ryot* is becoming increasingly acute and where discrimination against village A.K.s is still rampant. However, with the spread of legislation entitling tenants to ownership rights all over India, this problem will affect larger parts of the Union, particularly if decentralisation of industry continues. It seems therefore that the line of argument adopted here may have relevance far beyond the confines of Mysore and South India.

## THE POOR SHALL NOT BECOME POORER

The case studies in Wangala and Dalena clearly show that in both villages economic differentiation has become intensified. This happened in spite of the various legislative measures which are aimed to offer material help to village Scheduled Castes so as to effect their socio-economic uplift. The wealthiest Peasant farmers with the biggest wet landholdings benefited most; many of the middle-farmers gained only little or nothing from village economic development and landless labourers became worse off both relatively and absolutely.

Increasing economic differentiation accompanying rural development appears to be widespread throughout India. It occurs even in the North where the full impact of the green revolution has been felt. Kantowsky quotes from a report by Ladejinsky, in which he says: 'regardless of whether an observer probes deeply or ever so lightly into the Punjab scene, the single impression he is bound to carry away is one of the air of prosperity that permeates the State. . . . One must be careful, however, not to mistake illusion for reality, for meaningful though the process is, one has to remind oneself that the real sharing in it is restricted to relatively few, perhaps only 10, surely not more than 20 per cent of the farm households of Punjab. Not more than 10 per cent of the 73 per cent of the small farmers are in one way or another involved in the innovation process. The explanation is not in the lack of interest to partake of it, but in the restraint imposed by lack of resources and the failure of the co-operative credit system to help them breach this formidable barrier to any degree. . . . So far, in the discussions relating to the green revolution, the stress is on its additional labour requirements while giving little play to the widespread experience of other countries that as agricultural technology grows in sophistication it leads to less employment of labour' (1970:K7). It is highly likely, therefore, that even if the green revolution were to reach South India's paddy fields, economic differentiation in rural areas would continue to increase.

Western economists for the most part assume that a growing

concentration of wealth in the hands of a small *élite* is a necessary pre-condition for an increasing rate of economic development
among poorer peoples. In this context Myrdal says that 'they take
it for granted that *a price has to be paid for reforms* and often
this price is prohibitive for poor countries' (1971:68). He goes on
to challenge this assumption by first questioning the correctness
of the usual argument that inequality of income is a condition for
saving and then stressing the detrimental effect of poverty on
productivity of labour.

// Evidence from Wangala and Dalena does not lend full support
to Myrdal's first point : though village Peasant magnates undoubtedly spend a considerable proportion of their wealth on
conspicuous consumption, they also invest a lot of their funds in
productive assets. Radical reforms in India's taxation system
might help to reduce the rate of economic differentiation. Haswell
rightly points out that 'if the rate of economic development in
India is to be accelerated, bold tax reforms are necessary which
must include heavier agricultural taxation since this sector is
overwhelmingly large'. She goes on to sound a note of warning
that this tax should not take the form of 'a fixed levy on output
for this would penalise the efficient cultivator' (1967:90). Fixed
output levies are, of course, not the only way to raise agricultural
taxes. The standard rate of land tax could for instance be substituted by a rate which progressively increases with the size of
the landholding (Joshi, 1968:189), starting from as low a level as
three wet acres per farm unit. Some Indian Authorities seem to
regard five acres as the minimum size of viable holding (D.S.W.,
1969:124), but as Landejinsky correctly remarks 'not all the
farmers with five acres and less are necessarily small farmers – if
they have water' (1971:24).

I have shown that a South Indian farmer needs at present a
maximum of two or three wet acres to produce his household's
basic food requirements. While all *ryots* allocate first priority to
subsistence cultivation many are at the same time profit-oriented
for cash crops they grow on land surplus to their household food
needs. This should facilitate the introduction of a progressive land
tax for farm units of three or more wet acres. It is likely to
encourage farmers with larger holdings to increase the efficiency
of their cultivation. This, together with the possibility of utilising
the additional revenue for rural development, can be expected to

have beneficial effects on rural life. Therefore, increased land taxes may be used as a means to compel the wealthiest to spend less and redirect some of their savings. At the same time they should be offered tax concessions for increasing suitable productive investment.

Investment should be channelled, as far as possible, along lines where it helps to maximise yield per acre rather than where it substitutes machinery for brawn. In rural South India, where irrigated land and capital funds are extremely scarce factors of production, while labour is in abundant supply, it is not only wrong and immoral from a human point of view, but also uneconomic to mechanise productive processes unless this will result in greater yields per acre. Thus while Myrdal's claim that the richest do not save but rather squander their funds is not altogether borne out by my own data, it is an important consideration to keep in mind; more important still, the rich should be encouraged to invest in assets which will help labour to increase output rather than in machinery which operates in place of labour.

This leads straight on to Myrdal's second claim for which village studies provide ample evidence, namely that extreme poverty has a detrimental impact on the productivity of labour. First of all, undernourished workers naturally lack the stamina to sustain the physical effort necessary to work at the pace required by the criterion of maximum productivity. Second, one can hardly expect a casually employed field labourer to be prepared or able to perform his tasks with great efficiency while he is always worried how many days' wages he will be able to earn, for how long he will be able to feed his wife and children. Third, and possibly most important, since as we have seen, rural wages lag behind price rises in an inflationary period, labourers see farmers getting richer while they themselves find it harder to make ends meet. My own data for Mandya region indicate that real daily wage rates have been about halved between 1955 and 1970 while employment per labourer has also declined. Official reports admit that in Mandya district there has been a 14 per cent decline in real wage rates in the five years between 1962 and 1967. Moreover, available indications show that there has been only a small increase in labour employed in agriculture in that period (M.F.A.C., 1970:588). Thus not only real wage rates but also real wages per landless labourer have been declining in a period when agricultural productivity and crop prices have considerably increased.

The system of fixed annual rewards in kind, customary in South Indian villages, was well suited to static rural economies with little or no net increase in labour force. It assured at least a minimum subsistence to each; individual groups shared in the total village product according to their social status and the stake they had in the rural economy. Population growth resulting from natural increase as well as net immigration has upset the traditional balance between the supply of labour and its demand. The concomitant monetisation of rural economies as well as inflation made it easier for farmers to reduce real wage rates. The complete removal of rewards in kind, as has happened in Dalena, and their part substitution by daily cash wages, which is what happened in Wangala, has introduced the present instability and insecurity in intra-village labour relations.

Attempts to legislate for a minimum rural wage have so far failed in South India. Yet it may be possible to tie basic agricultural wages to an equivalent in kind. For instance, the reward for a day's work on harvesting paddy has remained stable over the years: it is still eight seers paddy which weigh altogether about 17 lb. and amount to about twice the daily real wage paid in cash for other field labour. It might thus be possible to prevent rural wage rates from declining any further by expressing them in real rather than in cash terms. When I discussed wages with some Wangala Peasant farmers and asked them if they knew how much rice or ragi a worker could buy with his daily wages they looked blank; they had obviously not thought of wages in these terms. All they were interested in was their labourers' performance. They seemed genuinely surprised when I put it to them that all the Rs. 2 daily wage would buy was 1.8 seer (= 3.7 lb.) rice, hardly enough to feed a family even for a day. They quickly added that the worker got a big midday meal of cooked rice and this therefore supplemented his cash wage. This is certainly true, but one meal is not sufficient to compensate for the decline in purchasing power of cash wages.

If, therefore, rural rewards are to keep up with rising food prices it would seem sounder to try and introduce agricultural minimum wages expressed in terms of a fixed quantity of the staple crop grown in the different areas; for instance, for paddy growing areas the minimum male daily wage might be fixed at eight seers. This is after all what Mysore farmers still give their labourers per day of paddy harvesting. Eight seers paddy produce approximately nine lb. rice which yield a total of about 11,000 calories. If in addition to this labourers were to continue to get a meal on every day they worked, which is likely, they could manage to feed their families provided they found work for at least 200 days each year. It is, of course, possible that an increase in real wage rates may result in a reduction of employment. However, I suspect that this would only be slight; past employment trends in Wangala and Dalena indicate a low demand elasticity for labour. There is no need to insist on payment in kind; as long as farmers undertake to pay their labourers either in kind or the appropriate cash equivalent, declining real wage rates can be avoided.

The main problem in implementing rural wages directly linked to the cost of living is to ensure that farmers will in fact adopt it. This may be difficult in the beginning, but I suspect that it should be a lot easier to get farmers to revert to a barter economy by persuading them to pay in kind, rather than legislate for a minimum cash wage which is likely to have to be continuously raised as prices go up. It may be argued against this suggestion that to make rural economies revert to barter is a retrogressive step. However, as we have seen, South Indian *ryots* are still largely subsistence-oriented and are subsidiary cash croppers only. Thus they fully appreciate the necessity for a household to have at least a minimum of basic foods. Farmers can, therefore, be expected to be prepared to give their labourers rewards in kind which will ensure at least a minimum survival. This after all has been their long-standing tradition. It is much easier for farmers to refuse to grant an increase in cash wages when prices are rising than it would be for them to reduce the quantity paid in kind, though this is precisely what a declining purchasing power of cash wages amounts to.

The immediate effect of a reversion to payment in kind would be an increase in the cultivation cost of labour. This is obviously the main reason why farmers may object to it. Competition among rural labourers for scarce employment might result in some of them undercutting agreed wage rates. To avoid this, jobs outside agriculture would have to be provided to reduce the pressure of surplus rural labour.

The interdependence of the different measures suggested here should now be clear. Just as the new improved varieties of seeds must be applied in conjunction with the necessary irrigation and fertiliser, so must the new development measures be adopted in appropriate 'packages'. Even if most surplus rural labour could be absorbed in employment outside agriculture this in itself would not automatically prevent further reductions in real agricultural wage rates. On the other hand, the stabilisation of rates of pay by tieing them to rewards in kind could not ensure agricultural workers a stable or rising income unless alternative employment opportunities were made available to them.

The package of new measures I am suggesting here consists in planning regionally integrated economies where landowners pay progressive land taxes and landless labourers are given priority in employment outside agriculture while applied research helps to increase the productivity of small holdings and rural wage rates are tied to rewards in kind. Such a package should help to reduce economic inequalities and make for greater social justice. As we have seen, India's officially expressed aims avow a casteless, egalitarian welfare society. In fact much in recent development trends points in the opposite direction. Measures of the kind I have been suggesting here may have a part to play in ensuring that India's poor shall not become poorer.

# Bibliography

## OFFICIAL PUBLICATIONS

B.E.S. Bureau of Economics and Statistics (1966). *Annual Season and Crop Report of Mysore State for the Year 1964–65.* Bangalore.

—— (1969). *Statistical Abstract of Mysore 1967–68.* Bangalore.

—— (1970). *Economic Development of Mysore 1956–69.* Bangalore.

D.S.W. (1969). Department of Social Welfare. Government of India. *Report of the Committee on Untouchability, Economic and Educational Development of the Scheduled Castes and Connected Documents.* Delhi.

Encyclopaedia Britannica (1961).

G.A.D. (1962). General Administration Department. Government of Mysore. *Scheduled Castes and Scheduled Tribes Appointments Committee Report.*

M.E. (1966). Bangalore. Ministry of Education, Government of India. *Report of the Education Commission, 1964–66.* Delhi.

M.F.A.C. (1970). Ministry of Food, Agriculture, Community Development and Co-operation (Department of Agriculture). *Modernising Indian Agriculture, Fourth Report on the I.A.D.P. (1960–68) Vol. II, District Chapters.* Delhi.

M.I.B. (1969). Ministry of Information and Broadcasting, Government of India, *India.* Delhi.

M.L.G.R. (1969). *Mysore Land Grant Rules.* Bangalore.

M.O.L. (1951). Ministry of Labour, Government of India Press. *Report on the Enquiry into the Conditions of Agricultural Workers in the Village Archikarahalli, Mysore State.* New Delhi.

M.P. (1962). Manager of Publications. *Report of the Commissioner for Scheduled Castes and Scheduled Tribes 1961–62.* Delhi.

M.S.C. (1969). The Mysore Sugar Co. Ltd. *36th Annual Report 1968–69.* Bangalore.

M.S.G. (1967). Mysore State Gazetteer, *Mandya District.* Bangalore.

P.C. Planning Commission, Government of India. (1952). *First Five Year Plan.*
—— (1956). *Second Five Year Plan.*
—— (1969). *Fourth Five Year Plan.* (Draft).
*The Constitution of India 1955*, Allahabad, Law Publishers.
*The Mysore Village Panchayat and District Board Act (1952).* Bangalore.


## OTHER REFERENCES

Agarwala, B. R. (1962). 'Nature and Extent of Social Change in a Mobile Commercial Community', *Sociological Bulletin*, II, Nos. 1 and 2.
Bailey, F. G. (1957). *Caste and the Economic Frontier* (Manchester : Manchester University Press).
—— (1960). 'The Joint Family in India : a framework for discussion', *Economic Weekly*, XII, No. 8, 20 February 1960.
Bardhan, P. (1970). ' "Green Revolution" and Agricultural Labourers', *Economic and Political Weekly*, V, Nos. 29–31, Special Number.
—— (1970). ' "Green Revolution" and Agricultural Labourers: a Correction', *Economic and Political Weekly*, V, No. 46.
Barth, F. (1967). 'Economic Spheres in Darfur', in *Themes in Economic Anthropology*, ed. R. Firth (Tavistock Press, London).
Beidelman, Thomas O. (1959). *A Comparative Analysis of the Jajmani System* (New York : J. J. Augustin).
Beteille, A. (1964). 'Family and Social Change in India and other South Asian Countries', *Economic Weekly*, XVI, Nos. 5, 6 and 7, Annual Number. February 1964.
—— (1965). *Caste, Class and Power* (Berkeley and Los Angeles: University of California Press).
—— (1967). 'The Future of the Backward Classes : The Competing Demands of Status and Power', in *India and Ceylon: Unity and Diversity*, ed. P. Mason (London : Oxford University Press).
Bhagwati, J. N. and Desai, P. (1970). *Planning and Industrialization. Industrialization and Trade Policies since 1951* (London : Oxford University Press).
Cohen, A. (1965). *Arab Border-Villages in Israel* (Manchester: Manchester University Press).

Dandekar, V. M. and Rath Nilakantha (1970). *Poverty in India* (New Delhi : The Ford Foundation).

Desai, I. P. (1956). 'The Joint Family in India – an Analysis', *Sociological Bulletin*, V, No. 2.

Douglas, M. (1962). 'Lele Economy Compared with the Bushong: A Study in Economic Backwardness', in *Markets in Africa*, eds. P. Bohannan and G. Dalton (Evanston : Northwestern University Press).

Driver, E. D. (1962). 'Family Structure of Socio-economic status in Central India', *Sociological Bulletin*, II, Nos. 1 and 2.

Dumont, Louis (1970). *Homo Hierarchicus* (London : Weidenfeld & Nicolson).

Durkheim, E. (1921). 'La famille conjugale', *Revue Philosophique*, XX.

Epstein, T. S. (1959). 'Industrial Employment for Landless Labourers only', *Economic Weekly*, XI, Nos. 28, 29 and 30, Special Number.

—— (1962). *Economic Development and Social Change in South India* (Manchester : Manchester University Press).

—— (1967). 'The Data of Economics in Anthropological Analysis', in *The Craft of Social Anthropology*, ed. A. L. Epstein (London : Tavistock Publications).

—— (1968). *Capitalism, Primitive and Modern – Some Aspects of Tolai Economic Growth* (Canberra : A.N.U. Press).

Firth, R. W. (1929). *Primitive Economics of the New Zealand Maori* (London : Routledge & Kegan Paul).

—— (1956). *Human Types*, Revised edition (London : Nelson).

—— (1959). *Social Change in Tikopia* (London : George Allen & Unwin).

Frankenberg, R. (1957). *Village on the Border* (London : Cohen & West).

Gallin, A. (1969). 'Political Factionalism and its Impact on Chinese Village Social Organisation in Taiwan', in *Local-level Politics*, ed. M. J. Swarts (London: University of London Press).

Gluckman, M. (1967). 'Introduction', in *The Craft of Social Anthropology*, ed. A. L. Epstein (London : Tavistock Publications).

Gupta, S. C. and Majid, A. (1965). *Producers' Response to Changes in Prices and Marketing Policies* (London : Asia Publishing House).

Haswell, M. R. (1967). *Economics of Development in Village India* (London : Routledge & Kegan Paul).

Isaacs, Harold R. (1964). *India's ex-Untouchables* (New York: John Day).

Joshi, T. M. and Anjanaiah, N. and Bhende, S. V. (1968). *Studies in the Taxation of Agricultural Land and Income in India* (Bombay : Asia Publishing House).

Kaldate, SMT, Sudha (1962). 'Urbanization and Disintegration of Rural Joint Family', *Sociological Bulletin*, II, Nos. 1 and 2.

Kantowsky, D. (1970). 'Social Aspects of a Green Revolution', in *Social Problems resulting from Industrialisation* (Berlin : German Foundation for Developing Countries).

Kolenda, P. M. (1968). 'Region, Caste and Family Structure : A Comparative Study of the "Joint Family" ', in *Structure and Change in Indian Society*, eds. M. Singer and B. S. Cohn (Chicago : Aldine Publishing Co.).

König, René (1970). 'Old Problems and New Queries in Family Sociology', in *Families in East and West*, ed. René König (Paris : Mouton).

Kropp, E. W. (1968). *Zur Mobilisierung ländlicher Arbeitskräfte im anfänglichen Industrialisierungsprozess* (Heidelberg: Dissertationsreihe des Südasiens-Instituts der Universität Heidelberg, No. 8).

Ladejinsky, W. (1971). 'Agrarian Reform in Asia, the "Green Revolution" and its Reform Effects', 28th International Congress of Orientalists, Canberra, in *The Impact of Technical Change in Asian Agriculture*, ed. R. T. Shand (forthcoming).

Lannoy, Richard (1971). *The Speaking Tree: A Study of Culture and Society* (London : Oxford University Press).

Mandelbaum, D. (1970). *Society in India* (Berkeley and Los Angeles : University of California Press).

Mason, P. (1967). 'Unity and Diversity – An Introductory Review', in *India and Ceylon – Unity and Diversity*, ed. P. Mason (London : Oxford University Press).

Mead, M. (1956). *New Lives for Old* (New York : William Morrow).

Miller, F. D. (1965). 'Factions in Indian Village Politics', *Pacific Affairs*, XXXVIII, No. 1.

Mitra, A. (1967). 'Internal Migration and Urbanisation in India, 1961', in *Report of the IUSSP Sydney Conference*.

Morris, M. D. (1960). 'The Labor Market in India', in *Labor Commitment and Social Change in Developing Areas*, eds. W. E. Moore and A. S. Feldman (New York : Social Science Research Council).

Myrdal, G. (1968). *Asian Drama* (London : Pelican Books).

—— (1971). *The Challenge of World Poverty – A World Anti-Poverty Programme in outline* (London : Pelican Books).

Nicholas, R. W. (1961). 'Economics of Family Types in Two West Bengal Villages', *Economic Weekly*, XIII, Nos. 27, 28 and 29. Special Number.

—— (1965). 'Factions : A Comparative Analysis', in *Political Systems and the Distribution of Power*, A.S.A. Monograph 2 (London : Tavistock Publications; New York : Praeger).

—— (1968). 'Structures of Politics in the Villages of Southern Asia', in *Structure and Change in Indian Society*, eds. M. Singer and B. S. Cohn (Chicago : Aldine Publishing Co.).

Parsons, T. (1961). 'Introduction to Part Two : Differentiation & Variation in Social Structures', in *Theories of Society*, eds. T. Parsons, E. Shils, K. D. Naegele and J. R. Pitts (New York : The Free Press of Glencoe).

Rosen, G. (1958). *Industrial Change in India* (Illinois : The Free Press of Glencoe).

—— (1966). *Democracy and Economic Change in India* (Berkeley and Los Angeles : University of California Press).

Rudolph, L. I. and Hoeber, Susanne (1967). *The Modernity of Tradition, Political Development in India* (Chicago : The University of Chicago Press).

Salisbury, R. F. (1962). *From Stone to Steel* (London : Cambridge University Press).

Schönherr, S. (1972). 'Berufliche Diversifikation and Führungsmodernisierung im ländlichen Indien', *SSIP – Schriftenheft* (Saarbrücken : D. Breitenbach).

Singer, M. (1968). 'The Indian Joint Family in Modern Industry', in *Structure and Change in Indian Society*, eds. M. Singer and B. S. Cohn (Chicago : Aldine Publishing Co.).

Smith, D. E. (1963). *India as a Secular State* (Princeton : Princeton University Press).

Spiro, M. E. (1969). 'Factionalism and Politics in Village Burma', in *Local Level Politics*, ed. M. J. Swartz (London : University of London Press).

Srinivas, M. N. (1952). *Religion and Society among the Coorgs of South India* (Oxford : Clarendon Press).

—— (a) (1955). 'Castes – can they exist in the India of tomorrow', in *Report of Seminar on Casteism and Removal of Untouchability* (Bombay : Indian Conference of Social Work).

—— (b) (1955). 'The Social System of a Mysore Village', in *Village India*, ed. McKim Marriott (Chicago : University of Chicago Press).

—— (1969). *Social Change in Modern India* (Berkeley and Los Angeles : University of California Press).

Thorner, D. and A. (1962). *Land and Labour in India* (New York : Asia Publishing House).

Van Velsen, J. (1967). 'The Extended-case Method and Situational Analysis', in *The Craft of Social Anthropology*, ed. A. L. Epstein (London : Tavistock Publications).

Watson, W. (1958). *Tribal Cohesion in a Money Economy* (Manchester : Manchester University Press).

Zachariah, K. D. (1968). *Migrants in Greater Bombay* (London: Asia Publishing House).

# Index